Grammar Builder

A grammar guidebook for students of English

4

CAMBRIDGE
UNIVERSITY PRESS

A. Amin

R. Eravelly

F.J. Ibrahim

CAMBRIDGE UNIVERSITY PRESS
Cambridge, New York, Melbourne, Madrid, Cape Town, Singapore, São Paulo

Cambridge University Press
10 Hoe Chiang Road, #08-01/02 Keppel Towers, Singapore 089315

www.cambridge.org
Information on this title: www.cambridge.org/9780521548625

© Cambridge University Press and Pan Asia Publications Sdn Bhd 2004

First published 2004
Fifth printing 2006

Printed in Singapore by Kyodo Printing Pte Ltd

Typeface Utopia. *System* QuarkXPress®

ISBN 0 521 54859 4 Grammar Builder Book 1
ISBN 0 521 54860 8 Grammar Builder Book 2
ISBN 0 521 54861 6 Grammar Builder Book 3
ISBN 0 521 54862 4 Grammar Builder Book 4
ISBN 0 521 54863 2 Grammar Builder Book 5

• • • • • • • • • • • • • • **INTRODUCTION** • • • • • • • • • • • • •

To the student

This book is designed to help you master key concepts in English grammar easily and quickly. Students who need to take written exams as well as those who wish to write well will find the *Grammar Builder* series helpful.

You may use this book for self-study and practice. An Answers section is located at the back of the book.

To the teacher

The *Grammar Builder* series is a useful supplement to any main English language course and is suitable for both classroom teaching and self-study. The series focuses on written grammar and the key grammar concepts that students need to know for written exercises.

How the book is organised

The *Grammar Builder* series comprises five books for beginner to upper-intermediate level learners of British English. Books 1 and 2 are intended for learners who need to acquire the basics of grammar. Books 3 to 5 are for learners who need to strengthen their proficiency in grammar and improve their written English.

Each book is made up of 42 to 56 units, and units dealing with related topics (e.g. prepositions) are grouped together for ease of use.

A unit covers three to five grammar concepts and includes four to six different types of exercises. Key grammar concepts (e.g. tenses) taught in the lower level books are re-visited and expanded upon in the other books of this series. For a list of units, refer to the *Contents* at the beginning of each book.

The books use a simple but effective three-step approach (error identification, correction, and practice) to help learners master English grammar.

There are four pages per unit, and each unit is divided into three sections: *Checkpoint*, *Grammar Points*, and *Practice*.

All units begin with a *Checkpoint* section containing several pairs of numbered examples that show common grammatical errors and then their corrected forms. These examples of correct and incorrect usage demonstrate to the student how slight differences in expression can result in grammatical errors.

The students can then refer to the corresponding *Grammar Points* in the next section which explain the grammar concepts highlighted under *Checkpoint*, show how to apply the grammar concepts correctly, and provide more examples.

In the third section, *Practice*, students revise the grammar concepts they have learned by completing a group of exercises. (The answers can be found at the back of the book.) This enables quick revision of each concept, and allows students to see if there are any aspects that they do not fully comprehend. Students may review what they have learned by going through the *Grammar Points* again after completing each exercise. The *Grammar Points* can also be used for quick reference purposes.

There are six revision and evaluation tests towards the back of every book. These tests deal with most of the *Grammar Points* covered in each book.

CONTENTS

CONTENTS

UNIT 1.1 VERBS

base form

Look at the **A** and **B** sentences below. Find out why **B** is correct and **A** is wrong in the **Grammar Points** section.

			GRAMMAR POINTS
1A	My parents **understands** my problem.	✗	
1B	My parents **understand** my problem.	✓	1
2A	**Moves** your car to the side, please.	✗	
2B	**Move** your car to the side, please.	✓	2
3A	Jeff **to give** us lunch.	✗	
3B	Jeff **wants to give** us lunch.	✓	3
4A	Everyone **must follows** the rules.	✗	
4B	Everyone **must follow** the rules.	✓	4

GRAMMAR POINTS

1 The base form of a verb is the simplest form. It does not have the 's', 'ed' or 'ing' ending. We use the base form for the present tense in these ways:

(a) with the pronoun subjects **I**, **you**, **we** and **they**
  EXAMPLES: I **remember** the robber's face very well.
  You **complain** about the weather all the time.
  We **prefer** a holiday in Spain rather than in Norway.
  They **manage** the whole company themselves.

(b) with plural noun subjects
  EXAMPLES: The immigration officers **check** the passport of every traveller.
  Those classrooms **lack** proper ventilation.

REMEMBER!

- The two basic types of verbs are main verbs and auxiliary verbs. The majority of verbs are main verbs. Auxiliary verbs are a small group of verbs including 'to be', 'to do', 'to have', **can**, **may**, etc. They are used in combination with main verbs. They cannot stand on their own in a sentence.
  EXAMPLE: I am going to the supermarket.
      (auxiliary verb) (main verb)

- The verbs 'to be', 'to do' and 'to have' can be used as main verbs as well as auxiliary verbs.
  EXAMPLES: He **does** the editing of that magazine.   (**do** as main verb)
      He **does like** her after all.   (**do** as auxiliary verb)

2

2 We have to use the base form of a verb when we give instructions, warnings, advice or commands to the person listening to us or when we make requests of that person.

EXAMPLES: **Fry** the fish in hot oil.   *(instruction)*
Move away from the cliff edge!   *(warning)*
Stay on good terms with everyone. *(advice)*
Go to bed at once.   *(command)*
Give me another form, please.   *(request)*

Take note that **you** (the listener) is the subject in each of the above sentences.

3 We call the base form of a verb together with **to** 'an infinitive' or 'a non-finite verb'. A sentence with an infinitive is not complete unless it contains a finite verb as well.

EXAMPLE: She <u>needs</u> to consult a doctor about her backache. ✓
(finite verb) (infinitive)

She to consult a doctor about her backache. ✗
(infinitive)

REMEMBER!

■ A verb is either finite or non-finite. A finite verb changes its form according to the tense and subject of the sentence. A non-finite verb does not change its form.

EXAMPLES: finite verb: like   non-finite verb: to play

Present tense : My parents like to play tennis at weekends.

Past tense   : My parents liked to play tennis in their younger days.

Singular subject : He likes to play tennis at weekends.

Plural subject   : We like to play tennis at weekends.

---

4 We use the base form of a verb with modals (such as **can**, **may**, **might**, **should**).

EXAMPLES: He **can answer** all the questions correctly.
(modal) (base form of verb)

You **should answer** all the questions at the interview.
(modal) (base form of verb)

PRACTICE | *A* | Underline the base forms in the sentences. Put **–** in the box if there are no base forms in a sentence.

1 The car veered to the left and collided with a truck.

2 Mary has to renew her driving licence tomorrow.

3 Open this can of peaches for me, please.

4 Larry should attend our meetings more regularly.

5 Janet is coming here to coach me in Science.

6 The airline staff must explain why there is a delay.

7 Telephone Evelyn and be friends again.

8 I go for computer classes on Mondays and Fridays.

9 John's foot bled profusely when he stepped on a piece of glass.

10 They always make sure that they send out their Christmas cards by the first week of December.

PRACTICE **B** Some of the sentences contain mistakes in verb forms. Underline the mistakes and write the correct verbs in the boxes.

1 Bend over and touch your toes.

2 The airline promises to compensates me for the loss of my suitcase.

3 I enjoys a cup of tea every morning before breakfast.

4 Please place an order for more office desks and chairs.

5 The children must wait for a while till the dentist is free.

6 Gets Mrs Rogers on the phone for me, please.

7 The chefs needs to thaw the frozen meat before they can cook it.

8 Our college will release the exam results on Monday.

9 They should informs Eric of the change in plans immediately.

10 Tony feels honoured to lead our delegation at the international conference.

PRACTICE **C** Fill in the blanks with the correct verbs in the brackets.

1 I used _____ pecan pie but now I prefer apple pie. (like / to like)

2 You should _____ to Macy for your thoughtlessness yesterday. (apologise / to apologise)

3 I can _____ suggestions on how to improve the menu. (give / gives)

4 _____ to cooperate with the others in the team. (Try / Tries)

5 We _____ to visit that factory to see how glass is recycled. (want / wants)

6 All sales assistants must _____ polite and helpful at all times. (be / being)

7 _____ out the washing before you leave for school. (Hang / Hanging)

8 The television stations _____ the news four times a day. (broadcast / broadcasts)

9 Those university students want _____ about lodgings for themselves. (enquire / to enquire)

10 He can _____ that T-shirt for something else of the same value. (exchange / exchanges)

PRACTICE *D* Underline the sentences with mistakes in the use of verbs and rewrite them correctly.

For a quick lunch, goes to 'Bennito's' in Holly Street. The notice on the café door reads, "We aims to please. Please to ring for service." Bennito himself will greet you at the door to take your order immediately. In less than 15 minutes, your food will arrives at your table. If it does not, Bennito will say to you, "Please be forgiving me, my wife, my chef and my café. We want you to enjoy our food. We wish you to have it free of charge now."

Bennito's café first opened for business three years ago. According to Alfredo, one of Bennito's waiters, Bennito had to gives away free food only twice in all those years!

1 *For a quick lunch, go to 'Bennito's' in Holly Street.*

2 _____

3 _____

4 _____

5 _____

6 _____

PRACTICE *E* Rewrite the sentences and change the description into instructions. Use the base form of the verbs.

First, I placed the printer on a flat surface. Then, I fixed the paper tray and paper rest to the printer. After that, I opened the front cover of the printer and inserted the colour cartridge into the cartridge holder. Next, I lowered the lock lever to make sure the cartridge was in place. Then, I connected the power cord to the back of the printer. Finally, I plugged the power plug into the power outlet.

1 *First, place the printer on a flat surface.*

2 _____

3 _____

4 _____

5 _____

6 _____

UNIT 1.2 VERBS

with 's' and 'ing' endings

Look at the **A** and **B** sentences below. Find out why **B** is correct and **A** is wrong in the **Grammar Points** section.

CHECKPOINT

			GRAMMAR POINTS
1A	Our company **donate** to charitable organisations every year.	✗	
1B	Our company **donates** to charitable organisations every year.	✓	1
2A	The waiter **taking** our orders.	✗	
2B	The waiter **is taking** our orders.	✓	2
3A	The women **wear** white uniforms are from the health department.	✗	
3B	The women **wearing** white uniforms are from the health department.	✓	3

GRAMMAR POINTS

1 We use the base form of a verb with the 's' ending for the present tense in these ways:

(a) with singular noun subjects and the pronoun subjects **he**, **she** and **it**
EXAMPLES: **He / She reaches** home later than 7 p.m. each day.
The machine / It makes a swishing sound when you press this switch.

(b) with uncountable or collective noun subjects
EXAMPLES: uncountable noun   collective noun
Water **flows** from the   The public **expects** the local council
rivers into the sea.   to use funds prudently.

REMEMBER!

■ Most base forms take 's' endings in the present tense. Those which end in 'ch', 'o', 'sh', 'ss', 'x' and 'zz' often take the 'es' ending. Those which end in 'y' often take the 'ies' ending.
EXAMPLES:

+ 's'	+ 'es'	...'y' 'i' + 'es'
quit → quit**s**	touch → touch**es**	hurry → hurr**ies**
shrink → shrink**s**	guess → guess**es**	worry → worr**ies**

■ An **uncountable noun** refers to things that cannot be counted. It always takes a singular verb form, even if it ends in 's'.
EXAMPLE: Physics **is** my weakest subject.

■ A **collective noun** refers to a group of people or things. It can take **both** a singular or plural verb. A singular verb is used to refer to the group as a unit. A plural verb is used to show that the focus is on the members that make up the group.
EXAMPLES: **The cast is** ready to perform.   (**cast** as a unit)
The cast are late for rehearsals.   (**cast** as members of the group)

6

- When the subject is a **noun phrase**, we decide whether to use a singular or a plural verb by looking at the **head word**. (A head word is usually the noun that is the most important part of a noun phrase.)

  EXAMPLE:

  noun phrase subject
  Their resistance to change **makes** it difficult to work with them.
  └── head word ──┘

2 We use the base form with the 'ing' ending together with the verb 'to be' in continuous tenses.

(a) present continuous tense : verb 'to be' (**am / is / are**) + base form with 'ing' ending

  EXAMPLE: Wendy **is distributing** the invitation cards.

(b) past continuous tense : verb 'to be' (**was / were**) + base form with 'ing' ending

  EXAMPLE: They **were arguing** just now.

(c) future continuous tense : verb 'to be' (**will be**) + base form with 'ing' ending

  EXAMPLE: Jean **will be contacting** you this evening.

3 The base form with the 'ing' ending is also called the present participle. (It is a non-finite verb.) We use it after a noun to describe or identify the noun. This type of 'ing' clause functions like a relative clause.

  EXAMPLES:

  'ing' clause
  The company **producing** teak furniture belongs to Gary's family.
  (noun) (present participle) (finite verb)

  relative clause
  The company which **is producing** teak furniture belongs to Gary's family.

  'ing' clause
  The students **waiting** at the bus stop are my classmates.
  (noun) (present participle) (finite verb)

  relative clause
  The students who **are waiting** at the bus stop are my classmates.

REMEMBER!

- Most present participles are formed by just adding 'ing' to the base form. When a base form ends in 'ie', the 'ie' is replaced by 'y' before 'ing' is added to it. Some base forms with vowel + consonant endings have their consonants doubled before 'ing' is added to them.

base form of verb + 'ing'	base form of verb ending in 'e' ('e̶' + 'ing')
EXAMPLE: explain → explain**ing**	EXAMPLE: measur**e** → measur**ing**

base form of verb ending in 'ie' ('i̶e̶'y' + 'ing')	base form of verb ending in a consonant + same consonant + 'ing'
EXAMPLE: tie → t**ying**	EXAMPLE: trave**l** → trave**lling**

PRACTICE *A* Tick the sentences that are correct.

1 Jessie realise she is late for her appointment.

2 We are willing to cooperate with you.

3 This reminds me of my trip to Florence last spring.

4 Seals those packing cases for me, please.

5 The crew has a lot of work to do each day.

6 That shop guarantee that its clothes do not shrink after a wash.

7 His vanity often irritates his friends.

8 They striving to improve their grades.

9 The boy grinning at you is Lucy's brother.

10 Helen icing the wedding cake now.

PRACTICE *B*   Underline the correct verb forms to complete the dialogue.

Receptionist :   Which type of room would you prefer, sir?

Sam   :   A room **1** (face / facing) the sea would be wonderful.

Receptionist :   **2** (Let / Lets) me see . . . We **3** (has / have) just one room left and it is one of our best. It **4** (give / gives) a breathtaking view of the sea at sunset.

Sam   :   I'll **5** (take / taking) it.

Receptionist :   All right . . . You will have Room 25. Here's your key. The porter **6** (wait / waiting) by the lift will escort you to your room, sir.

Porter   :   Here we are, sir . . . Room 25.

Sam   :   My goodness! This room **7** (smell / smells) of fish! Your receptionist said it's one of the best rooms in the hotel!

Porter   :   It is, sir, for viewing sunsets but it is also close to where our fishermen **8** (bring / brings) in their daily catch.

Sam   :   He failed **9** (tell / to tell) me that. I **10** (am leave / am leaving) this hotel at once!

PRACTICE *C*   Some of the sentences contain mistakes in verb forms. Underline the mistakes and write the correct verbs in the boxes.

1 Joan respond well to criticism.

2 That lecture on pollutants makes us want to be more careful.

3 Production have to stop because the raw materials have not arrived yet.

4 That child requires a lot of care and attention.

5 I be meeting Donna at the park at 6 p.m.

6 The Art Club holding its annual general meeting in November.

7 The journalist receiving the 'Journalist of the Year' award is Sarah Lane.

8 The despatch boy is running an errand for me now.

9 Police operate the roadblock are on the lookout for a grey sedan.

10 The consultant insists that the report will be ready by tomorrow.

PRACTICE $\boxed{D}$ Rewrite the sentences and correct them using the base form with 's' / 'ing' ending or the 'ing' clause.

1 He always bother about Kay's opinion.
He always bothers about Kay's opinion.

2 Your tiny handwriting giving me a headache.

3 The lady teach the girls to make patchwork quilts is Mrs Roberts.

4 Our college orchestra is take part in the inter-college music festival.

5 My favourite restaurant specialising in northern Indian cuisine.

6 Biology deal with the study of living things.

PRACTICE $\boxed{E}$ Underline the sentences with mistakes and rewrite them correctly using the base form of a verb, the base form with 's' / 'ing' ending or the 'ing' clause.

A four-year-old girl lies in a hospital bed with a broken arm is causing a lot of concern among the hospital staff. She speak a language no one understands. Her gestures baffles everyone. She points to her mouth so the staff offer her food and drink but she shakes her head and refuses both.

"She is try to tell us something. Unfortunately, we don't know what it is. No one knows who she is and where she is from," said Head Nurse McKinney. "She needs a lot of care and protection. Every day we get calls from reporters. The press want photograph her but I won't allow it until she gets better."

1

2

3

4

5

UNIT 1.3 VERBS

with 'ed' ending

Look at the **A** and **B** sentences below. Find out why **B** is correct and **A** is wrong in the **Grammar Points** section.

CHECKPOINT

				GRAMMAR POINTS
1A	Janet **was explain** the problem to me yesterday.	✗		
1B	Janet **explained** the problem to me yesterday.	✓		1
2A	They **have examine** the patient thoroughly.	✗		
2B	They **have examined** the patient thoroughly.	✓		2
3A	The hi-fi equipment **is loaded** into the van is for John's party.	✗		
3B	The hi-fi equipment **loaded** into the van is for John's party.	✓		3

GRAMMAR POINTS

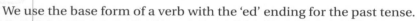

1 We use the base form of a verb with the 'ed' ending for the past tense.

EXAMPLES: Mr Thorne **coaxed** his son to share his toys with his cousin.
We **managed** to cross the swollen river after waiting for two days.
The playfulness of the students **annoyed** their teacher.
The health department **conducted** spot checks on eateries last week.

REMEMBER!

- The following are some ways of forming the past tense of regular verbs:

base form of verb + 'ed'	base form of verb ending in 'e' + 'd'
EXAMPLES: fail → fail**ed**	**EXAMPLES:** apologis**e** → apologis**ed**
inform → inform**ed**	exchang**e** → exchang**ed**

base form of verb ending in 'y' 'i' + 'ed'	base form of verb ending in a consonant + the same consonant + 'ed'
EXAMPLES: bull**y** → bull**ied**	**EXAMPLES:** pla**n** + **n** + ed → pla**nn**ed
quer**y** → quer**ied**	contro**l** + **l** + ed → contro**ll**ed

Note that the doubling of consonants does not apply to 'w', 'x' and 'y'.

- The past tense of an irregular verb does not consist of the base form of the verb with 'ed' ending.

  EXAMPLES: fe**el** → fe**lt**   g**ive** → g**ave**   go → **went**
  hurt → hurt   le**ave** → le**ft**   me**et** → met

---

2 We use the past participle in perfect tenses with the verb 'to have' and passive sentences with the verb 'to be'.

EXAMPLES: She **has solved** the problem.   (present perfect tense)
Kim and Donna **have booked** tickets for the show on ice.   (present perfect tense)
Twenty people **were injured**.   (passive sentence)
This tapestry **was woven** by my mother.   (passive sentence)

10

- The past participle is the base form of the verb with the 'ed' ending for a regular verb. It is formed in other ways for irregular verbs.

	Base form	**Past form**	**Past participle form**
Regular verbs	enter	entered	entered
	listen	listened	listened
Irregular verbs (Two forms the same)	catch	caught	caught
	sell	sold	sold
Irregular verbs (Three forms different)	sing	sang	sung
	write	wrote	written
Irregular verbs (Three forms the same)	cut	cut	cut
	hit	hit	hit

3 The past participle on its own is a non-finite verb. We use it after a noun to describe what happened to the noun. This type of 'ed' clause functions like a relative clause.

EXAMPLES:

'ed' clause

The flowers **ordered** by Mr Lee have arrived.

noun — past participle — finite verb

relative clause

The flowers which **were ordered** by Mr Lee have arrived.

'ed' clause

The document **kept** in this folder is missing.

noun — past participle — finite verb

relative clause

The document which **was kept** in this folder is missing.

- Present participles are active in meaning while past participles are passive in meaning.

EXAMPLES:

'ing' clause

The man **questioning** the security guard looks angry.   (**The man** is doing the action.)

present participle

'ed' clause

The man **questioned** by the security guard looks angry.   (**The man** is receiving the action.)

past participle

PRACTICE *A* Cross out the incorrect verb forms to complete the sentences.

1 Eric's team | challenged | was challenged | my team to a hockey match.

2 I | reprimanded | was reprimanded | by the management for poor timekeeping.

3 The shops | affected | were affected | by the power failure closed early yesterday.

4 Megan | remarked | was remarked | that no one was perfect.

5 We [have used | were used] only recycled material for our decorations.

6 Ram [approached | was approached] a policeman for directions to his hotel.

7 The oil tanker [developed | was developed] engine trouble on its way to a petrol station.

8 The shipment [has delayed | was delayed] for two days due to rough weather at sea.

9 The fashion collection [planned | has planned] for this summer uses a very light fabric.

10 The cars [involved | were involved] in the accident were towed away.

YOUR SCORE
10

PRACTICE *B* Underline the correct words in the brackets to complete the paragraph.

Last month, Dad **1** (surprised / was surprised) Mum with an unusual birthday gift—a *tandoor*, a type of clay oven used in India. The *tandoor* **2** (is shaped / shaped) like a large urn. Mum **3** (charmed / was charmed) by the gift. She **4** (hugged / was hugged) Dad again and again. He, in turn, **5** (delighted / was delighted) by her response.

Since her birthday, Mum **6** (has used / was used) the *tandoor* several times and we **7** (have enjoyed / were enjoyed) her *naan* and *tandoori* chicken tremendously. *Naan* is bread made from wheat and is usually oval in shape. It **8** (is pressed / pressed) against the inner wall of the oven and left there to bake. Chicken **9** (cooked / has cooked) in a *tandoor* is marinated first in yogurt and spices the previous day. An ingredient **10** (has also added / is also added) to the marinade to give the chicken a reddish colour.

YOUR SCORE
10

PRACTICE *C* Circle the letters of the correct sentences. There may be more than one answer for each question.

1 **A** Mr Moore addressed the large gathering at the community hall.
   B This letter addressed to you has a New Guinea postmark.
   C John was addressed the letter wrongly.

2 **A** The media raised a considerable amount of money for the boy with a kidney problem.
   B A lot of interest raised on the outcome of the boy's operation.
   C This private hospital has raised its charges for outpatient treatment.

3 **A** The diamonds have displayed in that showcase.
   B The diamonds displayed in that showcase are dazzling.
   C The diamonds displayed by Mr Hicks for the bride-to-be are dazzling.

4 **A** Our school has installed several drinking fountains along the corridors.
   B Our school installed several drinking fountains along the corridors last week.
   C Several drinking fountains installed along the corridors of our school last week.

5 **A** The chairman was promoted her to the post of financial adviser.
   B She was promoted to the post of financial adviser by the chairman.
   C The officer promoted to the post of financial adviser is Jean.

YOUR SCORE
10

12

Underline the mistakes in verb forms in the sentences. Write the correct verbs in the boxes.

line 1	
2	*enjoyed*
3	
4	
line 5	
6	
7	
8	
9	
line 10	
11	

I shopped for groceries online for the first time yesterday and enjoy it tremendously. The procedure was very simple. I just needed to register with the website. Then I was invited to browse through the list of items displaying on the screen. I was instructed to click on the food items I wanted to order and to state their quantity. I chose 'seafood' and immediately all types of seafood was appeared on the screen. The prices were state under the items. After I had finished my shopping, the price totalled for me. Then the website 'grocer' informed me that a delivery van would sent me my groceries the next day. I had really done my shopping without leaving home!

YOUR SCORE
10

PRACTICE `E` Fill in the blanks with the correct words in the box.

attracted	— was attracted		award	— were awarded
choose	— to choose		divided	— were divided
emerged	— was emerged		impressed	— were impressed
organised	— was organised		read	— to read
score	— scoring		selected	— selecting
walked	— walking			

Leela Menon, a dentist, and Mel Gates, a teacher, (1) _____*emerged*_____ the winners of the 'Read and Tell' contest (2) _____ by Reeds Book Centre. They each (3) _____ away with a voucher for $2000 to spend at the store.

The contest (4) _____ a total of 150 participants. They were required to select a book each from a range of newly-printed titles, scan it and make notes in half an hour. After that they (5) _____ into groups of 10. Each person in a group had to summarise the contents of the book (6) _____ and give his opinion of it. The group then awarded him a score ranging from 1–10. The person (7) _____ the most points moved on to the next round.

For the second round, 15 participants read a second title each. Then they broke up into groups of three (8) _____ the finalists. The final round saw five participants.

Each finalist had (9) _____ a third title each. Then they presented their speeches before seven judges. Leela Menon and Mel Gates (10) _____ the judges with their reading speed, clarity of thought, excellent summarising skills and humour. Both (11) _____ a perfect 10.

YOUR SCORE
10

UNIT 2.1 SUBJECT-VERB AGREEMENT

either . . . or, neither . . . nor, as well as, together with

Look at the **A** and **B** sentences below. Find out why **B** is correct and **A** is wrong in the **Grammar Points** section.

GRAMMAR POINTS

1A	Either Jane or her sisters **has** to buy the drinks for the party.	✗	
1B	Either Jane or her sisters **have** to buy the drinks for the party.	✓	1
2A	Neither report on the causes of the plane crash **were** accurate.	✗	
2B	Neither report on the causes of the plane crash **was** accurate.	✓	2
3A	The prime minister, as well as the members of his cabinet, **are visiting** the new airport.	✗	
3B	The prime minister, as well as the members of his cabinet, **is visiting** the new airport.	✓	3

1 When two subjects are joined by the words **either . . . or**, we use a singular verb when both subjects are singular, and a plural verb when both subjects are plural. If one subject is singular and the other is plural, the verb agrees with the subject that is closer to it.

EXAMPLES:

Either Nancy or Jill **is going** to manage the sales department.
(singular subject) (singular subject) (singular verb)

Either the supervisors or the workers **have gone** to see the manager.
(plural subject) (plural subject) (plural verb)

Either Kevin or his cousins **are** responsible for the mess in the room.
(singular subject) (plural subject) (plural verb)

2 When two subjects are joined by the words **neither . . . nor**, we use a singular verb when both subjects are singular, and a plural verb when both subjects are plural. If one subject is singular and the other is plural, the verb agrees with the subject that is closer to it.

EXAMPLES:

Neither Mr Sims nor his wife **likes** their new neighbours.
(singular subject) (singular subject) (singular verb)

14

<u>plural subject</u>   <u>plural subject</u>
Neither the seniors nor the freshmen **want** to take part in the race.
                                      ⌐plural verb⌐

<u>plural subject</u>   <u>singular subject</u>
Neither my aunts nor my mother **enjoys** seafood.
                               ⌐singular verb⌐

We can use **neither** with a singular noun subject and a singular verb to make a negative statement about two people or things.

EXAMPLE: singular
                   subject
Neither book by that author **is** on the bestseller list.
                            ⌐singular verb⌐

REMEMBER!

■ **Neither ... of** can be used with a plural pronoun or a plural noun group beginning with **the**, **these** or **those**. A singular verb must be used.

EXAMPLES: plural
                    pronoun   plural noun
Neither of them **enjoys** cricket.   Neither of those dresses **fits** me.
               ⌐singular verb⌐   ⌐singular verb⌐

---

3 When a singular subject is followed by an additional phrase beginning with words like **as well as**, **together with**, **besides**, or **along with**, we use a singular verb.

EXAMPLE: singular
                   subject
The director, along with several important officials, **was** present at the function.
                                                      ⌐singular verb⌐

PRACTICE *A* Fill in the blanks with the correct words in the boxes.

1 Either Ben or his friends _____ to the rugby finals tonight.

| are coming |
| is coming |

2 Neither the umpire nor the players _____ this pitch well.

| know |
| knows |

3 Neither of _____ is fit enough for the job.

| the man |
| the men |

4 Neither the crew nor the passengers _____ aware of the terrorists aboard the plane.

| was |
| were |

5 Neither of the _____ has been approved by our housing estate association.

| project |
| projects |

6 Our neighbour, as well as her children, _____ outside our gate.

| is standing |
| are standing |

7 Either the elephants or their trainer _____ to blame for the mishap.

| is |
| are |

15

8 Neither Mark nor his _____ is sure this is the right way.

brother
brothers

9 Either the scouts or their leader _____ a compass, so they will find the camp.

carry
carries

10 The mechanic, together with his assistants, _____

_____ my car.

is repairing
are repairing

YOUR SCORE
10

PRACTICE B Some of the underlined nouns or verb forms are incorrect. Write the correct words in the boxes provided.

1 Neither of the <u>box</u> of chocolates is suitable as a gift.

2 Neither Sally nor her friends <u>admits</u> that they are in the wrong.

3 The producer, along with the entire cast of actors, <u>have visited</u> the historic village.

4 Either the executive manager or his deputy <u>is going</u> to address the assembly.

5 Neither Selena nor her brother <u>likes</u> to be involved in club activities.

6 The surgeon, together with his medical team, <u>has begun</u> the operation.

7 Neither of those dresses <u>are</u> appropriate for evening wear.

8 Neither of these <u>pies</u> was prepared by my mother.

9 My aunt, as well as my cousins, <u>are planning</u> a trip to New Zealand.

10 Neither Peter nor <u>his sister</u> agrees with your suggestions.

YOUR SCORE
10

PRACTICE C Fill in the blanks to complete the dialogue.

Dad : Lyn, I can't find my fishing equipment. I think that (1) _____ you

(2) _____ your mum has taken it.

Lyn : Dad, we couldn't have taken your fishing equipment. (3) _____ Mum nor

(4) _____ like fishing.

Dad : I need to find it quickly. Are you sure you haven't seen it somewhere?

Mum : Yes, dear. (5) _____ of us (6) _____ seen it.

Dad : (7) _____ Uncle Paul (8) _____ John and Bill like to be kept waiting. I don't want to make them wait.

Mum : Hold on a second. I remember seeing something when I was spring-cleaning. Either the fishing rod or the tackle (9) _____ in the garage.

Dad : I hope you're right, dear. Uncle Paul, as well as my cousins, (10) _____ planned this trip for months. I can't disappoint them.

YOUR SCORE
10

16

PRACTICE *D*   Rearrange the words to form correct sentences. Add commas where necessary.

1 are — band — brothers — his — Kenny — neither — nor — of — part — the.

Neither _____

_____ band.

2 award — best — for — neither — of — performance — entered — the — them —has.

Neither _____

_____ award.

3 arrival — as — as — greeted — on — musicians — singer — the — the — warmly
   — was — well.

The _____

_____ arrival.

4 artist — by — commended — neither — painting — that — was.

Neither _____

_____ commended.

5 a — after — baby — how — knows — look — neither — of — them — to.

Neither _____

_____ baby.

YOUR SCORE
10

PRACTICE *E*   Rewrite the sentences and correct them.

1 Neither of these ties match my blue shirt.

_____

_____

2 Neither Grace nor her brothers intends to study overseas.

_____

_____

3 Either this houses at the junction or the one next to it belongs to my manager.

_____

_____

4 Neither articles on the efforts to protect wildlife gives a true picture.

_____

_____

5 The senior form teacher, along with her students, have painted a mural in the school
   canteen.

_____

_____

YOUR SCORE
10

17

UNIT 2.2 SUBJECT-VERB AGREEMENT

a lot of, any, every, none of, indefinite pronouns

Look at the **A** and **B** sentences below. Find out why **B** is correct and **A** is wrong in the **Grammar Points** section.

			GRAMMAR POINTS
1A	A lot of sawn timber **were piled** outside the paper mill.	✗	
1B	A lot of sawn timber **was piled** outside the paper mill.	✓	1
2A	Any of us **are** capable of organising the annual dinner.	✗	
2B	Any of us **is** capable of organising the annual dinner.	✓	2
3A	Nothing exciting ever **happen** in these isolated fishing villages.	✗	
3B	Nothing exciting ever **happens** in these isolated fishing villages.	✓	3
4A	None of the mail today **were** for us.	✗	
4B	None of the mail today **was** for us.	✓	4

GRAMMAR POINTS

1 When we use the words **a lot of** before an uncountable noun, we use a singular verb. When we use **a lot of** before a plural noun or pronoun, we use a plural verb.

EXAMPLES:

A lot of crude oil [uncountable noun] **has** already **seeped** [singular verb] into the sea due to the collision.

A lot of people [plural noun] **believe** [plural verb] that customs must change with time.

A lot of us [plural pronoun] **want** [plural verb] to do computer courses.

2 We use **any** and **every** before a singular noun, and **any of** before a plural noun or pronoun. All of them take singular verbs.

EXAMPLES:

Is [singular verb] any person [singular noun] here interested in joining our team?

Every item [singular noun] I bought **was marked** [singular verb] down in price.

18

plural
pronoun
Any of them **is** eligible for the post of secretary.

singular verb

3 We use singular verbs with indefinite pronouns.
EXAMPLES: indefinite pronoun
Somebody **has taken** my calculator.

indefinite   singular verb
pronoun
Everything **was laid** out elegantly on the table.

singular verb

4 When we use **none of** with an uncountable noun, we use a singular verb. When we place **none of** before a plural noun, we can use a singular or a plural verb.
EXAMPLES: uncountable noun
None of the furniture here **matches** my curtains.

singular verb

plural noun
None of the women **approve** / **approves** of the new fashions displayed.

plural verb   singular verb

PRACTICE *A* Fill in the blanks with the correct words in the boxes.

1 Something _____ to be wrong with our phone. There's no dialling tone.

appear	appears

2 Any of these fabrics _____ suitable for my evening gown.

are	is

3 Every candidate _____ to read the instructions carefully.

has	have

4 Anything toxic _____ the delicate balance of nature in the ocean.

affect	affects

5 A lot of music and singing _____ at our sister's wedding reception.

was heard	were heard

6 Somebody in this class _____ playing tricks on me.

enjoy	enjoys

7 None of the fish we bought _____ fresh.

was	were

8 Everyone here _____ that the weather today is going to be fine.

say	says

9 A lot of fresh lemonade _____ to quench the thirst of the runners.

was made	were made

10 Any of our students _____ able to do it for you.

are	is

YOUR SCORE
10

PRACTICE *B*   Cross out the incorrect words in the boxes to complete the sentences.

1 | None | No one | knows where Tom's car keys are.

2 | Someone | Anyone | is in the kitchen looking for food.

3 | Anything | Something | has happened on the highway to cause this massive traffic jam.

4 | Everyone | None of | the ladies have a key to the locker room.

5 | A lot of | Every | guest at the opening of the gallery was presented with a rose.

6 | Any | None of | the carpets at the auction are worth the prices quoted.

7 | Anything | Everything | has been sold out. There is no food left.

8 | A lot of | Any of | the money to be spent on subsidised housing has been misused.

9 | Any of | Every | these meals is all right for diabetic patients.

10 | All | Every | children taking part in the dances have to be in the stadium by 8 a.m.

YOUR SCORE

10

PRACTICE *C*   Some of the sentences contain mistakes in verb forms. Underline the mistakes and write the correct words in the boxes.

1   Any of us is likely to be chosen.

2   Something was moving silently in the bushes near the wall.

3   A lot of news have been heard about a possible global recession.

4   Any of our club members are able to cope with an emergency.

5   Every motorist has to obey the road safety regulations.

6   Everything was quiet when we arrived home late at night.

7   Nobody want to talk about the problem we had yesterday.

8   Someone was waiting for Mr Sharpe as he walked into the office.

9   None of the cattle were harmed when the barn caught fire last week.

10   Any increase in the prices of goods during the festive season are noted by the consumers' association.

YOUR SCORE

10

PRACTICE $\boxed{D}$ Underline the sentences that are incorrect and rewrite them correctly.

All the students were surprised at the announcement. Every class were asked to be present at a special assembly in the hall. Everybody were curious. A lot of rumours was circulating as everyone filed into the hall. Some even said that the principal was going to leave.

Any of the notions we had were quickly changed when the principal spoke. He wanted everyone to hear the good news. Our school, he said, had been selected by the Board of Education as the model school of the year. The teachers, as well as the students, was delighted. Everybody agreed that it was a very pleasant surprise.

1 _____

2 _____

3 _____

4 _____

5 _____

YOUR SCORE
10

PRACTICE $\boxed{E}$ Rewrite the sentences and correct them.

1 Everything about the operation of this company are being investigated.

_____

_____

2 A lot of the hi-tech equipment at the sports complex have not been fully utilised.

_____

_____

3 Every member of the hotel staff are instructed to give the best service possible to the guests.

_____

_____

4 Nothing concrete are being done to meet the needs of poor families.

_____

_____

5 Any of the women here are able to weave carpets.

_____

_____

YOUR SCORE
10

21

UNIT 2.3 SUBJECT-VERB AGREEMENT

all / all of, some / some of, each / each of, one / one of

Look at the **A** and **B** sentences below. Find out why **B** is correct and **A** is wrong in the **Grammar Points** section.

GRAMMAR
POINTS

1A	All the mud from the hillside **have swept** into the houses nearby.	✗	
1B	All the mud from the hillside **has swept** into the houses nearby.	✓	1
2A	Some of the things we bought at the sale **was** quite expensive.	✗	
2B	Some of the things we bought at the sale **were** quite expensive.	✓	2
3A	Each of the **horse** was taken to the paddock for the night.	✗	
3B	Each of the **horses** was taken to the paddock for the night.	✓	3

GRAMMAR POINTS

1 When we use **all** or **all of** before an uncountable noun, we use a singular verb.
When we use **all** or **all of** before a plural noun or pronoun, we use a plural verb.

EXAMPLES:
     uncountable noun
  All of the equipment in this studio **was bought** recently.
              (singular verb)

     plural noun
  All the speakers at the rally **were asked** to wear name tags.
          (plural verb)

2 When we use **some** or **some of** before an uncountable noun, we use a singular verb.
When we use **some** or **some of** before a plural noun or pronoun, we use a plural verb.

EXAMPLES:
     uncountable
      noun
  Some ice cream **is** still left in the bowl.
     (singular verb)

     plural
     pronoun
  Some of them **have explained** their problems to the director.
     (plural verb)

3 We use **each** or **one** before a singular noun, and **each of** or **one of** before a plural noun. All of them take singular verbs.

EXAMPLES:

Each | parent | has to take charge of his or her own child at the stadium.

singular noun

singular verb

One | person | was given a sum of money to be shared with the other members

singular subject

singular verb

of the group.

Each of | the new doctors | is assigned to a specific unit of the hospital.

plural noun

singular verb

One of | us | is sure to win the contest.

plural pronoun

singular verb

REMEMBER!

- **All** is used when we refer to people or things as a whole or in general.
  EXAMPLE: **All** security officers were placed on alert due to the bomb scare.

- **All of** is used to refer to a particular group of people or things.
  EXAMPLES: **All of us** are interested in joining the advanced cooking class.
  All of the flowers grown in this area are for export.

- **Some** or **some of** is generally used in positive sentences to refer to an indefinite number or amount.
  EXAMPLES: **Some girls** were reading in the library.
  Some of them want to leave the meeting early.

PRACTICE *A* Tick the correct sentences.

1 Some of the wet paint have stuck to my trousers.

2 All of us welcome Jane's ideas for the party.

3 Some of the food served today is very spicy.

4 One of my earrings are missing. Have you seen it anywhere?

5 Each of these novels contains true accounts of the war.

6 All the people in the audience were captivated by the children's performance.

7 Some of the orange juice have spilt onto the tablecloth.

8 Each orchid plant in the nursery is carefully tended.

9 One candidate have been selected to represent the team.

10 All the figures on the rate of accidents is accurate.

YOUR SCORE

10

Fill in the blanks with the correct form of the verbs in the brackets.

1 Some yeast _____ (be) added to the pancake batter to give it a smooth texture.

2 All the furniture in the kindergarten classes _____ (have) been brightly painted.

3 Some of the vegetation in this highland resort _____ (look) similar to the trees and shrubs in the valley.

4 Each official on duty at the games _____ (have) to wear a badge on his or her coat.

5 One of my office colleagues _____ (give) me a lift to work every day.

6 All the cotton grown locally _____ (be) exported overseas.

7 Each of us _____ (realise) the importance of getting a good education.

8 Some tomato soup _____ (be) still simmering on the stove. Help yourself if you're hungry.

9 Each of the dancers _____ (have) been given a bouquet of flowers.

10 One student from the senior class _____ (be) eligible for the scholarship.

YOUR SCORE 10

PRACTICE **C** Some of the sentences contain mistakes in the use of nouns or verbs. Underline the mistakes and write the correct words in the boxes.

1 Some extra seasoning was added to the chicken to improve its taste.

2 We all have to work very hard to increase the sale of our products.

3 One of the committee member has written a letter to the mayor.

4 Each hand-woven silk bedspread was displayed on the table.

5 Some of the construction works done in this house appears to be below standard.

6 All the traffics on the highway was diverted because of the massive accident.

7 Some of them believes that 13 is an unlucky number.

8 One of the zebra was fatally wounded by the hunter.

9 Each reporter was allotted five minutes to question the prime minister.

10 All the customs of these tribes have been practised for centuries.

YOUR SCORE 10

PRACTICE *D*   Underline the sentences that are incorrect and rewrite them correctly.

When the train reached the border, all the passengers were asked to disembark. Each of them were told to carry their bags to the customs checkpoint. Some of the women with young children was struggling to cope with their luggage. One of the officials noticed this and was kind enough to call his men to come to their help.

All of them were then directed to the immigration counter to have their passports checked. Some of the officers was ill-mannered and unfriendly. Each passenger were given careful scrutiny before his or her passport was cleared.

After two hours, the exhausted traveller were told to return to the train to continue their journey.

1 _____
   _____
2 _____
   _____
3 _____
   _____
4 _____
   _____
5 _____
   _____

YOUR SCORE
10

PRACTICE *E*   Rearrange the words to form correct sentences.

1 all — inherited — is — mortgaged — property — she — the.
   All _____
   _____ mortgaged.
2 is — blame — for — keys — misplacing — of — office — one — the — the — to — to — us.
   One _____
   _____ office.
3 downstream — each — is — logs — mill — of — sent — the — the — to.
   Each _____
   _____ mill.
4 choir — has — in — Lyn's — of — one — place — take — the — to — you.
   One _____
   _____ choir.
5 all — are — art — in — museum — works — priceless — of — the — this.
   All _____
   _____

YOUR SCORE
10

25

UNIT 2.4 SUBJECT-VERB AGREEMENT

abstract nouns, **there** + verb 'to be'

Look at the **A** and **B** sentences below. Find out why **B** is correct and **A** is wrong in the **Grammar Points** section.

			GRAMMAR POINTS
1A	The model's beauty **are** much admired in the fashion world.	✗	
1B	The model's beauty **is** much admired in the fashion world.	✓	1
2A	**Many** laughter helps to keep a person young.	✗	
2B	**Plenty of** laughter helps to keep a person young.	✓	2
3A	There **have been** severe famine in parts of Africa for a long time.	✗	
3B	There **has been** severe famine in parts of Africa for a long time.	✓	3

GRAMMAR POINTS

1 We use singular verbs with abstract nouns. (An abstract noun refers to a feeling, an idea or a quality. It may be something that cannot be seen or touched.)

EXAMPLES:
singular subject
Stress often **leads** to different kinds of illnesses.
(singular verb)

singular subject
His compassion **makes** him much loved by his people.
(singular verb)

2 Abstract nouns can be subjects by themselves, or they can come after words like **a lot of**, **a great deal of**, **plenty of**, and determiners like **much** or **little**.

EXAMPLES:
subject
A lot of excitement **is** in the air, as the children are going on an outing.
(singular verb)

subject
Much progress **was made** in the recent talks between the two countries.
(singular verb)

3 We can use the words **there** + the verb 'to be' when we want to state that something exists, or if we mention something for the first time.

When we begin a sentence with **there** + the verb 'to be', the subject comes after it. We use a singular verb if the subject is singular or uncountable, and a plural verb if the subject is plural.

EXAMPLES:

singular subject

There **is** a new book shop around the corner.

singular verb

singular subject

There **was** peace after the two sides agreed to a ceasefire.

singular verb

plural subject

There **are** several people waiting for the store to open.

plural verb

REMEMBER!

- The word **there** can be used with the verbs 'to have' and 'to be', and modals like **can be**, **may be**, and **should be**.

EXAMPLES: **There is** someone to see you.

There has been a lot of trouble in the country recently.

PRACTICE *A* Tick the correct sentences.

1 Patience is a useful virtue for everyone.

2 Mark's self-confidence have won him a promotion in his job.

3 The child's knowledge of the computer surprise all of us.

4 The darkness in the tunnel was frightening.

5 A lot of research have been done to find a cure for cancer.

6 Honesty is important in personal relationships.

7 Fear have prevented many oppressed people from seeking their freedom.

8 Little attention was paid to the children begging by the roadside.

9 Lucy's commitment to her job was observed by the management.

10 Her loyalty to her friends are very likeable.

YOUR SCORE

10

PRACTICE *B* Cross out the incorrect words in the boxes.

1 There | are | is | a lot of snow and ice on the mountaintop.

2 Information on the submarine disaster | hasn't been | haven't been | released to the press.

3 The young boy's intelligence | has enabled | have enabled | him to win an award.

4 Kate's generosity | has touched | have touched | the hearts of many people.

5 The despair of the stranded skiers | was changed | were changed | to joy when they saw the rescue team.

6 There | was | were | a great deal of happiness among the townsfolk when the enemy retreated.

7 A roar of applause | was heard | were heard | as the president and his wife entered the hall.

8 There | are | is | plenty of bread left. You don't have to buy any.

9 The courage of the battalion | has been praised | have been praised | by the general.

10 The fragrance of the flowers | captivate | captivates | all who pass by the nursery.

Fill in the blanks with suitable words in the box.

education	help	justice	skill	the suffering
there are	there is	there was	there were	violence

1 Her _____ at flower arrangement has won her many prizes.

2 _____ was sent immediately to the earthquake victims.

3 _____ silence in the reception hall when the distinguished guests arrived.

4 _____ plenty of hot water, so you can have a shower before dinner.

5 _____ demands that every individual gets a fair trial.

6 _____ many complaints regarding the poor service at the bank these days.

7 _____ of the orphans in the war-torn countries has evoked much sympathy.

8 _____ large crowds of excited onlookers at the parade yesterday.

9 _____ is a common theme in television programmes nowadays.

10 _____ plays an important role in moulding an individual's character.

Some of the sentences contain mistakes. Underline the mistakes and write the correct words in the boxes.

1 Relaxation helps to prevent stress-related illnesses.

2 Public anger against the vandals have increased in the past few days.

3 There were a lot of fun and laughter at the friendly hockey match.

4 Destruction of the forests have led to the extinction of certain animals.

5 Ben's strange behaviour makes us wary of him.

6 Poverty often result in malnutrition in young
   children.

7 There was a huge storm just now which damaged
   all the power lines in our area.

8 The hospitality shown by the villagers is typical of
   their culture.

9 There is few places of entertainment in these
   isolated towns.

10 Tom's sense of humour keeps us laughing all the
    time.

YOUR SCORE
10

PRACTICE E Rewrite the sentences and correct them.

1 Fog envelop the entire coast during the winter months.

2 There were great commotion in the departure terminal because of the flight delays.

3 The danger of a volcanic eruption have forced thousands to flee from their homes.

4 There were a variety of food and games at the charity carnival.

5 Depression affect many people who are lonely.

YOUR SCORE
10

29

UNIT 3.1 SIMPLE PRESENT AND PRESENT CONTINUOUS TENSES

Look at the **A** and **B** sentences below. Find out why **B** is correct and **A** is wrong in the **Grammar Points** section.

GRAMMAR POINTS

			GRAMMAR POINTS
1A	Nelly **is managing** a boutique in the city. She has been doing this for more than five years.	✗	
1B	Nelly **manages** a boutique in the city. She has been doing this for more than five years.	✓	1
2A	We **are living** in an apartment overlooking the park. We have lived there ever since the children were born.	✗	
2B	We **live** in an apartment overlooking the park. We have lived there ever since the children were born.	✓	2
3A	Mike **rents** Alice's beach cottage for the whole of next week.	✗	
3B	Mike **is renting** Alice's beach cottage for the whole of next week.	✓	3
4A	I **am promising** that I'll do my best in the science quiz. I won't let you down.	✗	
4B	I **promise** that I'll do my best in the science quiz. I won't let you down.	✓	4

1

Simple present tense	Present continuous tense
We can use this to refer to regular actions (habits), current situations or facts in general.	We can use this to refer to new habits (or repeated actions) which happen around the time of speaking or writing.
EXAMPLE: Poisonous gases **destroy** the ozone layer which protects the earth.	EXAMPLE: She **is skipping** every day to improve her stamina.

2

Simple present tense	Present continuous tense
We can use this to refer to more long-lasting or permanent situations.	We can use this to refer to situations which are temporary (lasting for a short time around the present).
EXAMPLE: Mark's ranch **stands** on twenty acres of rolling hills and plains.	EXAMPLE: I **am using** my brother's car until mine is repaired.

Simple present tense	Present continuous tense
We can use this to refer to actions which are going to happen very soon, or future actions which happen regularly according to a timetable or schedule.	We can use this to refer to planned future actions.
EXAMPLE: Hurry up! The tour bus **leaves** in five minutes.	**EXAMPLE:** We **are joining** Joe's team on their field trip next week.

4

Simple present tense	Present continuous tense
We can use this to refer to short actions happening at the time of speaking. We also use this in reviews of plays, films or books, and sports commentaries.	We can use this to refer to actions (especially longer actions) happening at the time of speaking or writing.
EXAMPLE: I **admit** that what I said earlier was inappropriate.	**EXAMPLE:** We **are grilling** sausages for breakfast now.

REMEMBER!

- These are some verbs used in the simple present tense to refer to short actions at the time of speaking:

accept	accuse	advise	agree	apologise	baptise	challenge	congratulate
forgive	nominate	object	order	promise	suggest	swear	wish

- The following verbs are not usually used in the present continuous tense:

feel	hear	see	smell

PRACTICE $\boxed{A}$ Circle the numbers of the sentences that are correct.

1 The Louvre in Paris contains some of the world's masterpieces of art and sculpture.

2 The defence witness is swearing that the accused was not there at the time the crime took place.

3 The whole neighbourhood carries out a clean-up campaign this Sunday.

4 We are staying up late tonight to watch the live telecast of the U.S. Open Golf tournament.

5 I tell you not to go into that section of the city because it is highly dangerous.

6 Ravi is using our gardening shears because he has lost his pair.

7 Ally works as a legal assistant in her uncle's firm. She joined the firm three years ago.

8 They are agreeing with our proposal that medical consultants should lower their fees.

9 We are electing a new parliamentary representative next month.

10 Eleven-year-old Jason Smith show great promise as an actor in his second film.

YOUR SCORE

10

PRACTICE *B*　Fill in the blanks with the simple present or present continuous tense form of the verbs in the brackets.

1　The workers _____ (demand) that the company provides compensation for making them redundant.

2　I _____ (look) for new lodgings as I have to move out of my flat in two weeks' time.

3　All motorists _____ (have) to pay the penalty for breaking regulations.

4　Julia _____ (work) as a fitness instructor in a sports club and enjoys it.

5　The book 'The Village by the Sea' _____ (describe) the physical and emotional struggle of surviving in a huge city.

6　Alan _____ (doubt) that the news he heard is accurate. There is nothing so far to confirm it.

7　The students' union _____ (hold) a meeting with the university council next Monday to discuss the issue of rising fees.

8　A variety of interesting creatures _____ (live) in the dry Australian outback.

9　In the financial world, a fall in the value of the Japanese Yen _____ (affect) all the other Asian currencies.

10　The townspeople _____ (lay) sandbags all along the river bank to stop the rising water from flooding their shops and homes.

YOUR SCORE
10

PRACTICE *C*　Underline the correct verbs to complete the dialogue.

Noel :　We **1** (are leaving / leaving) in 20 minutes. The taxi **2** (comes / is coming) to pick us up. Is everything packed and ready?

Joy　:　Yes, it is, but the children **3** (are still dressing / dress) in their rooms.

Noel :　Poor things! Since they usually **4** (are waking up / wake up) at 6.30, five o'clock in the morning **5** (is / are) an unearthly hour for them to be up!

Joy　:　I **6** (am feeling / feel) the same way they do. I had to drag myself out of bed.

Noel :　Our flight to Osaka **7** (is taking off / takes off) at 8 a.m. We **8** (have/ has) to be at the airport by 6 a.m. We really don't have much choice about the matter.

Joy　:　I **9** (am not grumbling / don't grumble), dear. I just **10** (am wishing / wish) international flights left a little later. That would give us more time to be fully awake!

YOUR SCORE
10

32

Some of the verb forms below are incorrect. Underline them and write the correct verbs in the boxes.

1 Melanie is helping out at a local grocery store until she leaves the town in September.

2 Grace objects to our choice of Mathew Gill as the new chairman.

3 The shareholders of the company are demand that the directors resign.

4 Sally's five-year term of office is coming to an end next month.

5 The auditors examine the school's accounts to find out the cause of the shortage of funds.

6 We are trying to contact him but there is no response from his handphone.

7 The main character in the novel strikes the reader as being witty and intelligent.

8 You have kept me waiting for more than an hour but I am forgiving you.

9 The lady across the street signalling to us. I think she wants to speak to us.

10 Zoologists are describing the black mamba as being one of the most dangerous of venomous snakes.

YOUR SCORE
10

PRACTICE $\boxed{E}$ Complete the passage with the correct form of the verbs in the box. Each word may only be used once.

bring	exist	help	introduce	manage
open	paint	show	toil	use

The story (1) _____ us to a world of poverty and despair. The two older children (2) _____ their wits to earn sufficient money to buy food. Cal, the boy, (3) _____ in the fields and (4) _____ unload the cargo from the fishing boats. He (5) _____ back a bundle of rice and scraps of fish for the family. His sister (6) _____ to cook a simple meal for their sickly mother and the younger ones.

In the book, we learn also about the other world, that of well-to-do families. They (7) _____ a total lack of concern for the misery around them. The author (8) _____ an authentic picture of the class differences which (9) _____ today and (10) _____ our eyes to the reality of life in many countries.

YOUR SCORE
10

UNIT 3.2 SIMPLE PAST TENSE

Look at the **A** and **B** sentences below. Find out why **B** is correct and **A** is wrong in the **Grammar Points** section.

GRAMMAR POINTS

1A	Once, these war-torn regions **enjoy** peace and stability.	✗	
1B	Once, these war-torn regions **enjoyed** peace and stability.	✓	1
2A	During my younger days, I **have dreamt** of being a pilot and doing daring things.	✗	
2B	During my younger days, I **dreamt** of being a pilot and doing daring things.	✓	2
3A	The mayor says that four decades ago, this busy metropolis **is** only a quiet inconspicuous town.	✗	
3B	The mayor says that four decades ago, this busy metropolis **was** only a quiet inconspicuous town.	✓	3

GRAMMAR POINTS

1 We use the simple past tense for an action or an event that occurred at a definite time in the past and is over at the time of speaking. To indicate the past, we use adverbs or phrases of time such as the following:

a long time ago	at one time	earlier
in those days	just now	later
last night	once	yesterday

EXAMPLE: In those days, before the motorcar was invented, people **travelled** from one place to another on horses, camels or donkeys.

2 We use the simple past tense to refer to an action which took place over a period of time in the past but is over, or which took place regularly and repeatedly in the past but does not happen anymore.

EXAMPLES: Throughout my university years, I **shared** a flat with five other students. *(past action lasting for a period of time)*

During the 1960s, my father **drove** to work daily in a rickety old Morris Oxford. *(repeated action in the past)*

3 We use the simple past tense when reporting certain past events or situations in newspapers, magazines or journals.

EXAMPLE: Two days ago, a fire **broke** out in a tyre shop. The fire **spread** swiftly and it was a matter of minutes before it **destroyed** all the other shops in the row.

PRACTICE *A*   Circle the numbers of the sentences that are correct.

1   Last night, we sat at the bus stop for more than an hour, waiting for the last bus home.

2   During the economic recession three years ago, thousands of people lose their jobs.

3   Josie used to eat Indian food when she was in college, but now she prefers Western cuisine.

4   When we were little, we love to sit by the railway tracks and watch the trains go by.

5   On Monday last week, the seniors began their higher school certificate exams.

6   The judge criticise the defence lawyers for wasting the court's time.

7   The cabinet approved a new pay scheme for the civil servants a fortnight ago.

8   At one time, the Roman empire stretch across Western and Eastern Europe.

9   Aaron used to flying into a rage when he didn't get his own way.

10   We almost froze because of the bitter cold last winter.

YOUR SCORE
10

PRACTICE *B*   Underline the correct verb forms in the brackets.

1   During my early years at school, I often (am getting / got) into trouble with my teachers.

2   Bernard (always finds / is always finding) fault with my work these days, although I have tried to do my best.

3   The models (are holding / held) their poses until the picture was taken.

4   The shepherd (guided / guides) the flock along the dangerous cliffs until they reach safe pastures.

5   Don't interrupt him now. He (is memorising / memorised) his lines for the play.

6   Tom and I (are frequently studying / frequently studied) together when we were at medical school.

7   John (use to practise / used to practise) playing on his bagpipes at night and irritated the rest of the boys in the dormitory.

8   At one time, the Miller family (almost frittered away / almost fritter away) their fortune, but fortunately their son saved the day.

9   This radio talk show (deals with / dealt with) teenage problems and is on the air every Tuesday at 6 p.m.

YOUR SCORE
10

10   Last summer, outdoor activities (keep / kept) our children busy all day.

PRACTICE *C*   Fill in the blanks with the simple present or past tense form of the verbs in the box.

| be | fascinate | fight | hire | intend |
| give | occupy | swing | take | work |

1   When I was a child, the lights of the carnival and the excitement of the ferris-wheel

_____ me.

2   The doors _____ open suddenly and three armed intruders ran into the crowded ballroom.

35

3 During the French Revolution, the people _____ for equality, justice and liberty.

4 Once, this sea of concrete, glass and steel buildings _____ a serene park full of brightly-coloured flowers.

5 When my father started his bakery years ago, we children _____ him all the help we could.

6 We _____ a car to drive from the west coast of Ireland to the green hills and plains of the scenic east coast.

7 Global News Network television now _____ you to the international airport where dignitaries await the arrival of the King and Queen of Thailand.

8 Celia _____ hard these days as she hopes to be promoted to the post of junior executive.

9 Nowadays, my mother's great interest in painting _____ her completely every afternoon.

10 The central bank _____ to lower interest rates next month to enable middle-income groups to obtain housing loans.

YOUR SCORE
10

PRACTICE _D_   Circle the correct words in the boxes to complete the sentences.

1 In those days, women _____ to play tennis rather than cricket.

| prefer | preferred |

2 For months the villagers _____ that some compensation would be given to them for the loss of their rice crops.

| have hope | hoped |

3 When we were growing up, our family _____ us the importance of good manners and integrity.

| taught | was teaching |

4 Joan _____ practising the piano every Saturday afternoon when she was in boarding school.

| disliked | dislikes |

5 Alexandria _____ an important position in ancient Egypt both as a port and centre of trade.

| occupy | occupied |

6 The climb up the sheer mountain cliff usually _____ four days but we did it in three.

| takes | took |

7 In the 1930s, people _____ it very difficult to get jobs because companies were closing down.

| were finding | found |

8 Lewis _____ the Olympic record when he ran the men's 200 metres race in under four minutes.

| broke | has broken |

9 Rita almost _____ over a chair just now when she was rushing out of the office.

| fell | was falling |

10 My friends _____ me daily about my accent.

| tease | were teasing |

YOUR SCORE
10

Rewrite the passage in the simple past tense.

Photography takes up much of Nick's time and energy. He derives a great deal of pleasure and satisfaction from capturing on camera the antics of animals in the wild. His pictures win him awards for his authentic presentation and originality.

Nick has inherited the talent from his father Martin Ross, a brilliant photojournalist. He hopes one day to produce documentaries both for the movie screen and for television.

_____

_____

_____

_____

_____

_____

_____

_____

YOUR SCORE
10

PRACTICE *F* Some of the sentences below are incorrect. Rewrite them correctly.

1 In those years when my father was in the foreign service, we are always moving from place to place and seldom had a chance to make good friends.

_____

_____

2 When Claire was about seven, her ambition is to be a doctor one day.

_____

_____

3 Kate's fears increase when she decided that the men on motorbikes were following her.

_____

_____

4 Last Friday, police recovered a cache of weapons and several rounds of ammunition from an assembly plant outside town.

_____

_____

5 Early this morning, a car crashed into a retaining wall. The impact cause the motorist and her companion to be flung out of the vehicle.

_____

_____

YOUR SCORE
10

UNIT 3.3 PAST CONTINUOUS TENSE

Look at the **A** and **B** sentences below. Find out why **B** is correct and **A** is wrong in the **Grammar Points** section.

			GRAMMAR POINTS
1A	At 11.00 yesterday morning, Joe **make** an oral presentation of his firm to the directors.	✗	
1B	At 11.00 yesterday morning, Joe **was making** an oral presentation of his firm to the directors.	✓	1
2A	We **took** orders from the customers while the cook was frying the noodles.	✗	
2B	We **were taking** orders from the customers while the cook was frying the noodles.	✓	2
3A	Sue was talking to us when George **interrupt**.	✗	
3B	Sue was talking to us when George **interrupted**.	✓	3
4A	The whole week while Dad was ill, Mum **worry** about him.	✗	
4B	The whole week while Dad was ill, Mum **was worrying** about him.	✓	4

GRAMMAR POINTS

1   We use the past continuous tense to show that an action was going on at a definite time in the past, or that an action or situation continued for a period of time in the past.

    EXAMPLES: At 6.30 yesterday evening, my friends and I **were planning** the activities for the rally next week. *(definite time in the past)*

                    Danny and I **were reminiscing** about old times for a couple of hours last night. *(continuous action in the past)*

2   We use the past continuous tense or the simple past tense for two actions that were going on at the same time in the past.

    EXAMPLES: Joy **was selecting** the seeds while Vic **was preparing** the vegetable patch.

                          (past continuous tense)

              Joy **selected** the seeds while Vic **prepared** the vegetable patch.

                         (simple past tense)

3 To show that something happened while a longer action was going on in the past, we use the past continuous tense for the longer action and the simple past tense for the shorter action.

EXAMPLE: Jennifer **was washing** her car outside when a stranger **came** to her gate.

(past continuous tense)   (simple past tense)

4 We use the past continuous tense to refer to repeated actions in the past.

EXAMPLES: My head **was hurting** the whole of yesterday.   *(repeatedly hurting)*
We **were looking** for her keys for an hour this morning.   *(repeatedly looking)*

PRACTICE *A*   Tick the correct sentences.

1 While I was studying for my exams last night, little Bobby was interrupting me all the time.

2 Sara and I window-shopped this afternoon when we bump into some of our former classmates.

3 The boys were arguing the whole night about who would win the football finals.

4 The men gather wood for the fireplace while the women scrubbed and cleaned the cabin.

5 Claire and I were listening spellbound for a couple of hours to Uncle Paul talking about his seafaring days.

6 We were cooking the whole morning to get lunch ready for our 150 guests.

7 When they came in to inspect the house, we still swept and dusted.

8 The officials announce the winners as soon as the competition was over.

9 People were running everywhere to take cover when the robbers opened fire.

10 Customs officers were searching through the bags thoroughly before they allow the passengers to proceed.

YOUR SCORE

10

PRACTICE *B*   Underline the correct verbs in the brackets to complete the sentences.

1 While the two motorists (argued / were arguing) on the road about who was to blame for the accident, a patrol car drew up.

2 Janet (is attending / was attending) a talk at the Royal Oaks Hotel next week.

3 While Sam explained the procedure to the participants at the seminar, Nell (handed out / hands out) the booklets to everyone present.

4 Mrs Lim (slipped / was slipping) and fell when she was hurrying to catch the bus.

5 Mike (is taking up / was taking up) a course in design management for the next three years at a local college.

6 My arm (throb / was throbbing) so badly this morning that I decided to go to the clinic for treatment.

7 Ann (graduated / was graduating) with an honours degree in English last month.

8 I (rummage / was rummaging) in a drawer for my keys while Lily was waiting outside for me.

39

9 The village girls (roasted / are roasting) the marinated lamb while the men baked bread over hot coals.

10 On Saturday night, police (arrested / were arresting) 20 youths who were involved in a brawl.

PRACTICE C Fill in the blanks with the simple present, present continuous, simple past or past continuous tense form of the words in the brackets.

1 While we were walking on the beach this morning, the fishing vessels _____ (come) into the port.

2 Judy _____ (move) into the apartment next to mine tomorrow and she will be here for a few months before she goes to Manila.

3 While David _____ (demonstrate) how the machine worked, the senior manager came in to listen and watch.

4 The doctors _____ (vaccinate) the children in the refugee camp against infectious diseases when three United Nations personnel arrived.

5 Rita _____ (frequently complain) about the high cost of medical and dental treatment nowadays.

6 We _____ (shovel) snow from our front porch for more than an hour last Friday morning.

7 The immigration officials _____ (examine) everyone's travel documents thoroughly before they allow them to drive on.

8 While the woman _____ (shout) for help, the thieves fled on motorbikes.

9 When the scouts _____ (climb) into the cave, they were startled to see fine paintings on the walls.

10 The current population explosion in parts of Asia _____ (cause) strain on the economies of these nations.

PRACTICE D Cross out the incorrect verb forms in the boxes to complete the passage.

It **1** | snow | was snowing | heavily while Mike **2** | drove | was driving | past the deserted Stewart mansion. He **3** | is thinking | thought | of the warmth of the blazing fire at home and the hot meal his mother **4** | prepares | was preparing | for dinner at that time.

Suddenly a swift movement **5** | caught | was catching | the corner of his eye. He **6** | wondered | was wondering | whether he **7** | dreamt | was dreaming | . He **8** | pulled up | was pulling up | sharply just before the junction. He **9** | is | was | sure that he had seen the blurred images of two girls at the door of the old house. While Mike **10** | is trudging | was trudging | through the deep snow, he looked up at the bedroom windows on the second floor and glimpsed a flickering light.

PRACTICE *E*   Some of the sentences below are incorrect. Rewrite them correctly.

1 While I was resting just now, I was hearing someone knocking at my door.

_____

_____

2 At midnight yesterday, Harun completed his assignment when he noticed a sleek black car stopping outside his gate.

_____

_____

3 When the lawyer revealed the serious nature of the problem, Tess wept bitterly.

_____

_____

4 May bargained with the stall-keeper for more than 20 minutes this afternoon and finally bring the price of the shawl down to 10 dollars.

_____

_____

5 The audience roaring with laughter at the jokes of the comedienne during the two-hour show last night.

_____

_____

YOUR SCORE
10

PRACTICE *F*   Rearrange the words to form correct sentences.

1 her — Mala — missing — purse — realised — she — shopping — that — was — was — when.

Mala _____

_____

2 about — complaining — he — his — morning — the — was — whole — workload.

He _____

_____

3 afternoon — buy — for — for — hours — people — queueing — show — the — this — tickets — to — up — were.

People_____

_____

4 at — history — I — last — my — night — notes — reading — still — ten — was,.

At _____

_____

5 after — at — Betty — children — had — hair — her — looked — salon — styled — the — the — Tom — while,.

While Tom _____

_____

YOUR SCORE
10

41

UNIT 3.4 PRESENT PERFECT TENSE

Look at the **A** and **B** sentences below. Find out why **B** is correct and **A** is wrong in the **Grammar Points** section.

CHECKPOINT

			GRAMMAR POINTS
1A	We **have driven** along the coastal road **last week** and the scenery was beautiful.	✗	
1B	We **drove** along the coastal road **last week** and the scenery was beautiful. / We **have driven** along the coastal road and the scenery is beautiful.	✓	1
2A	Mr Chen **took part** in the boat race since he was a young man. He wants to be in the race for a few more years.	✗	
2B	Mr Chen **has taken part** in the boat race since he was a young man. He wants to be in the race for a few more years.	✓	2
3A	He **already received** the acceptance letter for admission into university.	✗	
3B	He **has already received** the acceptance letter for admission into university.	✓	3

GRAMMAR POINTS

1 We use the present perfect tense, like the simple past tense, to talk about completed actions. However, unlike the simple past tense which is used with definite time phrases, we do not state the exact time of an action with the present perfect tense.

EXAMPLES:

SIMPLE PAST TENSE

We **attended** a seminar ⟨yesterday⟩.
(completed action at definite time)

PRESENT PERFECT TENSE

We **have just attended** a management seminar.
(completed action with no exact time given)

2 We use the present perfect tense with words like **since** and **for** to refer to an action that began in the past and is still going on at the point of speaking. (**Since** points to the start of a period of time, and **for** points to the entire period of time.)

EXAMPLES:

SIMPLE PAST TENSE

Sandra **worked** with our company till 2000. She **was** with us for four years.
(She is no longer working there.)

PRESENT PERFECT TENSE

Sandra **has worked** with our company since 1997. She **has been** with us for five years.
(She is still working there.)

3 We use the present perfect tense with adverbs of indefinite time such as **already** and **just** to refer to completed actions, and **yet** to refer to an action that is expected to happen at some point in the future. We do not use these words with the simple past tense.

EXAMPLES: We **have already made** reservations for the show. ✓

We **already made** reservations for the show. ✗

The band **has just signed** a contract with Unicorn Records. ✓

We **haven't received** any reply from them **yet**. ✓
We **have yet to receive** a reply from them. ✓
We **didn't receive** any reply from them **yet**. ✗

> **REMEMBER!**
> ■ **Yet** is usually used with a negative and is placed at the end of a sentence. However, for emphasis, **yet** can also be placed before a single verb or after an auxiliary verb and the negative.
> EXAMPLES: Mary **hasn't told** her parents about the incident **yet**.
> Mary **hasn't yet told** her parents about the incident.
> No one **yet knows** about the incident. *(single verb)*

PRACTICE *A* Circle the letters of the correct sentences.

1 A They have always enjoy our drama productions.
  B They always enjoy our drama productions.
  C They have always enjoyed our drama productions.

2 A Gwen has just returned home from overseas with a law degree.
  B Gwen returned home from overseas last week with a law degree.
  C Gwen just returned home from overseas last week with a law degree.

3 A I didn't finish my assignments yet and I have to hand them in today.
  B I haven't finish my assignments yet and I have to hand them in today.
  C I haven't finished my assignments yet and I have to hand them in today.

4 A I have known Lydia since we were young.
  B I know Lydia since we were young.
  C I am knowing Lydia since we were young.

5 A Two years ago, we have started a club to help underprivileged children.
  B Two years ago, we started a club to help underprivileged children.
  C Two years ago, we were going to start a club to help underprivileged children.

6 A She hasn't decided what to wear for the dance yet.
  B She didn't decide what to wear for the dance yet.
  C She hasn't yet decided what to wear for the dance.

YOUR SCORE
10

Underline the correct verb forms in the brackets.

1 Our grandparents (have looked after / were looking after) us since we were small.

2 George (chose / has chosen) to shift to a ground-floor apartment a month ago.

3 Steve (always encourages / always encouraged) us to do our best because he cares about us.

4 She (was forever threatening / forever threatened) to resign unless she was given a raise.

5 Prices of stationery (have risen sharply / rose sharply) these days because of the shortage of quality paper.

6 We (have lived / lived) in this large rambling bungalow ever since I can remember.

7 I (hung / was hanging) up the picture when I lost my balance and fell.

8 Mum (didn't scold / hasn't scolded) me yet for breaking her expensive crystal vase.

9 Sheila (has already seen / already saw) the coach about a place in the basketball team.

10 She (grew / has grown) up to be the confident young woman we see today.

YOUR SCORE
10

PRACTICE C Some of the sentences contain mistakes in verb forms. Underline the mistakes and write the correct verbs in the boxes provided.

1 They have already tracked down the gang involved in the cyberfraud scandal.

2 Just two weeks ago, Amy has discovered a little restaurant which serves excellent seafood.

3 The insurance company hasn't yet told us why our claims have not been paid.

4 He just eat all the cake that was on the plate and hasn't left us any.

5 The organisers of the marathon didn't announce the results yet.

6 Since we came to this town some 10 years ago, we have received nothing but kindness and support from people.

7 I waited for more than a month for a letter from the bank but I have received no reply from them.

8 No one yet see the problems the way we do.

9 Karen has just announced her engagement to Simon who she met two years ago.

10 Some time ago, the couple has bought the house next door to mine.

YOUR SCORE
10

PRACTICE D Fill in the blanks with the correct forms of the verbs in the brackets.

It (1) _____*has been*_____ (be) a long time since Joanne and I saw each other. For many years I (2) _____ (often wonder) if she still remembers me. I (3) _____ _____ (change) so much since the 1990s when we (4) _____ (be) two giggling schoolgirls. Today Joanne (5) _____ (hold) an executive position in her company. In fact she (6) _____ (just become) the manager for the Asia-Pacific region. Since then, I, on the other hand, (7) _____ (earn) a university degree, got married and settled down.

As I stood waiting, my eyes suddenly (8) _____ (focus) on an elegant young woman standing there in front of me. It was unmistakably Joanne! She (9) _____ (throw) her arms around me and hugged me. Since our schooldays, time (10) _____ (lead) us down different paths in life, but our bond of friendship (11) _____ (remain) as strong as ever even after all these years.

PRACTICE E The sentences below are incorrect. Rewrite them correctly.

1   I have misplace my house keys. I hope I find them soon or I will have to climb in through a window.

    _____

    _____

2   Sue already distribute the booklets to the participants at the seminar, so everyone should have his or her own copy.

    _____

    _____

3   The workmen have stacked up all our furniture yesterday because they are going to paint the house today.

    _____

    _____

4   Our friends didn't reply to our wedding invitation yet.

    _____

    _____

5   Peggy and I are close friends since we were children. We enjoy doing things together like going shopping and watching movies.

    _____

    _____

UNIT 3.5 PAST PERFECT TENSE

Look at the **A** and **B** sentences below. Find out why **B** is correct and **A** is wrong in the **Grammar Points** section.

CHECKPOINT

			GRAMMAR POINTS
1A	When I visited Tess last night, she **went** to bed.	✗	
1B	When I visited Tess last night, she **had gone** to bed.	✓	1
2A	World Bank officials **already studied** the situation in the country before they approved the loan.	✗	
2B	World Bank officials **had already studied** the situation in the country before they approved the loan.	✓	2
3A	We **have warned** him **more than once** not to drive recklessly but he didn't listen to us.	✗	
3B	We **had warned** him **more than once** not to drive recklessly but he didn't listen to us.	✓	3

GRAMMAR POINTS

1 When we refer to completed actions in the past, we can use different past tense forms to indicate what we mean.

EXAMPLES:

SIMPLE PAST TENSE	+	SIMPLE PAST TENSE
They **came** immediately		when we **called** them.
When we **entered** the hall,		the lecture **began**. *(We were just in time.)*

We use the past perfect tense for an action or situation that happened earlier and the simple past tense for the action or situation that happened later.

EXAMPLE:

SIMPLE PAST TENSE	+	PAST PERFECT TENSE
When we **entered** the hall,		the lecture **had begun**. *(We were late for the lecture.)*

2 We use the past perfect tense with words like **already** and **just** to refer to actions which were completed before a specific time in the past.

EXAMPLES: Before we **left** for the airport, Dad **had already confirmed** our flight schedules.

Delia **had just sat down** to have her dinner when the phone **rang**.

3 We use the past perfect tense with indefinite time words and phrases like **always** and **more than once** to refer to repeated actions in the past.

EXAMPLES: I **had always suspected** that Brian was to blame for the accident.

Before I left the workshop, the mechanic **had reminded** me **more than once** to check the tyres.

PRACTICE **A** Circle the numbers of the sentences that are correct.

1 The class came up with excellent ideas after we had discussed the problem for more than an hour.

2 We take the wrong turning and spent some time trying to get our bearings right.

3 The shouts of the people indicated that the match already start.

4 I had just written a note to tell Mike that I would be late when he called me.

5 The students had already assembled in the hall when the principal walked in.

6 Grace sewn the new curtains for the dining room and we are going to help her hang them up.

7 Everyone had expected Mrs Tindall to give a farewell speech but she declined politely.

8 We stood at the back of the auditorium and had admired the flower decorations on the stage.

9 Elaine hopes to pursue a career in music but she needs to practise much more.

10 The intruder silently open the French windows and slipped into the bedroom.

YOUR SCORE

10

PRACTICE **B** Cross out the incorrect verb forms to complete the sentences.

1 They | have emphasised | had emphasised | the importance of the course to all those present before they introduced the speakers.

2 We | passed | were passing | through the entrance of the monastery when we heard the continuous ringing of bells.

3 Tom and I | always disagreed | had always disagreed | about the methods used to fight child abuse when we were working for the welfare department.

4 The intricate beaded patterns sewn by hand on clothes | had fascinated | have fascinated | visitors to the villages of Thailand since the early sixties.

5 Sam | hadn't done | haven't done | the song sheets yet so we didn't hold the choir practice.

6 Ben | hadn't had | hasn't have | time for a coffee break this morning, so we went out and bought him soup and sandwiches for lunch.

7 The queue at the cab stand | became | has become | even longer but still there was no cab in sight.

8 The two children | have fallen | had fallen | ill after the trip and were taken to the clinic for treatment.

9 The teachers | have seen | had seen | a tremendous change in Jason since his sessions with the coach these last four months.

10 The beauty of the English countryside | have inspired | inspired | many nineteenth-century poets.

YOUR SCORE

10

PRACTICE $\boxed{C}$ Fill in the blanks with the correct forms of the verbs in the brackets.

Bullfighting (1) _____ (be) a national pastime of Spain for more than a hundred years. Last year, we decided to watch a bullfight when we were in Spain. When we arrived at the arena, hundreds of people (2) _____ (already flock) there from all over the country. As the matador (3) _____ (sweep) into the ring with a red cape flung over his shoulder, the crowd cheered and (4) _____ (shout) 'Ole!'.

The matador (5) _____ (have) years of training before he (6) _____ (find) the courage to stand in the ring and face a two-ton raging bull! He (7) _____ (stand) proudly in the centre of the ring and (8) _____ (swing) his cape to entice the bull to charge at him. Each time the angry animal charged, the spectators applauded to encourage this master performer. We (9) _____ (never see) anything like that before.

When it came to the peak of the fight, the bull was pierced with two swords. We (10) _____ (already close) our eyes tightly so we didn't really see what happened. We felt weak at the knees as we left the arena.

YOUR SCORE
10

PRACTICE $\boxed{D}$ Some of the verbs in the sentences are incorrect. Underline them and write the correct verbs in the boxes.

1 We had heard today that next week's exams would be postponed.

2 We had reminded ourselves more than once that failure should not deter us from trying again.

3 These files had already been checked last week before they were placed in the cabinet.

4 On my way home from work today, I had decided to stop by to see how my Aunt Letty was coping in her new house.

5 There had been a deluge of mail for Richard after his story had been published in the newspapers.

6 It had took us several weeks to compile all the letters and photographs which we included in our book.

7 Jane had always believed that her friends thought very little of her cooking but she was mistaken.

8 We had torn open the parcel before we realised that it was addressed to our neighbours.

9 The stone cottage surrounded by green hills was everything we ever hope for.

10 The weather bureau had predicted bright sunshine this morning but it had been drizzling since 6.30 a.m.

PRACTICE **E** Fill in the blanks with suitable words in the box.

had broken down	had taken	had worked	hadn't decided
hadn't given	has raised	has willed	have ignored
had burnt	delights		

1 When I registered at college, I _____ which courses to take yet.

2 We expected Neil to come for dinner but he _____ a wrong turning and got completely lost.

3 My finger was extremely painful as I _____ it while cooking dinner.

4 The four boys were waiting by the kerb for a taxi as their car _____ on the way to college.

5 The community project failed because they _____ much thought to the consequences it would have on the residents.

6 The committee thinks that the authorities _____ the proposals they had put forward.

7 Celia _____ her life savings towards the cancer research foundation of the hospital.

8 Nine-year-old Ryan _____ more than US$20,000 to help refugees.

9 Her warmth and concern for others _____ all who come to know her.

10 The concert was excellent because the producer _____ hard to make sure everything was perfect.

UNIT 3.6 PRESENT AND PAST PERFECT CONTINUOUS TENSES

Look at the **A** and **B** sentences below. Find out why **B** is correct and **A** is wrong in the **Grammar Points** section.

			GRAMMAR POINTS
1A	I **was waiting** at the taxi stand since 1.30 p.m. but no taxi has come by so far.	✗	
1B	I **have been waiting** at the taxi stand since 1.30 p.m. but no taxi has come by so far.	✓	1
2A	Scientists **have done** research on drugs to combat AIDS for over 20 years with some success.	✗	
2B	Scientists **have been doing** research on drugs to combat AIDS for over 20 years with some success.	✓	2
3A	The boys came in covered with mud and grime. They **have been playing** football.	✗	
3B	The boys came in covered with mud and grime. They **had been playing** football.	✓	3

GRAMMAR POINTS

1 We use the present perfect continuous tense for an action or a situation which began in the past and continues up to the point of speaking. The action may or may not be finished.

We use the present perfect tense to refer to an action which began in the past and continues to the present. The action is finished at the point of speaking.

EXAMPLE:

It is 2 p.m.
Ann begins to write letters.

It is 3.30 p.m.
Ann is still writing letters.

Ann **has been writing** letters since 2 p.m.   (*act of writing is not over*)
Ann **has written** four letters since 2 p.m.   (*act of writing is over*)

2 We use the present perfect continuous tense to refer to a series of repeated actions or situations that began in the past and continues to the present.

EXAMPLE: Bob **complained** of a backache recently but he is much better now. (*action is over*)
Bob **has been complaining** of a backache for the past three weeks.
(*action is not finished – Bob is still suffering*)

3 We use the past perfect continuous tense to refer to an action which had been going on continuously up to that time in the past that we are talking about.

EXAMPLE: We **had been driving** for more than four hours before we **found** a small hotel

(continuous earlier action)   (later action)

off the highway to spend the night.

PRACTICE *A*   Circle the numbers of the sentences that are correct.

1 Sam had supervised the building project for the last five years until it was taken over by a huge company.

2 My motorcycle had broken down this morning. I'll have to wheel it to the mechanic.

3 The children are hot and hungry. They have been playing on the beach all morning.

4 The plumber has been trying to seal the leak in the main pipe for more than an hour.

5 We have watched an exciting movie on television. It is going to end in half an hour's time.

6 Connie had been calling Mark's office several times but he doesn't seem to be in.

7 The enemy planes have been dropping bombs on the area all night.

8 Our family lived in this wooden bungalow since the time Dad retired from the army nine years ago.

9 My hands are covered with grease because I have been cleaning the kitchen stove.

10 The director talked about pay increments for the past two years but wages remain low.

YOUR SCORE

10

PRACTICE *B*   Cross out the incorrect verb forms in the boxes to complete the sentences.

1 Betty was surprised when she found out that her office mates | had been planning | had planned | a birthday party for her for months without her knowledge.

2 The management | already saw | has already seen | our proposals and has promised to give us an answer soon.

3 Julian and his friend were involved in an accident because they | had been drinking | had drunk | and driving.

4 The team | had been designing | has designed | new marketing strategies to boost the sales of our products.

5 Mr Tan | has been working | has worked | at two jobs to support his family since his wife lost her job in May last year.

6 The number of students playing truant from school dropped recently as parents | had been cooperating | have cooperated | closely with the disciplinary board these past few months.

51

7 The man who masterminded the bank robbery was finally caught. The police had been investigating | had investigated | his activities for months.

8 Everything is in a mess because we had rearranged | have been rearranging | the furniture in the hall.

9 The garden looks beautiful now. We have been trimming | have trimmed | and planting since four this afternoon.

10 Alex had just finished | had just been finishing | cooking dinner when we dropped in to see him last night.

PRACTICE **C**   Fill in the blanks with the present perfect, past perfect, present perfect continuous or past perfect continuous tense form of the verbs in the brackets.

1 During the last two years, the government _____ (restore) old historic buildings.

2 Dad's 12-year-old car _____ (show) signs of fatigue for more than six months before it finally broke down last week.

3 The health authorities _____ (indicate) that a dangerous outbreak of cholera may occur.

4 Tom's overalls were splattered with paint. He _____ (paint) the fence all morning.

5 Benny _____ (run) around the playground all morning. He looks sweaty and breathless.

6 Those people who _____ (queue) in front of the bank since 8.30 this morning are getting irritated because it is already past 9.30 a.m. and the bank has not opened yet.

7 They _____ (not tell) Ben yet that he had been posted to Seoul when he went in to see the directors.

8 For the past few years, China _____ (make) a great effort to save the giant pandas from extinction.

9 By nightfall yesterday, the committee _____ (already put up) most of the decorations in the hall.

10 When the refugees staggered into the village at night, they found that the people _____ (wait) several hours for them with food and blankets.

PRACTICE **D**   Some of the sentences below contain incorrect verb forms. Underline them and write the correct verbs in the spaces provided.

My friends and I all want to go to Australia. We had been trying to arrange a holiday there for several years but something always goes wrong.

The year before last, we have all been working hard for months and really wanted a good holiday. We sent for brochures and started to make bookings but then one friend became ill and another suddenly had to move house.

Last year somebody said, "We had been talking about an Australian holiday for such a long time. Let's just go!" We agreed, but found that it was difficult to make bookings at the resorts that interested us. After we have been phoning and emailing for two weeks, we became discouraged and took a local holiday.

This year we may be successful. We have found a good travel agent who specializes in trips to Australia and she had been working hard at the arrangements. She says she'll phone us tomorrow and let us know what is available. I do hope we make it this time!

1 _____

2 _____

3 _____

4 _____

YOUR SCORE

5 _____

/10

PRACTICE E Rewrite the sentences below correctly.

1 Since early this morning, water was gushing out of the burst mains and no one has come to repair it.

_____

_____

2 They came back from the forest covered with insect bites. They have caught butterflies all afternoon.

_____

_____

3 I usually keep my letters in a drawer but now they are scattered all over the place. Someone was reading my mail.

_____

_____

4 That lady has stared at us ever since we sat down. I wonder whether we know her.

_____

_____

5 Kate was postponing going to the dentist's for months but this morning her toothache was so bad that she had to rush off to the dental clinic.

_____

YOUR SCORE

_____

/10

UNIT 3.7 SIMPLE FUTURE TENSE

will and **going to** forms

Look at the **A** and **B** sentences below. Find out why **B** is correct and **A** is wrong in the **Grammar Points** section.

		GRAMMAR POINTS
1A In 10 years' time, many countries **experience** great changes in their economic and social structures.	✗	
1B In 10 years' time, many countries **will experience** great changes in their economic and social structures.	✓	1
2A Australia certainly **win** the coming cricket test series against England.	✗	
2B Australia **will** certainly **win** the coming cricket test series against England.	✓	2
3A It feels stuffy in here. I **switch** on the air-conditioner to help cool the room.	✗	
3B It feels stuffy in here. I **will switch** on the air-conditioner to help cool the room.	✓	3
4A I **going to do** a computer course to upgrade my skills.	✗	
4B I **am going to do** a computer course to upgrade my skills.	✓	4

GRAMMAR POINTS

1 We use the simple future tense to refer to actions or events that will happen in the future.
> **EXAMPLE:** We still have a long way to go. We **will** only **reach** the resort late at night.

2 We use the simple future tense with **will** to make predictions or refer to events which we think are highly possible in the future.
> **EXAMPLES:** Liverpool **will beat** all the other teams to win the FA Cup this year. *(prediction)*
> The sky looks gloomy. There **will be** a storm this afternoon. *(highly possible event)*

3 We can also use the simple future tense with **will** to refer to something which we decide to do at the time of speaking.
> **EXAMPLE:** Rose, how about having dinner with us this evening? Yes, I **will join** you for dinner.

4 We use the **going to** form for actions which we have already planned to do in the future and events which we think are possible in the future.
> **EXAMPLES:** That school **is going to hold** a workshop on counselling during the August holidays. *(action planned for the future)*
> Asian share markets **are going to perform** better at the end of the year because of brighter prospects for the world economy. *(possible event)*

PRACTICE *A* Circle the numbers of the sentences which are correct.

1 The sports club will distribute food coupons to the competitors later today.

2 Why don't you take a rest, Kate? I finish the reports for you.

3 The outlook for the banking and finance industry going to be brighter next year.

4 The weather seems quite chilly today. I think I go in and find my jacket.

5 They are going to approve the construction of a multi-level car park behind the office blocks.

6 Sandra is doing very well in the company. I believe she will receive an offer to go for further training overseas.

7 Because of the heavy rain recently, the river is going to bursts its banks and flood the low-lying areas.

8 The rise in the price of oil is going to cause a simultaneous rise in the prices of all other commodities.

9 Our guests are going to be here soon. I run upstairs to take a shower and change.

10 George and Alice get on so well with each other. I think they will get married before the year is over.

YOUR SCORE

10

PRACTICE *B* Fill in the blanks with the simple future, present perfect or past perfect tense form of the verbs in the brackets.

1 Come on, Dad. We have to leave now or we _____ (miss) the first part of the movie.

2 We had better get off the streets. There is going to _____ (be) a clash between the police and the demonstrators.

3 I can't reach the top shelf to get the bags down. Sam, please _____ (climb) up and get them for me.

4 When Jean called me last Sunday, she _____ (just move) to an apartment near the college.

5 Lucy _____ (be) going to have a shock when she walks into the surprise farewell party we have planned for her.

6 We have lectured Maisie so often about her untidiness but it _____(not do) her any good.

7 The clouds have cleared at last. We _____ (have) beautiful sunshine for our picnic this afternoon.

8 "The doctor is busy, sir. Would you like to take a seat and wait?" "Yes, I _____ (wait) and see him. I need to consult him about my medication."

9 Bill's shop was only partially damaged by the fire. Fortunately, the neighbours _____

_____ (alert) the Fire Department as soon as they noticed the smoke.

10 The children _____ (be) so excited about the trip.
They have never been on a riverboat before.

YOUR SCORE
10

PRACTICE **C** Cross out the incorrect verb forms to complete the sentences.

1 Anna | is going to receive | will received | the parcel we sent her in 10 days' time.

2 The situation in the village is tense. We think there | will be | will being | a struggle for power between the rival factions.

3 "We have a choice of pastries and sandwiches. What would you like?" "I | am having | will have | a sandwich, please."

4 That crystal vase | fall | is going to fall | . It is too near the edge of the table.

5 The government | going to approve soon | will soon approve | the construction of a dam to generate electricity for the villages in the valley.

6 Consumers | think | will think | seriously before buying imported goods when prices of these items increase.

7 My bank | has frozen | will froze | all applications for housing loans with immediate effect.

8 They | are going to close | were closing | the post office when I dashed in to buy some stamps.

9 The club president | is going to officiate | will be officiate | the opening of the annual general meeting this Saturday.

10 Future water shortage | has dominates | will dominate | the discussion at the conference next week.

YOUR SCORE
10

PRACTICE **D** The sentences below contain incorrect verb forms. Write the correct verbs in the boxes.

1 "I need to send these letters today."
"I'm going past the post office later. I <u>am going to</u> <u>mail</u> them for you."

2 Mrs Jones <u>already agreed</u> to the auction, so we will itemise the things tomorrow.

3 Adam <u>is going to scoring</u> straight 'A's in the coming exams. He has been studying hard for months.

4 Aunt Sue, why don't you take a rest? We <u>were washing</u> and dry the dishes for you.

5 The family <u>had been watching</u> a live telecast tonight so they haven't had time for dinner.

56

6 The director <u>will insisted</u> that Eddy come for the rehearsals today. We only have a week left before the concert.

7 Henry <u>isn't going to be reveal</u> the secret plan but we managed to coax him to give us some clues.

8 Beth and David are planning to buy a house next year as they think property prices <u>are going to came down</u> by that time.

9 Economists can't really predict which direction the global economy <u>will taking</u> in the next two years.

10 As oil resources are rapidly being depleted, geophysicists <u>has been searching</u> for alternative sources of energy.

YOUR SCORE
/ 10

PRACTICE *E* Some of the sentences in the passage are incorrect. Underline them and rewrite them correctly.

The World Wildlife Foundation—WWF—has chosen the giant panda as its logo for a good reason. Their numbers rapidly dwindling in their native China.

In the next few years, China will embark on a programme to save the pandas from extinction. Concerned Chinese scientists going to take steps to increase the panda population. The Chinese government will intensified efforts to protect the young cubs, monitor their growth and feed them. Food will being of the utmost importance in this case, as the staple diet of these animals consists of young bamboo shoots which used to grow in profusion in parts of China. Forest clearance has led to a loss of habitat for the pandas. Many of these animals will face starvation unless something is done quickly. China is going to ban logging and officially announce that pandas are a protected species. These measures helped to safeguard the environment in which the pandas live.

1 _____

_____

2 _____

_____

3 _____

_____

4 _____

_____

5 _____

YOUR SCORE
/ 10

_____

UNIT 3.8 FUTURE CONTINUOUS TENSE

Look at the **A** and **B** sentences below. Find out why **B** is correct and **A** is wrong in the **Grammar Points** section.

GRAMMAR POINTS

				GRAMMAR POINTS
1A	On Friday morning, the Prime Minister **leading** a trade delegation to China.	✗		
1B	On Friday morning, the Prime Minister **will be leading** a trade delegation to China.	✓	1	
2A	In two weeks' time, James **will be gone** into hospital for surgery.	✗		
2B	In two weeks' time, James **will be going** into hospital for surgery.	✓	2	
3A	**You playing** tennis at the club this evening, Tony?	✗		
3B	**Will you be playing** tennis at the club this evening, Tony?	✓	3	

GRAMMAR POINTS

1 We use the future continuous tense to refer to actions or events which will be going on at a certain time in the future.

EXAMPLE: We **will be setting off** early tomorrow morning on our study tour of the National Park.

2 We use the future continuous tense to refer to actions or events in the future which have already been planned or which will take place regularly.

EXAMPLES: The management **will be attending** an urgent meeting with union leaders this morning to settle the ongoing dispute. *(action already planned for the future)*

Kathy and I won't be free today to join you. We **will be visiting** our grandparents as we usually do. *(action which takes place regularly)*

3 We use the future continuous tense in a question when we want to enquire politely about someone's plans, particularly when we want that someone to do something for us.

EXAMPLE: A: **Will you be seeing** Jean this evening, Ben?
B: Yes. Why do you ask?
A: Could you give her a message from me?

REMEMBER!

■ The future continuous tense is formed in this way:

will be + base form of verb + 'ing'

EXAMPLES: will be investigating
will be settling

58

PRACTICE *A*   Tick the correct verbs in the boxes.

1   At 5.30 this evening, Grant | was flying / will be flying | in from Wellington.

2   Three days ago, while I | was studying / will be studying | at home I heard several gunshots in the distance.

3   The orchestra | have been rehearsing / will be rehearsing | all morning for their performance this Saturday. They are tired now and need to take a break.

4   John, | will you be using / you are using | your car tonight? I wonder whether I could borrow it for a while.

5   Cheryl won't be coming for the function tonight. She | has been attending / will be attending | a French class. at the language centre.

6   The cashiers | have been working / were working | for more than 10 years with our firm. I don't think they would make a serious mistake.

7   The nurses | are keeping / will be kept | a close watch over the baby to see if there is any change in her condition.

8   The audience | were listening / will be listening | to a splendid rendition of Mozart in a short while.

9   Donna | is going to preparing / will be preparing | lunch for us all tomorrow morning. She has asked us to be there by 12.30.

10 | Will you be taking / You will take | me to the gym for my practice, Dad?

YOUR SCORE
10

PRACTICE *B*   Fill in the blanks with the future continuous or past perfect continuous tense form of the verbs in the brackets.

1   My parents are sure to be at home. They _____ (watch) a Cantonese movie on television at this time.

2   Engineers _____ (drill soon) under the Caspian Sea for oil and this will lead to an increase in traffic in the Straits of Bosphorus.

3   Sarah's colleagues were sad when they found out she _____ (apply) for other jobs.

4   They _____ (surely attend) the rock star's concert this Sunday as they are his long-time fans.

5   The police surveillance unit _____ (keep) watch on the apartment for more than three weeks before they arrested the criminals.

6 "_____ (you meet) Darren today?" "Yes, why?" "Could you hand him these brochures, please?"

7 The club _____ (host) a creative workshop on 'Décor for the Home' this afternoon at 4.30.

8 We _____ (expect) a poor turnout for the PTA meeting today but the good response from both parents and teachers surprised us.

9 "I am extremely busy this morning. _____ (you go) out to buy lunch?" "Yes, why?" "Do you think you could get me some sandwiches?"

10 Anita _____ (spring-clean) her room just now. Let's drop in and surprise her!

PRACTICE C Some of the sentences below contain incorrect verb forms. Underline them and write the correct verbs in the boxes provided.

1 We are going to move to the suburbs last month but we changed our minds and decided to stay where we were.

2 Mr Stoner will be directing our play scheduled for next month. We will begin rehearsals on Friday.

3 Mum, you will be going down to the shops this afternoon? Could you please get me a box file and some black marker pens?

4 A number of executives will resign from the company once they learn that the directors are planning to cut back on salaries.

5 I not be sharing the cost of Carol's wedding gift with you. I've made up my mind to buy her something on my own.

6 They have invaded the movie star's privacy by taking secret pictures of her .

7 By early this afternoon, the defence lawyers will be presenting their case before the grand jury.

8 "The coach will be making the final selection for the junior basketball team on Friday?"
"Yes, why?"
"I want to ask him to consider giving me a chance."

9 Sam and I looking forward to seeing you again in Melbourne next year.

10 These squatters haven't had electricity and piped water for more than 10 years.

PRACTICE D Complete the sentences using suitable endings in the box.

> are going to play the role of ambassadors when they go on tour abroad.
> were firing randomly into the crowd to disperse them.
> will be stopping at the lakeside to allow us time to enjoy the scenery.
> into the complaints about the poor quality of food in the cafeteria.
> for the Prime Minister's comments about the situation.
> as it looks like there is going to be a storm.
> because of the thick smoke in the room.
> will be distributing water to the drought-stricken areas.

1 The reporters have been waiting all morning _____

_____

2 The squads of soldiers _____

_____

3 The welfare committee will be looking _____

_____

4 We had better leave now _____

_____

5 Everyone will soon be spluttering and coughing _____

_____

YOUR SCORE
10

PRACTICE E Rewrite the sentences correctly.

1 Our parents will be celebrate their 30th wedding anniversary this Sunday.

_____

_____

2 The lifeguards here will be putting through rigorous training to ensure that they are
fully prepared to deal with emergencies.

_____

_____

3 Will she releasing the results of the competition to the participants soon?

_____

_____

4 We going to speak to the doctor today about Dad's ear problem.

_____

_____

5 The sales season has hitting the town again. Many people can be seen queueing up
early outside stores to get the best bargains.

_____

_____

YOUR SCORE
10

UNIT 3.9 **FUTURE PERFECT TENSE**

Look at the **A** and **B** sentences below. Find out why **B** is correct and **A** is wrong in the **Grammar Points** section.

GRAMMAR POINTS

				GRAMMAR POINTS
1A	By the middle of next year, my brothers **have come** back home from overseas.		✗	
1B	By the middle of next year, my brothers **will have come** back home from overseas.		✓	1
2A	This group of Pacific islands **will already gain** their independence by December this year.		✗	
2B	This group of Pacific islands **will have already gained** their independence by December this year.		✓	2

GRAMMAR POINTS

1   We use the future perfect tense to refer to actions or events which will be completed by a definite time in the future.

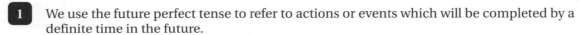

EXAMPLE: The developers will have cleared this pineapple plantation to make way for houses by the year 2004.   *(The clearing of the pineapple plantation has not been done yet.)*

The developers have cleared a pineapple plantation to make way for houses. *(The clearing of the pineapple plantation has been done but we don't know when.)*

The developers had cleared a pineapple plantation in 2000 and by 2001 they were building houses on it.   *(The clearing of the pineapple plantation was done in 2000 and the building of houses started a year later.)*

2   We use the words **already** and **just** with the future perfect tense to refer to actions or events which will be finished by an approximate time in the future.

EXAMPLES: By June, James **will have already completed** his degree in music.

Mrs Lim's grandson **will have just turned** one at the end of this year.

Tick the sentences which are correct.

1 This coming Saturday, we are going visiting the historical buildings in this city.

2 Brian and I will have arrive in Spain for our vacation by this time next week.

3 Our parcels will have reached Carol by Monday.

4 By the planting season, the farmers will built these irrigation canals.

5 Vincent will hear from us the moment we land in Jakarta.

6 By the middle of next year, we will have already moved to Hong Kong.

7 Brenda has finished her exams. She will be joined her brother in Perth in three months' time.

8 The workers are still repairing the bridge over the highway. They will have finished the job by Monday.

9 I haven't managed to speak to Chris yet. By this evening I will have passed him your message.

10 We will have to cut back on our expenditure or we will be spent all our money by the end of the year.

YOUR SCORE
10

PRACTICE *B* Cross out the incorrect verb forms to complete the sentences.

1 The songs he wrote │ have made │ will have made │ an impact on thousands of young people these past few years.

2 Miss Holmes │ had retired │ will have retired │ as the principal of the college by the end of December.

3 Mum │ had just done │ will have just done │ the grocery shopping when I came home from the office.

4 We won't come in. Your family │ has already gone │ will have already gone │ to bed by now.

5 The boys │ hadn't realised │ won't have realised │ how worn out they were until they finally got home and collapsed.

6 The police │ has succeeded │ will have succeeded │ in solving the puzzle and arresting the culprit by the end of the year.

7 The storm │ has damaged │ will have damaged │ several boats anchored in the marina and wrecked the boathouse.

8 I │ hadn't accepted │ won't have accepted │ the truth about the affair until I read the whole story in the newspaper.

9 By early autumn, the leaves on the trees │ have turned │ will have turned │ red and gold and gradually begun to fall.

10 An amazing fact about salmon is that they │ will have swum │ will swim │ upstream against the current to return to the same spot yearly to lay their eggs.

YOUR SCORE
10

PRACTICE *C* Fill in the blanks with the correct verbs in the box.

had already left	have been cleaning	have seen	lost
will have closed	will have established	will have fitted	
will have returned	will have sold	will rain	

1 They _____ the kitchen cabinets by this Saturday so I can rearrange my collection of spices and crockery.

2 In recent years, parts of Asia _____ an increase in the per capita income due to a renewed interest in cottage industries.

3 Laura _____ most of her life savings in the economic crash because she had invested heavily in the stock market.

4 That young designer _____ a name for himself by the time his next fashion collection is shown.

5 By six tomorrow evening, when the garage sale is over, we _____ most of our furniture.

6 We had better pack our picnic things and leave. It looks like it _____ soon.

7 Peter is going to call Dad in half an hour. He _____ home from work by then.

8 Anne will be free to go hiking in mid-July. Her college _____ for the holidays by that time.

9 The students deserve a break now. They _____ the school compound all morning.

10 When we drove up to Barbara's house, we found that she _____ for a committee meeting.

YOUR SCORE

10

PRACTICE *D* Some of the sentences below contain incorrect verb forms. Underline them and write the correct verbs in the boxes provided.

1 The children will rested sufficiently by this afternoon. We can take them sightseeing after that.

2 The store manager has just announced a discount on all shoes in the shop.

3 This evening, the village women have come down to the well to fill their vessels with fresh water.

4 When the rescue helicopters arrived, hundreds of houses had already been swept away by the floods.

5 The youngsters will have explored the caves by the end of their trip, so they will have an exciting story to tell.

6 The little pine tree that Grandpa planted when I was born will have grow to a height of six feet or more by now.

7 David will break all records if he manages to clear the nine-metre hurdle in next week's international track meet.

8 We were driving around in circles for the last half an hour and we still haven't found the old cotton mill marked on this map.

9 By the time we arrive at the wedding reception, dinner will already been served.

10 Julia will be coaching the junior women's swimming team from this week onwards.

YOUR SCORE
10

PRACTICE *E* Rewrite these sentences correctly.

1 Southeast Asian countries have experience an economic recovery by the end of next year if the global situation improves.

_____

_____

2 Before the end of the year, welfare officials have find foster homes for the orphans.

_____

_____

3 Our holiday will be ended this week. We will have returned to the business world by Monday.

_____

_____

4 The president will announcing the names of the incoming board of the club at this evening's official dinner.

_____

_____

5 Mrs Thomas never saw such strange behaviour before in her life.

_____

_____

YOUR SCORE
10

65

UNIT 4.1 **ACTIVE AND PASSIVE VOICE**

tense and agreement, phrasal verbs

Look at the **A** and **B** sentences below. Find out why **B** is correct and **A** is wrong in the **Grammar Points** section.

1A Active voice : John washes the cars every week. Passive voice : The cars **is washed** every week by John.	✗		
1B Active voice : John washes the cars every week. Passive voice : The cars **are washed** every week by John.	✓	1	
2A Active voice : The girls will bring the posters for the exhibition on Saturday. Passive voice : The posters **will be bring** by the girls for the exhibition on Saturday.	✗		
2B Active voice : The girls will bring the posters for the exhibition on Saturday. Passive voice : The posters **will be brought** by the girls for the exhibition on Saturday.	✓	2	
3A Active voice : The village elders handed down the art of silk-weaving to their children. Passive voice : The art of silk-weaving **was handed** by the village elders to their children.	✗		
3B Active voice : The village elders handed down the art of silk-weaving to their children. Passive voice : The art of silk-weaving **was handed down** by the village elders to their children.	✓	3	

GRAMMAR POINTS

1 When we change a sentence from the active voice to the passive voice, the tense of the verb has to remain the same and the verb has to agree with the subject in number.

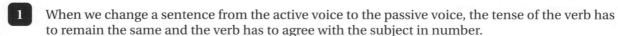

EXAMPLES: Sam usually **sends** the car to the workshop once every four months. (*active voice, present tense*)

The car **is usually sent** to the workshop once every four months by Sam. (*passive voice, present tense*)

The guide **took** the visitors on a tour of the palace gardens. (*active voice, past tense*)

The visitors **were taken** on a tour of the palace gardens by the guide. (*passive voice, past tense*)

2 We form passive verbs in the simple present tense, the simple past tense and the simple future tense in this way: the verb 'to be' + past participle of main verb

EXAMPLES:

Tenses	Active Verbs	Passive Verbs
simple present	inform / informs	am / is / are informed
simple past	informed	was / were informed
simple future	will inform	will be informed

3 When we change a phrasal verb (verb + preposition or verb + adverb) from the active voice to the passive voice, we must not omit the adverb or preposition that is a part of it.

EXAMPLE: *Active voice :* Some burglars **broke into** our house last night.
(verb) (preposition)

Passive voice : Our house **was broken** last night. ✗

Our house **was broken into** last night. ✓
(verb) (preposition)

> **REMEMBER!**
> ■ Sometimes, a passive sentence does not contain an agent (the person or thing that does the action).
> EXAMPLE: Our house was broken into ~~by someone~~ while we were on holiday.
> ■ The following are some examples of phrasal verbs:
> look after   catch up   hand down   take over

PRACTICE *A* Underline the correct verbs in the brackets.

1 The florist (delivers / is delivered) flowers to my office every day.

2 Bob (took over / taken over) the marketing department when Mr Sim left.

3 The preparations for the carnival (kept / was kept) us busy for the last two weeks.

4 Everything in the town (shut down / was shut down) and the people were evacuated.

5 The children (looked after / are looked after) by their grandmother.

6 We (will be tied / will tie) up the old newspapers in bundles and keep them for recycling.

7 The rock band (will be met / will meet) by thousands of fans at the airport.

8 The piano (moved / was moved) to the lobby so that everyone could enjoy the music.

9 The swift water of the Nile (is removed / removes) tons of debris and deposits it in the delta.

10 The authorities (banned / were banned) all assemblies in the city square.

YOUR SCORE
10

PRACTICE B | Tick the correct sentences.

1 James dismissed from his job because of misconduct.

2 The delicious aroma of fresh cookies is attracted many customers.

3 We were offered refreshments after a hard day's work.

4 Larry's ideas were added fun and gaiety to the event.

5 Peggy will be surprised with the gift we sent her.

6 Terry's name was struck off the list because of his frequent absences.

7 A timetable will draw up so the seniors will get more time to study.

8 We were kept waiting for more than an hour.

9 Stella's address taken out of the directory for security reasons.

10 Tony is required to produce strong evidence before the judge can make a decision.

YOUR SCORE
10

PRACTICE C | Fill in the blanks with the correct active or passive form of the verbs in the brackets.

1 They _____ (put off) plans for the building of the highway due to a shortage of funds.

2 A lot of our time _____ (take up) yesterday by the listing of items for the jumble sale.

3 The city mayor _____ (declare) open the new Performing Arts Complex next week.

4 The meeting with the shareholders _____ (schedule) for today.

5 The automobile plant _____ (employ) more than a thousand workers at present.

6 The site for the new airport terminal _____ (decided) soon.

7 The townspeople usually _____ (launch) the wine festival with music and dancing.

8 The fury of the hurricane _____ (feel) all along the coastal areas last week.

9 Hannah _____ (smell) the cookies baking as soon as she entered the kitchen.

10 The irate customer _____ (hold up) the long queue of people at the bank.

YOUR SCORE
10

Some of the sentences below are incorrect. Rewrite them correctly.

1 Joan was agreed with us that our volleyball team needed more training.

_____

_____

2 The rumble of an avalanche startled the skiers on the mountain slopes.

_____

_____

3 The pounding of drums to warn of an imminent attack woken up the entire village.

_____

_____

4 The marines made to do difficult manoeuvres while they are in training with the navy.

_____

_____

5 Our plans for the evening was forgot when unexpected visitors arrived.

_____

_____

YOUR SCORE

10

PRACTICE E Rewrite the passage on the making of paper in the passive voice.

Machines crush wood into small pieces. They mix the pieces with water and chemicals to produce pulp. Other machines spin the resulting pulp into fine sheets of paper.

When we recycle paper, we repeat the process. We use different chemical processes to produce the various required grades of paper.

_____

_____

_____

_____

_____

_____

_____

_____

_____

_____

YOUR SCORE

10

UNIT 4.2 ACTIVE AND PASSIVE VOICE

present and past continuous tenses, the passive with **by** or **with**

Look at the **A** and **B** sentences below. Find out why **B** is correct and **A** is wrong in the **Grammar Points** section.

GRAMMAR POINTS

1A	Active voice :	The men are repairing my car at the moment.	✗	
	Passive voice :	My car **is being repairing** at the moment.		
1B	Active voice :	The men are repairing my car at the moment.	✓	1
	Passive voice :	My car **is being repaired** at the moment.		
2A	Active voice :	They just told us of the flight delay.	✗	
	Passive voice :	We were just told of the flight delay **by them**.		
2B	Active voice :	They just told us of the flight delay.	✓	2
	Passive voice :	We were just told of the flight delay.		
3A	Passive voice :	The target was shot **by** a high-powered, long-range rifle.	✗	
3B	Passive voice :	The target was shot **with** a high-powered, long-range rifle.	✓	3

GRAMMAR POINTS

1 When we change a sentence in the present or past continuous tense to the passive voice, we do it in this way:

the verb 'to be' + **being** + past participle of main verb

EXAMPLES: present continuous tense: **am** / **are** / **is** + **being** + past participle

The workers **are taking down** the flags in the stadium.   (*active voice*)

The flags in the stadium **are being taken down** by the workers.   (*passive voice*)

past continuous tense: **was** / **were** + **being** + past participle

Dr Jones **was giving** the opening speech when we arrived.   (*active voice*)

The opening speech **was being given** by Dr Jones when we arrived.   (*passive voice*)

2 We can omit the agent (the person or thing that does the action) when we change a sentence from the active voice to the passive voice if the agent is unknown or unimportant.

We include the agent when we want to emphasise the person or thing that caused the action. We have to use **by** before the agent.

70

EXAMPLES: At lunchtime **they were distributing** pamphlets at the bus station.

<u>pronoun subject</u> *(active voice, past continuous tense)*

Pamphlets **were being distributed** at the bus station at lunchtime ~~by them~~.
(passive voice, past continuous tense)

Hundreds of people **were injured by a bomb blast** in the marketplace.
(passive voice) <u>thing that caused the action</u>

---

3 We use **with** instead of **by** in a passive voice sentence when the verb refers to a state of things rather than to an action, or when we refer to an instrument that is used by someone.

EXAMPLES: The stadium **is crowded with people** today. *(refers to state of the stadium)*

My mailbox **was flooded with junk e-mail** over the weekend. *(refers to instrument used by someone)*

> **REMEMBER!**
> - These are some verbs which use **with** in the passive voice:
>
>   cram   crowd   decorate   fill   throng

PRACTICE *A*   Cross out the incorrect words to complete the sentences.

1 The kitchen | is being tiled | is tiled | so we cannot use it yet.

2 The entire collection of dresses shown | was being created | was created | by a reputable fashion house.

3 The bank vault had been blown open | by | with | dynamite.

4 Carbon dioxide | is being produced | is produced | in great quantities now because of the great increase in industrial plants.

5 The priceless diamond was stolen | by | with | a professional thief.

6 Historical buildings | are being given | are giving | a new lease of life by the Heritage Trust as part of their restoration project.

7 The ranches in the valley | are being sold | are selling | as their owners are in financial difficulties.

8 The banquet last night | was being attended | was attended | by a number of distinguished guests.

9 A lot of new technology | is being introduced | are introduced | into schools to make learning more effective.

10 A traditional breakfast was prepared | by | with | the chef for the hotel's special guests.

YOUR SCORE

10

71

PRACTICE *B* Fill in the blanks with the correct active or passive form of the verbs in the brackets.

1 The visiting World Bank official _____ (interview) by a reporter at the moment.

2 I _____ (chat) with Pam on the phone when I was interrupted by the sound of the doorbell.

3 Ann is busy now. She _____ (design) the sets for the new play.

4 The sports arena _____ (pack) with people who are eagerly waiting for the match to begin.

5 Our work _____ (complete) last night so we can relax this morning.

6 The room _____ (fill) with the fragrance of perfume as the women entered.

7 The comedy on television _____ (keep) everyone in the lounge entertained at the moment.

8 The finishing touches to the arrangements for the reception _____ (add) by Sue now.

9 Passersby _____ (dazzle) by the fireworks display on Main Street yesterday evening.

10 The lights in the porch _____ (check) by the electrician right now.

PRACTICE *C* Some of the sentences below are incorrect. Rewrite them correctly.

1 The cafeteria was crowding with so many people that we couldn't find a place to sit.

_____

_____

2 The construction worker was strike by a falling beam while he was building the attic.

_____

_____

3 The agenda is being discussed now, so members are free to voice their opinions.

_____

_____

4 At 8.30 last night, technicians were tried to reconnect the damaged power lines and restore electricity in our area.

_____

_____

5 The cupboard crammed with so many things that everything fell out when I opened it.

_____

PRACTICE $\boxed{D}$ Rewrite the sentences in the passive voice.

1 The demonstration turned violent and the people were burning cars on the streets.

_____

_____

2 The soldiers fired several shots to disperse the mob.

_____

_____

3 The police overpowered many demonstrators with batons.

_____

_____

4 They led scores of detainees to waiting trucks.

_____

_____

5 The TV crew was filming the incident despite the angry protests from the soldiers.

_____

_____

YOUR SCORE
10

PRACTICE $\boxed{E}$ Rewrite the passage in the passive voice.

Everyone is busy now. We are preparing the stage for our play on Saturday night. Mani and Chan are setting up the sound system. Pete and Halim are testing the lights to ensure they are working. Polly, our stage coordinator, is putting up the backdrop. Polly and her team completed all the props just two days ago. Now, we are checking everything to make sure there will be no last-minute problems on opening night.

Everyone is busy now. The stage is being prepared for our play on Saturday night.

_____

_____

_____

_____

_____

_____

_____

_____

_____

YOUR SCORE
10

UNIT 4.3 ACTIVE AND PASSIVE VOICE

present, past and future perfect tenses, **be supposed to**

Look at the **A** and **B** sentences below. Find out why **B** is correct and **A** is wrong in the **Grammar Points** section.

<table>
<tr><td></td><td></td><td></td><td colspan="2" align="right">GRAMMAR POINTS</td></tr>
<tr><td>1A</td><td>No news is heard from them since they moved to Auckland last May.</td><td>✗</td><td></td></tr>
<tr><td>1B</td><td>No news has been heard from them since they moved to Auckland last May.</td><td>✓</td><td>1</td></tr>
<tr><td>2A</td><td>The questionnaire had completed by most of the participants before the workshop began.</td><td>✗</td><td></td></tr>
<tr><td>2B</td><td>The questionnaire had been completed by most of the participants before the workshop began.</td><td>✓</td><td>2</td></tr>
<tr><td>3A</td><td>All flights to the island will have resumed by the airlines next week.</td><td>✗</td><td></td></tr>
<tr><td>3B</td><td>All flights to the island will have been resumed by the airlines next week.</td><td>✓</td><td>3</td></tr>
<tr><td>4A</td><td>The judge is suppose to give the verdict anytime now.</td><td>✗</td><td></td></tr>
<tr><td>4B</td><td>The judge is supposed to give the verdict anytime now.</td><td>✓</td><td>4</td></tr>
</table>

GRAMMAR POINTS

1 We form the passive voice of the present perfect tense in this way:
has been / have been + past participle of main verb

EXAMPLES: Wilson **has been nominated** to head the new advisory council.
They **have** frequently **been criticised** for refusing to listen to others.

2 We form the passive voice of the past perfect tense in this way:
had been + past participle of main verb

EXAMPLE: The proposal for a shopping mall in our vicinity **had been discussed** before we met yesterday.

3 We form the passive voice of the future perfect tense in this way:
will / shall + **have been** + past participle of main verb

EXAMPLE: The song Winnie composed **will have been recorded** by the beginning of next month.

> **REMEMBER!**
> ■ All three perfect tenses (present, past and future) are used with adverbs of indefinite time and frequency, such as **already**, **just**, **since**, **never** and **yet**.

4 When we want to refer to an action or event which is expected or was expected to happen, we do it in this way:

verb 'to be' + **supposed to** + base form of main verb

EXAMPLES: Brenda **is supposed to come** at 8.30 tonight. *(Brenda has promised to come.)*

My parents **are supposed to drive** to the beach next week.
(action planned beforehand)

Bill **was supposed to see** us off at the station but he didn't come.
(action that was expected to take place but did not)

PRACTICE *A* Fill in the blanks with the correct form of the verbs in the brackets.

1 We _____ (already register) for the management course which begins on Monday.

2 The economic improvement _____ (feel) in most Asian nations by this time next year.

3 The film show _____ (not begin) yet when Tom and I arrived.

4 The staff meeting _____ (just postpone) as the principal has fallen ill.

5 It _____ (be supposed to rain) today but so far we have only had sunshine.

6 Valuable natural forests _____ (cut down) before the government passed the conservation laws this year.

7 Vicki _____ (already tell) that she will be the new executive secretary to the manager.

8 The entire coastline _____ (cover) by smog by tomorrow unless something is done to clean up the air.

9 None of my letters _____ (deliver) to Vera since her change of address.

10 My cousins _____ (be supposed to visit) us last week but they did not come.

YOUR SCORE
10

PRACTICE *B* Underline the correct words in the brackets.

1 The dusk-to-dawn curfew (will have lifted / will have been lifted) by the end of the week.

2 The baby (has been looked after / had been looked after) by Dr Young before he retired as a paediatric consultant.

3 The glass windows (were shattered / had been shattered) and their house burgled by the time Mr and Mrs Davies returned from a party.

4 He (will have undergone / will undergo) surgery by Tuesday this week.

5 They (are supposed to lend / supposed to lend) us their domino sets for the competition.

75

6 These special lights using solar energy (are suppose to illuminate / are supposed to illuminate) the garden at night.

7 Linda (has been ridiculed / is been ridiculed) by insensitive friends for the strange colour of her hair.

8 Fellow scientists (have been recognised / have finally recognised) Dr Hall's research findings on cancer.

9 The directors (had been briefed / had briefed) the prime minister before he inspected the construction of the dam.

10 Kate (will have been spent / will have spent) most of her money by the time she goes back home.

YOUR SCORE
10

PRACTICE *C* Five of the underlined verb forms in the passage are incorrect. Circle them and write their numbers and the correct verbs in the spaces provided.

In some countries, women (1) <u>had come</u> a long way from what they (2) <u>were</u> in the past. A half-century ago, many women (3) <u>were</u> contented to remain at home. They (4) <u>have not yet been exposed</u> to the challenges which professional work (5) <u>offered</u> them.

In some places there was a change in the early 1960s, with the movement for equal treatment of men and women. This movement (6) <u>caused</u> many women to reexamine their traditional roles as mothers and homemakers. Since then, many of them (7) <u>went</u> out to work. Nowadays, as women in greater numbers pursue professional qualifications, the theory that the man (8) <u>is suppose</u> to be the sole family breadwinner (9) <u>had been laid</u> to rest.

In these countries, women (10) <u>have been employed</u> in almost every field of work. Their capabilities as being equal to that of their male co-workers (11) <u>has been proved</u>.

(*1*) *have come* _____   (   ) _____

(   ) _____   (   ) _____

(   ) _____   (   ) _____

YOUR SCORE
10

PRACTICE *D* Some of the sentences are incorrect. Rewrite them correctly.

1 We are supposed to be left for the island this afternoon but there might be a delay due to weather conditions.

We are supposed to leave for the island this afternoon but there might be a delay due to

weather conditions.

2 Kevin will have graduated with a degree in law by June this year.

_____

_____

76

3 Pat has been supported by her parents for two years before she was awarded a scholarship.

_____

_____

4 You were supposed to treated us to dinner if we did well in our exams.

_____

_____

5 A couple of passengers have been cancelled their names from the waiting list so we are able to get seats on the next flight.

_____

_____

6 We have submitted our report to the chairman long before he asked for it.

_____

_____

PRACTICE E Rewrite the sentences in the active or passive voice.

1 The visiting dignitaries have been escorted to a number of places by the club president.

The club _____

_____

2 Mrs Jones had taught us for five years before she returned to the her own country.

We _____

_____

3 She is supposed to tell the candidates the requirements of the interviewing board.

The candidates _____

_____

4 The secretary will have posted the agenda for the meeting to all the shareholders by Friday.

The agenda _____

_____

5 Stella has been highly commended by the city authorities for informing the police about the robbery she witnessed.

The city _____

_____

UNIT 5.1 DIRECT AND INDIRECT SPEECH

positive and negative statements

Look at the **A** and **B** sentences below. Find out why **B** is correct and **A** is wrong in the **Grammar Points** section.

			GRAMMAR POINTS
1A	"I was waiting outside for two hours," **said he**.	✗	
1B	"I was waiting outside for two hours," **he said.**	✓	1
2A	"Lately," said Aunt Nelly**, you** have been so busy."	✗	
2B	"Lately," said Aunt Nelly**, "you** have been so busy."	✓	2
3A	Kate said to us, "I don't have Pat's telephone number." Kate told us that she **don't have** Pat's telephone number.	✗	
3B	Kate said to us, "I don't have Pat's telephone number." Kate told us that she **didn't have** Pat's telephone number.	✓	3

GRAMMAR POINTS

1 In direct speech, we put the actual words of the speaker or writer within quotation marks. We can place the reporting clause before or after the quote.

EXAMPLE:

Betty said **,** " I'm going to the bank. "

- reporting clause
- comma after reporting clause
- quote

"I'm going to the bank," said Betty.

- quote
- reporting clause

When the reporting clause comes after the quote, we can place the subject after the verb unless the subject is a pronoun.

EXAMPLE:

"I'm going to the bank," said Betty. ✓
- noun subject

"I'm going to the bank," said she. ✗
- pronoun subject

"I'm going to the bank," she said. ✓
- pronoun subject

2 We use two sets of quotation marks when we present the quote in two parts. We can place the reporting clause between the first and second parts of the quote in these ways:

(a) after a noun group

EXAMPLE: " My boss ," said Rose , " is a hardworking woman. "

noun group — reporting clause — second part of quote

(b) after an adverb

EXAMPLE: " Later ," said Tom , "we will go for a swim."

adverb — reporting clause

(c) after names or terms of address

EXAMPLE: " My dear ," said Mr Wells , "we don't want to be late for the show."

term of address — reporting clause

(d) after a clause

EXAMPLE: " We stood there for an hour ," said Dave , "but no one came."

clause — reporting clause

3 In indirect speech, we report what someone has said using a **that**-clause. We usually change the tense of the verb, pronouns, possessive adjectives and time expressions when we convert from direct speech to indirect speech.

EXAMPLES: Bob said to his wife, " **I made** a few changes to **our** plans. "

Bob told his wife that **he had made** a few changes to **their** plans .

reported clause

Colin said to me, " **I don't** think **I can** attend **your** party **tomorrow**. "

Colin told me that **he didn't** think **he could** attend **my** party **the next day** .

reported clause

REMEMBER!

■ If a statement in the quote (direct speech) is true at the time of reporting (indirect speech), there is no need to change the tense of the verb for indirect speech.

EXAMPLE: Sally said, "I **work** in a legal firm."
Sally said that she **works** in a legal firm.

PRACTICE | *A* | Tick the correct sentences.

1 "Ryan isn't coming," said Mary, because he had an urgent phone call."

2 "Sometimes," said Jane, "I feel so weary after work."

3 "I can't understand what all the fuss is about," he said.

4 The girls said "We would like to discuss the problem."

5 "I'm not as active as I used to be," said Mr Jones.

6 "I suggest you have a complete rest, Mrs Lance," said he.

7 "My dear Sally," said Steve, "you have taken the wrong route.

8 "This café has a beautiful ambience," said Ben to us, "but terrible service."

9 "The concert pianist," said the theatre manager "has fallen ill."

10 Jean said, "I'm sure I've seen that man somewhere."

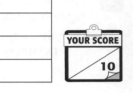

PRACTICE **B** Underline the correct words in the brackets.

1 ("Those women" / "Those women,") said Janet, "would like to see the director."

2 "There's a queue at the bank," said David, ("so we'll come back later" / "so we'll come back later.")

3 ("I'm tired and hungry said Sara," / "I'm tired and hungry," said Sara,) "because I've walked a long way."

4 Mum said to Dad, ("we'll be ready in half an hour" / "We'll be ready in half an hour.")

5 ("Hello, Sandra" / "Hello Sandra,") said Mr Smith. "I've not seen you for quite a while."

6 ("Gradually said Karen," / "Gradually," said Karen,) "we managed to get out of the cave."

7 ("My dear Kate," / "My dear Kate,) said Ann, "please write to me often."

8 (Recently, / "Recently,") said Uncle Pete, "there's been a lot of talk about re-employing retired teachers."

9 "I'd like some medication for my cold," (said Sally, to the doctor. / said Sally to the doctor.)

10 "I've been here for an hour," said Mr Sims, ("and the counter is still closed". / "and the counter is still closed.")

PRACTICE **C** Tick the correct words to complete the sentences.

1 Justin said to me, "I will talk to you next Friday."

Justin told me that [ ] he / [ ] I [ ] will talk / [ ] would talk to me the following Friday.

2 "This book," said Eddy, "fascinates me greatly."

[ ] That / [ ] This book, said Eddy, [ ] fascinated / [ ] had fascinated him greatly.

3 Brian said to us, "I need you to help me decorate the hall tomorrow."

Brian told us that he [ ] needs / [ ] needed [ ] them / [ ] us to help him decorate the hall the next day.

4 The elderly couple said to me, "We didn't hear the announcement."

The elderly couple told me that [ ] they / [ ] we [ ] hadn't heard / [ ] didn't hear the announcement.

5 "It's a wonderful party," said Sue, "but I have to leave now."

It [ ] is / [ ] was a wonderful party, said Sue, but she [ ] has / [ ] had to leave then.

PRACTICE *D* Rewrite the sentences in direct speech or indirect speech.

1 "Sara has so many things to do," said Tom, "that she doesn't know where to begin."

_____

_____

2 "We may come for the meeting tomorrow," said the workers.

_____

_____

3 Bill told Julie that his sister was going to visit her on Saturday.

_____

_____

4 Miss Wong said, "The Chao Praya River provides the Thai people with water for consumption and irrigation."

_____

_____

5 Philip told us that we hadn't missed much as the match had just begun.

_____

_____

YOUR SCORE 10

PRACTICE *E* Some of the sentences below are incorrect. Rewrite them correctly.

1 They said to us, "We will have submitted our designs by next week."
They told us that they would submit their designs by next week.

_____

_____

2 Mrs Potts complained to the manager that his salesman had been rude to her.
Mrs Potts said to the manager, "His salesman was rude to me."

_____

_____

3 "Mr President," said the Mayor, "your guests are waiting in the banquet hall."
The Mayor told the President that his guests were waiting in the banquet hall.

_____

_____

4 Connie told me that she hadn't worn an evening gown before.
Connie said to me, "I hadn't worn an evening gown before."

_____

_____

5 "A long time ago," said Mum, "I used to read you bedtime stories."
A long time ago, said Mum, I used to read you bedtime stories.

_____

_____

YOUR SCORE 10

UNIT 5.2 DIRECT AND INDIRECT SPEECH

positive and negative questions

Look at the **A** and **B** sentences below. Find out why **B** is correct and **A** is wrong in the **Grammar Points** section.

GRAMMAR POINTS

1A	"Is this the book you want"**?** said the salesman.	✗	
1B	"Is this the book you want**?**" said the salesman.	✓	1
2A	Peter said to me, "**Are** you busy today?" Peter asked me whether I **am** busy that day.	✗	
2B	Peter said to me, "**Are** you busy today?" Peter asked me whether I **was** busy that day.	✓	2
3A	Mr Dale said to Ann, "Where did I put my blue file?" Mr Dale asked Ann **where had he put** his blue file.	✗	
3B	Mr Dale said to Ann, "Where did I put my blue file?" Mr Dale asked Ann **where he had put** his blue file.	✓	3
4A	Scott asked, "Aren't the boys coming to help us?" Scott asked **the boys whether or not** were coming to help us.	✗	
4B	Scott asked, "Aren't the boys coming to help us?" Scott asked **whether or not the boys** were coming to help us. / Scott asked **whether the boys** were coming to help us **or not**.	✓	4

 **GRAMMAR POINTS**

1 In a direct question, we put the actual words of the speaker as well as the question mark within quotation marks. We can place the reporting clause before or after the quote.

EXAMPLE:

The lawyer said, " Did you see the incident**?** " ✓

reporting clause — quote

The lawyer said, "Did you see the incident"**?** ✗

" Did you see the incident**?** " said the lawyer. ✓

quote — reporting clause

2 In an indirect question, we do not use a question mark or quotation marks. We do the following in the reported clause:

(a) we always place the subject before the verb (just like in a statement).

EXAMPLE: *Direct speech:* David said to me, "**Is** Mark **coming**?" ☑

verb · subject · verb

Indirect speech: David asked me if Mark **was coming**. ☑

subject · verb

David asked me if **was** Mark **coming**. ✗

verb · subject · verb

(b) we usually change the tense of the verb as well as pronouns, possessive adjectives and time expressions.

EXAMPLE: Tom said to Sue, "**Are you going** to the play **next week**?"

verb · subject

Tom asked Sue whether **she was going** to the play **the following week**.

subject · verb

REMEMBER!

■ When a direct question has a **yes** or **no** answer, **whether** or **if** is used in its indirect question.

EXAMPLES: He said, "Would you like a hot drink?" "Is she waiting for a lift?" he said.
He asked **if** I would like a hot drink. He asked **whether** she was waiting for a lift.

---

3 When a direct question begins with the verb **do** or **did**, or a wh-word + **do** or **did**, we omit the verb **do** or **did** for the indirect question.

EXAMPLES: Kelly said to me, "**Do** you **want** some tea?"

Kelly asked me **if** I **wanted** some tea. ☑

Kelly asked me **did** I **want** some tea. ✗

Her husband said, "**What did** you **buy** from the shop?"

Her husband asked her **what** she **had bought** from the shop. ☑

Her husband asked her **what did** she **buy** from the shop. ✗

4 When a direct question begins with the negative form of the verb 'to be' or the verb 'to do', we use **whether** and **or not** in the indirect question.

EXAMPLE: He said to James, "**Don't** your parents live here?"

He asked James **whether** his parents lived there **or not**. ☑

He asked James **whether or not** his parents lived there. ☑

PRACTICE ▢*A* Rewrite the direct questions and put in the correct punctuation marks.

1 The cashier said to Mrs Singer, do you prefer to open a new account?

_____

_____

83

2 "How much did those shoes cost" said Jill to Nina?

_____

3 The principal said to the coach "isn't the school team playing on Friday?"

_____

_____

4 Simon said to us, Where would you like to go for dinner"

_____

5 "did you hear the doorbell ring?" said Mary to me

_____

PRACTICE _B_ Cross out the incorrect words to complete the questions.

1 "Can you pick up my clothes from the cleaners?" Mum said to John.
Mum asked John if he [can | could] pick up [her | your] clothes from the cleaners.

2 The doctor said to me, "What kind of medication did you take?"
The doctor asked me what kind of medication [I | you] [took | had taken] .

3 James asked Linda if she knew the way to the station.
James said to Linda, " [Do | Does] [she | you] know the way to the station?"

4 Mabel asked Joanna whether that mixture needed more sugar or not.
" [Doesn't | Don't] [this | that] mixture need more sugar?" said Mabel to Joanna.

5 "Why does Jill want to leave early?" Sam said.
Sam asked [why | why did] Jill [had wanted | wanted] to leave early.

PRACTICE _C_ Rewrite the sentences using indirect questions.

1 The lady said to me, "Why are you shivering?"
The lady asked me why I was shivering.

2 "Did you finish your homework?" Mum said to Linda.

_____

3 Mrs Law said to us, "Do you want some lemonade?"

_____

4 "When are we starting work?" Tom said to me.

_____

5 Sally said to us, "Doesn't the birthday cake look lovely?"

_____

6 Eddy said, "Why do you want to see me?"

_____

Some of the sentences below are incorrect. Rewrite them correctly.

1 "Why are you playing in the rain?" Ken said to the children.
   Ken asked the children why were they playing in the rain.

   _____

   _____

2 He asked his daughter, Sandra, if she liked the dress he had bought her.
   He said to his daughter, Sandra, "Do you like the dress I had bought you?"

   _____

   _____

3 The science teacher said to us, "Do you know how to set up the equipment?"
   The science teacher asked us do we know how to set up the equipment.

   _____

   _____

4 "Is there enough petrol in the car?" Dinah said to me.
   Dinah asked me if there was enough petrol in the car.

   _____

   _____

5 "Didn't you switch on the porch lights?" we said to Jenny.
   We asked Jenny whether or not she switch on the porch lights.

   _____

   _____

YOUR SCORE
10

PRACTICE E   Rewrite the questions in the dialogue below in indirect speech.

Dave : Libby, aren't the invitation cards for the club dinner and dance ready?
Libby : I sent them out to the various schools last week.
Dave : Have you got any replies?
Libby : More than 70 people have said they are coming.
Dave : Do you think there will be a good turnout?
Libby : I think we will have a crowd of about 200.
Dave : Has John finalised the arrangements for the food?
Libby : He has already spoken to the caterers. Dave, I think we should have
         a meeting to make sure everything is going smoothly.
Dave : Are you going to contact the committee members?
Libby : Dave, you can do that.

1 Dave asked Libby _____

2 Dave asked Libby _____

3 Dave asked Libby _____

4 He asked her _____

5 He asked her _____

YOUR SCORE
10

85

UNIT 6.1 MODALS

positive statements

Look at the **A** and **B** sentences below. Find out why **B** is correct and **A** is wrong in the **Grammar Points** section.

			GRAMMAR POINTS
1A	Joanna needs to **informs** the college immediately about the incident.	✗	
1B	Joanna needs to **inform** the college immediately about the incident.	✓	1
2A	They should **announcing** the results of the elections soon.	✗	
2B	They should **be announcing** the results of the elections soon.	✓	2
3A	Why did he go by bus? We could have **gave** him a lift.	✗	
3B	Why did he go by bus? We could have **given** him a lift.	✓	3
4A	The posters ought to **design** by Emily.	✗	
4B	The posters ought to **be designed** by Emily.	✓	4

GRAMMAR POINTS

1 We always use the base form of a verb with a modal. We do not use the 's' or 'es' forms for singular subjects.

EXAMPLES:

David **ought to** spend more time with his family.
subject — modal — base form of main verb

We **should** share the cost of the meal.
subject — modal — base form of main verb

John Sullivan **could** be the next prime minister.
subject — modal — base form of verb 'to be'

2 We use a present participle with a modal to indicate something is possibly (**could**, **may**) or very likely to be (**must**, **should**) happening at the time of speaking, or will probably (**could**, **may**) or very likely (**shall**, **will**) be happening in the future.

> **REMEMBER!**
>
> ■ Modals are a type of auxiliary verb. The following are modals:
>
> | | | |
> |---|---|---|
> | can | could | may |
> | might | must | shall |
> | should | will | would |
>
> | | | |
> |---|---|---|
> | have to | need to | ought to |
>
> *Note:* **Have to** and **need to** are the only modals that must agree with the subject.
> **EXAMPLES:**
> I/We **have to/need to** . . .
> Joan/She **has to/needs to** . . .
>
> ■ Modals are usually used in statements to express the following:
> ability – can, could
> advice – had better, ought to, should
> certainty or intention – shall, will, would
> necessity – must, need to
> obligation – ought to, should
> permission – can, may
> possibility – could, may, might
> willingness – shall, will, would

We use the base form of the verb 'to be' with the present participle in this way:

Subject + modal + **be** + present participle

EXAMPLES: The college **could** be processing our application forms now.
modal
subject   base form   present participle
(possible event now)

Lynn **may** be staying with her cousin when she goes to India.
modal
subject   base form   present participle
(probable event in the future)

3 We use a past participle with a modal to indicate the speaker thinks it is possible (**could**, **might**) or very likely (**must**, **would**) that something happened in the past. We use it in this way:

Subject + modal + **have** + past participle

EXAMPLES: They **could** have forgotten that the meeting was cancelled.
modal
subject   base form   past participle
(possible event in the past)

The clerk **must** have shredded the documents by mistake.
modal
subject   base form   past participle
(likely event in the past)

4 We can use passive verbs with modals in this way:

Subject + modal + **be** + past participle

EXAMPLE: *Active voice:* You **must** take the medicine three times a day.
modal
subject   active verb

Passive voice: The medicine **must** be taken three times a day.
modal
subject   passive verb

PRACTICE *A* Underline the correct words in the brackets.

1 It may (be / to be) too late to call Louise.

2 I (can / could) have left my mobile phone in the car.

3 You (should get / could getting) your electrician to check the thermostat of your fridge.

4 The company (may be considering / may be consider) John for the post of marketing manager.

5 The president's speech (would read / would be read) out to the whole assembly.

6 The authorities need to (put / puts) up a sign warning motorists about the dangerous bend ahead.

7 That man waving from the balcony could be (try / trying) to get your attention.

8 The cleaners would (have completed / completing) the job by now.

9 The brochures (must be placed / must place) in a prominent place.

10 The council ought to (spray / sprays) the area because of mosquitoes.

YOUR SCORE

10

PRACTICE *B*   Circle the letters of the correct sentences. There may be more than one answer for each question.

1   **A**   He ought apologised to Mr Woods for his mistake.
    B   He ought to apologise to Mr Woods for his mistake.
    C   He ought to apologised to Mr Woods for his mistake.

2   **A**   You could have informed me earlier that you would be late.
    B   You could had informed me earlier that you would be late.
    C   You could have inform me earlier that you would be late.

3   **A**   Mrs Larson may be staying late to finish some work at the office.
    B   Mrs Larson may stay late to finish some work at the office.
    C   Mrs Larson may be stay late to finish some work at the office.

4   **A**   The accused must jailed for a minimum of four years if he is found guilty.
    B   The accused must be jail for a minimum of four years if he is found guilty.
    C   The accused must be jailed for a minimum of four years if he is found guilty.

5   **A**   The writing desk you ordered will delivered to your office tomorrow afternoon.
    B   The writing desk you ordered will be delivering to your office tomorrow afternoon.
    C   The writing desk you ordered will be delivered to your office tomorrow afternoon.

6   **A**   We need to holds the function in a hall that can accommodate about a thousand guests.
    B   We need to hold the function in a hall that can accommodate about a thousand guests.
    C   We need hold the function in a hall that can accommodate about a thousand guests.

7   **A**   The search teams would have entered the jungle by now to look for the missing scouts.
    B   The search teams might enter the jungle by now to look for the missing scouts.
    C   The search teams may be entering the jungle now to look for the missing scouts.

8   **A**   The distress signal should have been spot by the marine patrol boats.
    B   The distress signal should have been spotted by the marine patrol boats.
    C   The distress signal should be spot by the marine patrol boats.

YOUR SCORE

10

PRACTICE *C*   Fill in the blanks with the correct words in the box.

be	been	cancelled	cancelling	elect	elected
forgot	forgotten	read	reading	remember	remembered
run	running	take	taking		
use	be used	want	wanting		

1   This could _____ the missing necklace Nancy is looking for.

2   Malachite is a bright green ore which can _____ to make beads.

3   They may be _____ a workshop on effective speaking next week.

4   Water is flowing into the living room! You must have _____ to turn off the kitchen tap!

5   The vice-chancellor will be _____ disciplinary action against the students who vandalised the stage.

6   The members might have _____ David Carr as chairman when they considered his vast experience in the private sector.

7   He would have _____ his flight to New York after hearing about his sister's accident.

88

8 You ought to _____ that Elaine supported you last year.

9 She might _____ to see the original documents before she decides whether or not to employ you.

10 House buyers need to _____ the fine print before signing the contract.

PRACTICE *D* Rewrite the sentences in the passive voice.

1 You must keep your cheque book in a safe place.
Your cheque book must be kept in a safe place.

2 Helen should tell Mr Nelson the good news.

_____

3 You ought to remind your grandfather about his next medical appointment.

_____

_____

4 The factory may dismiss about a hundred workers next month.

_____

5 Julie has to finalise the tour arrangements this afternoon.

_____

6 Speedy Caterers can organise a buffet dinner for five hundred guests in two days.

_____

_____

PRACTICE *E* Five other verb forms in the conversation are incorrect. Underline them and write the correct verbs in the spaces provided.

Julia : Mike, I see a building ahead. That <u>could been</u> Windsong Hotel.

Mike : It must be the hotel we're looking for. We haven't seen a building for miles around and we must have been travelled more than five kilometres by now.

Julia : Yes, it is the hotel. I can see its signboard now.

Mike : Good . . . . Hey, why is the gate locked? Hotels ought to leaving their gates open so guests can drove right up to their front doors. I will complain to the hotel manager about this. Yes, and I'll also tell him that a new and bigger signboard should provide so hotel guests can find his place easily.

Julia : Mike, you need to be more understanding. For all you know, the hotel owner could planning to renovate the place. I can see bricks and a pile of sand near the gate.

1 *could be* _____ **4** _____

2 _____ **5** _____

3 _____ **6** _____

UNIT 6.2 **MODALS**

negative statements

Look at the **A** and **B** sentences below. Find out why **B** is correct and **A** is wrong in the **Grammar Points** section.

1A	You **must not to** visit me because I have chickenpox.	✗	
1B	You **must not / mustn't** visit me because I have chickenpox.	✓	1
2A	He **shouldn't making** fun of people all the time.	✗	
2B	He **shouldn't make** fun of people all the time. / He **shouldn't be making** fun of people all the time.	✓	2
3A	Sue **might not seen** you when you waved to her.	✗	
3B	Sue **might not have seen** you when you waved to her.	✓	3
4A	That document **cannot signed** by anyone but Tim.	✗	
4B	That document **cannot be signed** by anyone but Tim.	✓	4

GRAMMAR POINTS

1 We use **not** or its contraction **n't** to change a modal to its negative form. We drop **to** when we form the negative of **need to**. However, we keep **to** when we form the negative of **ought to**. The verb that follows has to be in its base form.

EXAMPLES:

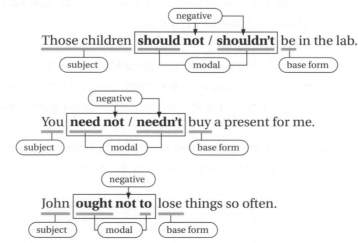

You **must not / mustn't** use the telephone when there's lightning or thunder.
subject — modal — base form — negative

Those children **should not / shouldn't** be in the lab.
subject — modal — base form — negative

You **need not / needn't** buy a present for me.
subject — modal — base form — negative

John **ought not to** lose things so often.
subject — modal — base form — negative

2 When we use a present participle with the negative form of a modal, we have to include the base form of the verb 'to be' in this way:

Subject + modal + **not** / **n't** + **be** + present participle

EXAMPLES:

negative modal

He **shouldn't** be taking such long lunch breaks.

subject — base form — present participle

negative modal

Sue **won't** be vying for the post of chairperson this year.

subject — base form — present participle

3 When we use a past participle with the negative form of a modal, we have to include the base form of the verb 'to have' in this way:

Subject + modal + **not** / **n't** + **have** + past participle

EXAMPLES:

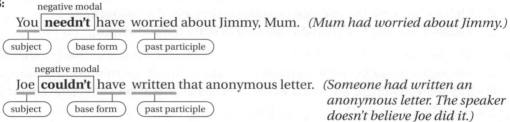

negative modal

You **needn't** have worried about Jimmy, Mum. *(Mum had worried about Jimmy.)*

subject — base form — past participle

negative modal

Joe **couldn't** have written that anonymous letter. *(Someone had written an anonymous letter. The speaker doesn't believe Joe did it.)*

subject — base form — past participle

4 We use passive verbs with the negative form of modals in this way:

Subject + modal + **not** / **n't** + **be** + past participle

EXAMPLE:

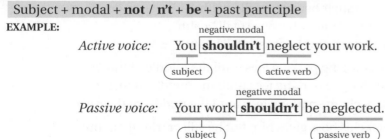

negative modal

Active voice: You **shouldn't** neglect your work.

subject — active verb

negative modal

Passive voice: Your work **shouldn't** be neglected.

subject — passive verb

PRACTICE [*A*] Fill in the blanks with the correct modals in the boxes.

1 You _____ be meticulous but you _____ be finicky.

| ought to |
| ought not to |

2 He _____ stay with Simon because Simon's relatives are here. He _____ stay at Hogan's Inn which isn't very expensive.

| can |
| can't |

3 Sylvia _____ splurging on clothes and cosmetics every month. She _____ trying to save some money.

| should be |
| shouldn't be |

4 I _____ tell anyone what you told me. I _____ keep it a secret between us.

| shall |
| shan't |

5 They _____ let him go out at night on his own in a foreign city. They _____ gone with him.

| would have |
| wouldn't have |

PRACTICE [*B*] Circle the letters of the correct sentences.

1 **A** We needn't make dinner reservations at that restaurant.
   B We needn't made dinner reservations at that restaurant.
   C We needn't to make dinner reservations at that restaurant.

2 **A** The angry crowd couldn't restrained so the riot police had to be brought in.
   B The angry crowd couldn't restraining so the riot police had to be brought in.
   C The angry crowd couldn't be restrained so the riot police had to be brought in.

3 **A** You can't be cleaned your room so soon!
   B You can't cleaned your room so soon!
   C You can't have cleaned your room so soon!

4 **A** Those who come late shouldn't be allowing to enter the auditorium.
   B Those who come late shouldn't be allowed to enter the auditorium.
   C Those who come late shouldn't allowed to enter the auditorium.

5 **A** The secretary ought not to have made a decision without consulting the chairman.
   B The secretary ought not have made a decision without consulting the chairman.
   C The secretary ought not to has made a decision without consulting the chairman.

6 **A** Jaime and Anna would not consoled by anyone.
   B Jaime and Anna would not be consoled by anyone.
   C Jaime and Anna would not be console by anyone.

7 **A** He might not attended the seminar because of ill health.
   B He might not be attending the seminar because of ill health.
   C He might not be attended the seminar because of ill health.

8 **A** The supermarket won't be charging parking fees until the middle of this year.
   B The supermarket won't be charged parking fees until the middle of this year.
   C The supermarket won't have charge parking fees until the middle of this year.

9 **A** Mark may not like the orders his boss gives him but he still carries them out.
   B Mark mayn't like the orders his boss gives him but he still carries them out.
   C Mark may not liked the orders his boss gives him but he still carries them out.

10 A These canisters mustn't be leaving in the sun.
    B These canisters mustn't left in the sun.
    C These canisters mustn't be left in the sun.

PRACTICE *C* Rewrite the sentences in the passive voice.

1 You ought not to discard these boxes and files.
   These boxes and files ought not to be discarded.

2 The company can't dismiss John without good reason.
   _____

3 My friend could not eat the spicy food at the restaurant.
   _____

4 She might not ask Steve to explain his whereabouts yesterday.
   _____

5 The girls needn't carry the heavy rucksacks and poles.
   _____

6 Your employer shouldn't discourage you from attending evening classes.
   _____

PRACTICE *D* Underline the mistakes in verb forms in the conversation. Fill in the blanks with the correct verbs.

Paula : Jack, you're using your handphone while driving! You <u>mustn't breaking</u> the law!

Jack : You needn't worry. I can drive perfectly well with one hand on the wheel.

Paula : You ought to be using a hands-free kit so you won't endangering our lives!

Jack : The hands-free kits are unreliable. All my friends say so.

Paula : I can't understand why you listen more to your friends than to the law. Just last week a celebrity and her companion suffered massive internal injuries in a road accident. It is possible that they might not live and this is all because of her chauffeur. The police say he shouldn't answered his handphone when it rang. The news report also says that it's not just dialing a number or holding a handphone that causes car accidents. When you're talking on the phone, you can't concentrated fully on the road. I really think it's about time the law ruled that any motorist caught holding a handphone while driving will not allowed to drive for a month. That should make lawbreakers like you take notice.

Jack : You wouldn't have a driver to take you around if I got caught.

Paula : That needn't bother me. At least I wouldn't lying on a hospital bed somewhere because of your silly ways!

1 *mustn't break* _____   4 _____

2 _____   5 _____

3 _____   6 _____

UNIT 6.3 MODALS

positive and negative questions

Look at the **A** and **B** sentences below. Find out why **B** is correct and **A** is wrong in the **Grammar Points** section.

			GRAMMAR POINTS
1A	**Can take** this pamphlet?	✗	
1B	**Can I take** this pamphlet?	✓	1
2A	**You will** contact me later?	✗	
2B	**Will you** contact me later?	✓	2
3A	Shouldn't John **leaves** now?	✗	
3B	Shouldn't John **leave** now?	✓	3
4A	Can't the children **taught** by Anne?	✗	
4B	Can't the children **be taught** by Anne?	✓	4

GRAMMAR POINTS

1 Every question beginning with a modal must have a subject.

EXAMPLES: **Must I** write my name in block letters on this form?   ✓

Must write my name in block letters on this form?   ✗

Should the committee recommend that he be suspended?   ✓

Should recommend that he be suspended?   ✗

REMEMBER!

■ Modals are used in questions for various purposes, such as the following:

to find out about a person's ability – can/can't, could/couldn't (for the past)

to get suggestions or advice – shall, should/shouldn't, ought to/ought not to

to find out if something is the right thing to do or is necessary – must/mustn't, should/shouldn't, ought to/ought not to

to offer something – can, could, may, shall

to ask for permission or help – can/can't, could/couldn't, may/might (more tentative)

to get an opinion – will/would, won't/wouldn't

to express uncertainty – could, might, would

to request for help or information – can/can't, could/couldn't, may, will/won't, would

to express obligation – must, should, ought to, shall

to express possibility – could/couldn't, might (more formal)

Note: **May** is normally used with the subjects **I** and **we** in questions.

■ The modal **shan't** is not used in questions.

2 In a statement, we use a modal and the base form of a verb after the subject of the sentence. In a question, we use a modal at the beginning and the subject between the modal and the base form in this way: Modal + subject + base form of main verb / the verb 'to be'

EXAMPLES:

Statement   Sandra **would** like to attend the holiday camp.
subject   modal   base form

Timothy **can** be relied upon at all times.
subject   modal   base form

Question   **Would** Sandra like to attend the holiday camp?
modal   subject   base form

Can Timothy be relied upon at all times?
modal   subject   base form

3 We use only the base form of a verb with a modal.

EXAMPLES: **Could** Cathy **take** charge of the costumes for our play?   ✓
base form

Could Cathy **takes** charge of the costumes for our play?   ✗
finite verb (present tense)

Won't he **object** to our suggestion to postpone the trip?   ✓
base form

Won't he **objecting** to our suggestion to postpone the trip?   ✗
present participle

4 We have to use the base form of the verb 'to be' + past participle with a modal when the question is in the passive voice.

EXAMPLES: **Must** the cough syrup **be taken** after meals?   ✓

Must the cough syrup **taken** after meals?   ✗

Must the cough syrup **takes** after meals?   ✗

Must the cough syrup **taking** after meals?   ✗

Must the cough syrup **took** after meals?   ✗

PRACTICE *A* Tick the correct sentences.

1 May I be excused from attending tomorrow's committee meeting?

2 Can that band make it to the top of the charts with their latest release?

3 Must answer all four questions in this section of the test paper?

4 Shouldn't they stay to help us arrange the exhibits?

5 Shall I signalled to the waiter to bring us our bill?

95

6 Ought Jason to eating so much fried food?

7 Would you like an extra blanket?

8 Should we discouraged Richard from buying a motorcycle?

9 Couldn't you get someone to babysit your children yesterday?

10 Would you fancied a trip to Portugal or to Spain?

YOUR SCORE
10

PRACTICE *B* Circle the letters of the correct questions.

1 to ask for advice
   A Should Mrs Burns be notified about this matter?
   B Shall I buy this pair of court shoes or that pair of slingbacks?
   C Ought he to lodged a complaint with the management of that company?

2 to invite
   A Could I interest you in a game of tennis?
   B Would you like to join me at the gym this evening?
   C Can your family comes for our barbecue on Saturday, 21st July?

3 to object to someone's behaviour
   A Must you let Sam bullies you every time?
   B Must Mum remind you every day to take the dog for a walk?
   C Must they frighten the little children with their shouting?

4 to express uncertainty
   A Would Kim ever do a thing like that?
   B Could Sally kept something from us?
   C Might Fiona be the one who told Mrs Brown about us?

5 to enquire about a person's ability
   A Can you solved this crossword puzzle for me?
   B Could Joanna see the boat through her telescope?
   C Can Mr Smith resolve the deadlock between management and the union?

YOUR SCORE
10

PRACTICE *C* Underline the correct words in the brackets to complete the sentences.

1 Would your company (agree / agreed) to donate a prize for our annual lucky draw?

2 Shouldn't Pamela (apply / applied) for a promotion? She is such a good worker.

3 Might Mrs Richards (override / overriding) your decision to go on unpaid leave?

4 Will the new king's coronation (be televised / televised) worldwide?

5 Must (get / we get) the council's approval before putting up these posters?

6 (Can / Would) you change a punctured tyre? I'd like you to teach me how to do it.

7 May I (be exempted / exempted) from sitting for this qualifying test?

8 Shouldn't you (look over / be looked over) the report before you sign it?

9 Can (use this ointment / this ointment be used) to ward off mosquito bites?

10 (Should Maggie be / Should be Maggie) the one to lead the debating team?

YOUR SCORE
10

PRACTICE D Rearrange the words to form correct questions.

1 a — call — committee — for — I — immediately — meeting — shall ?
Shall I call for a committee meeting immediately?

2 a — extinguisher — fire — have — his — in — John — kitchen — shouldn't ?

3 a — against — chance — have — our — Red Riders — team — the — will ?

4 be — before — can — Monday — printer — repaired — the ?

5 go — into — out — shouldn't — sun — sunblock — the — use — when — you — you?

6 at — be — contacted — couldn't — her — home — Tina — yesterday ?

YOUR SCORE
10

PRACTICE E Write questions using one of the modals given in brackets and the words in the boxes.

be	be sent
complain	like
pay	post

a cup of tea	a fussy person
by cheque	a friend's house
the electricity company	
the organisers of the competition	

1 A: Here are the class entries for the story-writing competition, Mrs Smith.
   B: Request for help (Could / Wouldn't) *Could you post the entries to the organisers of the*
   competition?

2 A: I'm so sorry. We've been so busy chatting that I forgot to get you a drink.
   B: Offer something (Must / Would)

3 A: Excuse me, Madam, here's your bill for these items.
   B: Request for information (Can / Shouldn't)

4 A: Oh dear! This is the third time we have had a power failure this week!
   B: Suggest (Will / Should)

5 A: Jeff, you're such an inconsiderate man! I just tidied your cupboard and now it's in a mess!
   B: Complain (Must / Won't)

6 A: What shall we do about our dog if we want to go on a vacation?
   B: Suggest (Can't / Mustn't)

YOUR SCORE
10

UNIT 7.1 PREPOSITIONS

> ## with ages, lists, numbers, weights, etc.

Look at the **A** and **B** sentences below. Find out why **B** is correct and **A** is wrong in the **Grammar Points** section.

			GRAMMAR POINTS
1A	These toys are not suitable for children **less than** / **lower than** three years of age.	✗	
1B	These toys are not suitable for children **below** / **under** three years of age.	✓	1
2A	Your name is **on top of** mine.	✗	
2B	Your name is **above** mine.	✓	2
3A	The temperature today is **up** 30 degrees Celsius.	✗	
3B	The temperature today is **above** 30 degrees Celsius.	✓	3
4A	The things on sale are 20 per cent **down**.	✗	
4B	The prices of things on sale have been reduced **by** 20 per cent.	✓	4

GRAMMAR POINTS

1 We can use the prepositions **at**, **above**, **below**, **over** and **under** to describe a person's age. We use them differently in these ways:

(a) **at** – refers to the exact age of a person
EXAMPLES: Children in many countries go to school **at** the age of six.
Mrs Hemmings opted for early retirement **at** the age of 45.

(b) **above** and **over** – refers to ages higher than a specific age level
EXAMPLES: The bank has provided special services for those **above** the age of 55.
Only those **over** 21 can apply for membership to the club.

(c) **below** and **under** – refers to ages lower than a specific age level
EXAMPLES: Children **below** 7 years cannot enter the pool unless accompanied by an adult.
Those **under** 55 are not considered to be senior citizens.

(d) **between** – refers to a range of ages
EXAMPLES: The spelling competition is for children **between** the ages of 5 and 7.
(Those who are 5, 6 and 7 years of age can take part in the competition.)

2 We can use **above** and **below** to refer to the position of someone or something in a group or list.
EXAMPLES: Yvonne is the senior officer in the Accounts Department. She has two other officers working **below** her.
You can find Sam's phone number just **above** Sarah's in my telephone book.

3 We can use **above**, **below**, **between**, **over** and **under** to refer to numbers or quantities. We use them differently in these ways:

(a) **above**, **below**, **over**, **under** – refers to numbers in relation to scales of measurement (such as price, speed, weight, etc.)

EXAMPLES: We need to bring down his temperature. It is **above** 100°F.
(higher than 100°F)
Those who scored **below** 50 marks are to see Mrs Chan for more coaching.
(lower than 50 marks)

(b) **over** – refers to numbers in relation to people or heights

EXAMPLES: The computer fair attracted **over** 2,000 people this weekend.
Jonathan is **over** six feet tall.

(c) **between** – refers to an approximate number or amount by stating first the smaller number and then the bigger one

EXAMPLES: That company suffered losses of **between** 1 and 1.5 million dollars last year.
I think **between** 50 and 60 people came to the opening of the new art gallery on Stonor Road.

REMEMBER!

■ The preposition **between** may or may not have to be accompanied by **and**.
It could also involve more than three people or things.

EXAMPLES: The little girl walked **between** her father **and** mother. *(three people involved)*
The little girl walked **between** her parents. *(three people involved)*

Zambia lies **between** Angola, Zimbabwe, Malawi, Tanzania **and** the Congo.
The millionaire divided his assets **among** / **between** his five children.
The retired colonel spends his time **between** gardening, playing golf, running errands for his wife **and** watching TV.

---

4 We can use **at** to refer to an exact number or quantity, and **by** to refer to an increase or decrease in quantity, or the difference between two quantities.

EXAMPLES: The grandfather clock was priced **at** $1,000 but the shop brought it down to $800 during the sale.
The baby's weight increased **by** another pound last week.

PRACTICE *A* Underline the correct words in the brackets.

1 Those (above / after) the age of 50 and those in poor health are strongly advised not to go on the Runaway Train ride at the theme park.

2 Colin is the head of the crime unit. He has 20 detectives working (below / by) him.

3 Don't buy from that supermarket. Their prices are way (above / up) those in other supermarkets in the area.

4 It's a good day for a hike. The temperature is (below / down) 20°C.

5 You can join our expedition if you're (at / over) 20.

6 (Between 20 youths / Between 20 and 25 youths) were arrested yesterday for vandalising billboards around the city.

7 Kim was upset that she missed getting a perfect score on her Maths test (below / by) just 4 marks.

8 (At / Under) the age of 80, Mr Burns was still able to carry out demanding duties on the farm.

9 Mrs Johnson's son is (before / under) five years of age so he should join the younger group over there for the games.

10 My sister prefers to teach children who are (below / between) the ages of 12 and 15.

PRACTICE *B* Complete the sentences with the correct words in the boxes.

1 The prices of stocks are falling. ABC Holdings which was trading _____ $4.50 on Friday went down _____ another dollar yesterday.

at
by

2 The weather was fine in the last few days, with the temperature _____ 80 degrees. Today, however, it's so stiflingly hot. I'm sure the temperature is _____ 90 degrees.

above
below

3 The housing agent told Mr Myers that pricing his old house _____ $400,000 was unrealistic because the more modern designs she was dealing with were _____ $250,000 and $350,000.

at
between

4 Please abide by the speed limit, Jeremy. You're so fond of driving _____ 120 kph. We were warned about crosswinds so do drive _____ 80 kph.

over
under

5 Each of the two castles is _____ 600 years old. It is said that in summer _____ 500 and 700 tourists visit the castles weekly.

between
over

PRACTICE *C* Circle the letters of the correct sentences. There may be more than one answer for each question.

1 A The Akashi-Kaikyo bridge in Japan is longer than the StoreBaelt bridge in Denmark by 390 m.
B The Akashi-Kaikyo bridge in Japan is longer than the StoreBaelt bridge in Denmark above 390 m.
C The Akashi-Kaikyo bridge in Japan is longer than the StoreBaelt bridge in Denmark over 390 m.

2 A Among the Hunzas, it is not unusual for women above the age of 50 to bear children.
B Among the Hunzas, it is not unusual for women over the age of 50 to bear children.
C Among the Hunzas, it is not unusual for women between the ages of 50 and 60 to bear children.

3 A The Dead Sea is the lowest point on the Earth's surface. It is about 1,200 feet after sea level.
B The Dead Sea is the lowest point on the Earth's surface. It is about 1,200 feet at sea level.
C The Dead Sea is the lowest point on the Earth's surface. It is about 1,200 feet below sea level.

4 A Maria weighed over 70 kilos last year but she is now under 50 kilos.
B Maria weighed above 70 kilos last year but she is now below 50 kilos.
C Maria weighed over 70 kilos last year but she is now before 50 kilos.

5 A Death Valley in California is one of the hottest places in the world. The temperature there is sometimes over 125°F.

B Death Valley in California is one of the hottest places in the world. The temperature there is sometimes above 125°F.

C Death Valley in California is one of the hottest places in the world. The temperature there is sometimes after 125°F.

6 A The Crime Desk is headed by Peter Ward. He has eight crime reporters working by him.

B The Crime Desk is headed by Peter Ward. He has eight crime reporters working after him.

C The Crime Desk is headed by Peter Ward. He has eight crime reporters working below him.

YOUR SCORE
10

PRACTICE *D* Fill in the blanks with suitable words in the box. Each word may be used more than once.

at	below	between	by	over

Mum : Where did you get that lovely pink jumper, Kathy?

Kathy : I bought it from a little shop on Beet Street, Mum. Mrs Hill, the owner, is very nice. She helped me choose it and she even reduced the price (1) _____ five dollars. It was priced (2) _____ 25 dollars to begin with.

Mum : What other colours does she have? Does she have grey?

Kathy : This was the only one she had. Here, Mum, you take it.

Mum : No, no. I shouldn't be wearing pink at my age.

Kathy : Mum, where did you get the idea that (3) _____ 55 you shouldn't wear pink?

Mum : I just read in the latest issue of Second Life that women (4) _____ 50 should dress with dignity and leave bright colours to those (5) _____ the ages of 21 and 49.

Kathy : Let me say this, Mum, and trust my words even though you are older than me (6) _____ 35 years. You have always been able to wear any colour. Getting a year older doesn't in any way change that. You should meet Mrs Hill. She must be (7) _____ 60 but you should see how elegant she is! She was wearing a red suit. She said (8) _____ 30 and 40 people visit her shop daily. Most of her regular customers are (9) _____ the age of 40 and she has helped them to stop worrying about their wrinkles and start living. She has set up an exclusive group called 'The Autumn People' and no one (10) _____ the age of 50 can gain membership to it. I think you should join it, Mum. It would be fun for you.

YOUR SCORE
10

UNIT 7.2 PREPOSITIONS

with situations and things

Look at the **A** and **B** sentences below. Find out why **B** is correct and **A** is wrong in the **Grammar Points** section.

			GRAMMAR POINTS
1A	This pretty picture frame is made **by** silver.	✗	
1B	This pretty picture frame is made **from / of / out of** silver.	✓	1
2A	Please complete the application form **with** ink.	✗	
2B	Please complete the application form **in** ink.	✓	2
3A	He got **in** trouble with the police when he tried to make an illegal U-turn.	✗	
3B	He got **into** trouble with the police when he tried to make an illegal U-turn.	✓	3

GRAMMAR POINTS

1 We can use the prepositions **from**, **of** and **out of** to refer to the origin of an object or a person, or state what something is made of. We use them differently in these ways:

(a) **from** – refers to the sender or giver, the place of origin, or the material used to make something

EXAMPLES: This card is **from** Ellen.
These oranges are **from** California.
You can make mats **from** straw.

(b) **of** – refers to the content of something, or the substance or material used to make something

EXAMPLES: The new set of encyclopaedia consists **of** 20 volumes.
This cardigan is made **of** 100 per cent wool.

(c) **out of** – refers solely to the substance or material used to make something

EXAMPLES: This lantern is made **out of** papier mâché.
Rick made this unusual puppet **out of** an old sock.

2 We can use **by**, **in** and **with** to refer to how something is done. We use them differently in these ways:

(a) **by** – refers to ways of travelling, sending or receiving something, or doing things

EXAMPLES: We travelled to Thailand **by** air.
I sent you the documents **by** courier service.
Keep the dough moistened **by** covering it with a damp muslin cloth.
(*Note:* The verb after **by** in a sentence like the above must have an 'ing' ending.)

(b) **in** – refers to the medium used when saying or doing something

EXAMPLES: Melanie sang us a beautiful song **in** French.
That artist does portraits **in** crayon.

(c) **with** – refers to the object or tool used when doing something

EXAMPLES: The workers brought down the wall **with** sledgehammers.
The doctor checked the patient's breathing **with** a stethoscope.

REMEMBER!

- A preposition can have more than one function. It can refer to position as well as time, situation, speed, etc.

EXAMPLES: Mum is **at** the door waving to Mrs Lim. *(position)*
We arrived **at** five to eight, just before the concert began. *(time)*
The countries have been **at** war for 10 years now. *(situation)*
The young man was driving **at** 140 kph when the patrol car set off after him. *(speed)*

- For some situations involving the use of objects or tools, other prepositions are used instead of **with**.

EXAMPLES: After the accident, Mike had to be **on** crutches for three weeks. *(He leans on them.)*
Grandpa can't walk now so he moves around **in** a wheelchair. *(He sits in it.)*

---

3 We can use **in**, **into** and **out of** to refer to situations. We use them differently in these ways:

(a) **in** – refers to the situation a person or thing is in already

EXAMPLES: Since October 2000, that company has been **in** financial difficulties.
We had an office party yesterday and left the whole place **in** a mess.

(b) **into** – refers to someone's getting involved or caught in a situation

EXAMPLES: The swimmer got **into** difficulties when he was about 100m from the shore.
Peter always got **into** scrapes with his neighbour's son.

(c) **out of** – refers to a person or thing no longer being in a certain situation

EXAMPLES: Carol is **out of** a job. *(She had a job earlier but now she doesn't.)*
The heart patient is **out of** danger now. *(He was critically ill earlier
but now he isn't.)*

PRACTICE *A* Circle the correct words in the boxes to complete the sentences.

1 I received the items I ordered from the catalogue _____ special delivery.

by	from

2 Mandy's great-grandmother slipped _____ a coma late last night.

in	into

3 I bought these old volumes _____ the second-hand bookstore down the road.

from	out of

4 She speaks fluently _____ both Mandarin and Tamil.

in	with

5 My dream house is one built entirely _____ timber.

by	out of

6 The prize-winning confectionery was made _____ egg white, icing sugar and lemon juice.

into	of

7 Mum improved the flavour of the salad dressing _____ adding in some parsley flakes.

by	with

8 That country is _____ a state of emergency and needs food and medical supplies.

in	out of

9 Jonathan managed to remove the stain on his shirt _____ bleach.

| of | with |

10 Your request for a transfer is _____ my hands now. Mr Lane is dealing with it.

| from | out of |

PRACTICE *B* Tick the correct sentences.

1 My naughty brother showed he was repentant by volunteer to run errands.
2 Vince got into a quarrel with Marie because of the political party she supports.
3 I bought some plaster and paint with the new hardware store.
4 The fire department removed the dangerous animal from Joe's garden out of a large net.
5 Tina restored the sheen to her dining table by polishing it with linseed oil.
6 Ben communicates with his hearing-impaired friends in sign language.
7 My great-aunt makes lovely pot holders out of scraps of material and old towels.
8 Our country imports basmati rice out of India and Pakistan.
9 The hunter stood with a gun in his hand as he waited for the wild dogs to reappear.
10 For several years, our government has been working from collaboration with other countries to end drug trafficking.

PRACTICE *C* Mark with ∧ where the prepositions should be in the sentences.

1 That dolphin understands instructions given English .

| in |

2 Do you know where these imported chocolates come ?

| from |

3 Paul makes lovely miniature furniture used matchsticks .

| out of |

4 Joanna went stocks and shares and now she regrets it .

| into |

5 I have been touch with what has been happening in the scientific field .

| out of |

6 Larry promptly put out the fire in the kitchen a fire extinguisher .

| with |

7 Their son got trouble during the time they were away .

| into |

8 Jennifer's creative work glass and ceramic caught the attention of an art reviewer .

| in |

9 Her time the world of modelling led to her setting up a modelling agency .   in

10 She eventually finished the project getting assistance from her close friends.   by

YOUR SCORE

10

PRACTICE *D*   Circle the letters of the correct sentences. There may be more than one answer for each question.

1 A That art lecturer enjoys doing batik in silk.
  B That art lecturer enjoys doing batik from silk.
  C That art lecturer enjoys doing batik into silk.

2 A This urn is made from copper and iron.
  B This urn is made of copper and iron.
  C This urn is made by copper and iron.

3 A You can reduce the saltiness with adding some water.
  B You can reduce the saltiness out of adding some water.
  C You can reduce the saltiness by adding some water.

4 A Could you mend the broken vase out of the strong glue I gave you?
  B Could you mend the broken vase by the strong glue I gave you?
  C Could you mend the broken vase with the strong glue I gave you?

5 A He played badly yesterday so he's out of the semi-finals.
  B He played badly yesterday so he's in the semi-finals.
  C He played badly yesterday so he's into the semi-finals.

6 A They have been of the shoe-making business for 20 years.
  B They have been from the shoe-making business for 20 years.
  C They have been in the shoe-making business for 20 years.

7 A I made you a Christmas candle out of paraffin wax and crayons.
  B I made you a Christmas candle from paraffin wax and crayons.
  C I made you a Christmas candle in paraffin wax and crayons.

8 A Michael got into photojournalism by chance when he photographed a bomb explosion and sold the photo to a newspaper company.
  B Michael got in photojournalism by chance when he photographed a bomb explosion and sold the photo to a newspaper company.
  C Michael got from photojournalism by chance when he photographed a bomb explosion and sold the photo to a newspaper company.

YOUR SCORE

10

UNIT 7.3 PREPOSITIONS

with people and things

Look at the **A** and **B** sentences below. Find out why **B** is correct and **A** is wrong in the **Grammar Points** section.

			GRAMMAR POINTS
1A	He usually eats crackers **and** cheese.	✗	
1B	He usually eats crackers **with** cheese.	✓	1
2A	Susie's mother is a woman **with** great courage.	✗	
2B	Susie's mother is a woman **of** great courage.	✓	2
3A	You are **same like** me.	✗	
3B	You are **like** me.	✓	3
4A	The angry woman threw a tea towel **to** her son and told him to dry the dishes.	✗	
4B	The angry woman threw a tea towel **at** her son and told him to dry the dishes.	✓	4

GRAMMAR POINTS

1 We use the preposition **with** to refer to two or more people being together or two or more things being used at the same time.

EXAMPLES: Since Tina was unsure of the way to Bill's house, I went **with** her.
I knew you liked bananas but I didn't know you ate them **with** chillies!

2 We can use **with** and **of** to show possession. We use them differently in these ways:

(a) **of** – to describe the characteristics a person or thing possesses

EXAMPLES: She has a heart **of** gold.
That sculpture is an object **of** great beauty.

(b) **with** – to describe the physical features or behaviour of a person or thing, or to state what is attached to that person or thing

EXAMPLES: Janet's sister is that lady **with** long, curly hair.
Since its fall from a tree, my cat has been walking **with** a limp.
Tom is the boy **with** an eye-patch.
They have a house **with** a beautiful view of the sea.

REMEMBER!

■ The preposition **without** is the opposite of **with**.

EXAMPLES:

He is a man **without** a conscience. *(He does not have a conscience.)*

May was finally able to walk **without** her crutches. *(She does not need to use the crutches.)*

---

3 We use **from** and **like** as opposites when we make comparisons between people or things. We use them differently in these ways:

(a) **like** – to show similarity

   EXAMPLE: This chest of drawers looks exactly **like** the one I saw in Paradise Mall except that this isn't made of teak.

(b) **from** – to show lack of similarity

   EXAMPLES: You are very different **from** your sister. You are outgoing but she is an introvert.
   Your signature on this cheque differs **from** that on your other cheque.

REMEMBER!

■ A verb can go with two different prepositions. The preposition which is to be used depends on whether the object is a person or thing.

   EXAMPLES: Your first essay **differs from** your second essay in style and maturity of thought.
   I **differ with** you on the issue of corporal punishment for children.

Verbs and also adjectives that take different prepositions for person and thing include the following:

Verbs		Adjectives	
person	**thing**	**person**	**thing**
agree with	agree about / on / to	angry with	angry about
apologise to	apologise for	disappointed with	disappointed about / at / with
complain to	complain about	pleased with	pleased at / about / with

---

4 We use **for** or **against** to show whether or not we support someone or something.
We use **at** with verbs like **shout** to show negative attitudes or actions towards someone or something, and **to** with some verbs to show neutral or positive attitudes or actions.

   EXAMPLES: I voted **for** school hours to be shortened but Jessie voted **against** school hours being shortened. (*I wanted less school hours but Jessie didn't.*)

   Mrs Hanson shouted **at** the cow which had wandered into her garden.
   Mrs Hanson shouted **to** her children to be careful when crossing the road.

PRACTICE *A* Fill in the blanks with the words in the box. Each word may be used more than once.

> against   at   for   from   like   of   to   with

1 She amazes me because she does her housework _____ such enthusiasm.

2 That tall young man walks _____ a stoop.

3 Sue is exactly _____ her mother in her mannerisms.

4 The unkind boys laughed _____ me when I fell into the pond.

5 I like spaghetti _____ lots of sauce and cheese on it.

6 The watchmaker is unable to distinguish the fake watches _____ the genuine ones.

7 She never forgives those who go _____ her wishes.

8 He is a man who has gone through a period _____ great suffering.

9 I am _____ the motion to introduce religion as a subject in schools as this promotes understanding between students of different faiths.

10 James tossed a ball _____ his dog and watched as it cleverly leapt up and caught it.

PRACTICE **B** Circle the letters of the correct sentences. There may be more than one answer for each question.

1 **A** Tom argued against the proposal to make 20 employees redundant.
 B Tom argued at the proposal to make 20 employees redundant.
 C Tom argued with the proposal to make 20 employees redundant.

2 **A** The chairman described the guest speaker as a man to his word.
 B The chairman described the guest speaker as a man like his word.
 C The chairman described the guest speaker as a man of his word.

3 **A** Sally accepted the challenge to lead the team with any hesitation.
 B Sally accepted the challenge to lead the team from any hesitation.
 C Sally accepted the challenge to lead the team without any hesitation.

4 **A** Sarjit has a sense of humour like his father.
 B Sarjit has a sense of humour from his father.
 C Sarjit has a sense of humour with his father.

5 **A** The public was for the total conservation of the forested area.
 B The public differed with the land office on the issue of logging permits in the area.
 C The public spoke out against those who wanted the land office to issue logging permits.

6 **A** Paul snapped to the little girl who was throwing a tantrum.
 B Paul snapped at the little girl who picked up his glass trophy.
 C Paul snapped against the little girl who refused to go to bed.

7 **A** Children's stories of long ago differ greatly with those written by authors of today.
 B Children's books of today have lots of illustrations, just like those of long ago.
 C The books we read as children are so different from those read by children nowadays.

PRACTICE **C** Rewrite the sentences that are incorrect.

1 Ever since her illness, she has had difficulty of her breathing.

_____

_____

2 The criticisms levelled against the building of the dam were valid.

_____

_____

3 Joe's dream is to go on a cruise ship of its own swimming pool, cinema, restaurants and video games arcade.

_____

_____

4 I love animals so I'm with all scientific experiments that subject them to pain.

_____

_____

5 The tour guide yelled against her tour group members not to sit too close to the edge of the pool.

_____

_____

PRACTICE [**D**]   Some of the places marked with ⋀ require prepositions. Write the correct prepositions in the boxes.

1 My father is ⋀ a man of great talent.

2 Wherever he goes outside of work hours, he takes ⋀ his briefcase, tool set and saxophone with him.

3 Even as a guest in someone's house, he will not hesitate ⋀ to offer to repair a burst pipe or change a fuse.

4 In these ways he is very much ⋀ his late father, my grandfather.

5 My grandfather, Dad once told me, was a person everybody found different ⋀ from anybody else they had met.

6 He was multi-talented and he always offered help to anyone ⋀ a problem.

7 He also never hesitated to speak out ⋀ anything he found unjust, unethical or dishonourable.

8 His favourite people were children. He never spoke harshly ⋀ them and he never allowed anyone to ill-treat them.

9 When he died, even those who had disliked him came ⋀ to pay their respects.

10 They said he was a man ⋀ fear who lived a life of integrity.

PRACTICE [**E**]   Read the passage. Mark with ⋀ where a preposition is missing and write the preposition above the line.

Ladies and gentlemen. Here ⋀*on* my right are the proposers the motion 'Science has brought more evil than good to mankind .' On my left are those debating against the motion . Each team has come prepared lots of 'ammunition' to 'fire' at their opponents . I think we are going to have an exciting time this evening because both teams have made it to the finals losing a single debate along the way . I have been told they are Mark Anthony and Brutus , two historical figures such stature that they could sway crowds with their oratory , passion and logic . So let us give our finalists here all our attention .

109

UNIT 7.4 PREPOSITIONS

with issues, purposes, reasons

Look at the **A** and **B** sentences below. Find out why **B** is correct and **A** is wrong in the **Grammar Points** section.

			GRAMMAR POINTS
1A	The prime minister spoke **about** the need for racial harmony.	✗	
1B	The prime minister spoke **on** the need for racial harmony.	✓	1
2A	Nikko refused to speak in English **because** fear of being laughed at.	✗	
2B	Nikko refused to speak in English **because of** fear at being laughed at. / Nikko refused to speak in English **for** fear of being laughed at.	✓	2
3A	He telephoned me **for to get** the latest news on Mike's accident.	✗	
3B	He telephoned me **for** the latest news on Mike's accident. / He telephoned me **to get** the latest news on Mike's accident.	✓	3

GRAMMAR POINTS ───

1   (a)   We use the prepositions **about** and **on** when we are dealing with topics or issues. We usually use **about** in informal situations and **on** in formal contexts.

           EXAMPLES: Nita and I were talking **about** our primary school days just now.
                          Mr Lim's talk was **on** creating opportunities for new businesses.

     (b)   We use **of** to refer to the content that is expressed by two nouns, the first noun being an aspect of the topic indicated by the second noun.

           EXAMPLES:

                                topic
                 The teachers discussed the good performance **of** some students at their weekly meeting.
                                  (aspect of topic)

                          topic
                 He emphasised the importance **of** discipline .
                        (aspect of topic)

2   We use **because of** or **for** to refer to the cause of or reason for something happening.

     EXAMPLES: James is very upset **because of** his boss's refusal to let him go on leave next week.
                    That restaurant is well-known **for** its mouth-watering desserts.

3   We use **at** to refer to a goal and **for** to refer to the purpose of doing something.

     EXAMPLES: He worked hard **at** improving his public image.
                    Rashid designed the entry forms **for** the slogan-writing competition.

PRACTICE $\boxed{A}$ Tick the correct sentences.

1 Are you whispering at Robert's atrocious haircut?

2 That actor is famous of his biting sarcasm and dry wit.

3 He feared for his family because of the threat of a hurricane coming their way.

4 Why don't you make another attempt on finishing your novel?

5 It was the skill of the beautician that brought out Maggie's fine features.

6 We're rushing around to get everything ready at Wednesday's event.

7 It is not every day that we get a respected politician to address our group.

8 I think Paula's hasty retreat into the kitchen was because her sister's unexpected appearance at our party.

9 Tina wrote to me about her frightening experience when she got lost in the jungle.

10 The professor was notorious for his reluctance to give students high scores.

YOUR SCORE
10

PRACTICE $\boxed{B}$ Underline the correct prepositions to complete the sentences.

1 She underwent surgery (on / for) the removal of a cataract in her left eye.

2 The others complained to me yesterday (about / on) the mess in my room.

3 They are often in Eric's house (because of / for) a game of cards.

4 Both parties are required to abide by the terms (of / on) the agreement.

5 Cracks began to appear on the walls of many houses (because of / for) poor workmanship.

6 The members of the panel expounded (on / about) the consequences of global warming.

7 They are against the destruction (for / of) rainforests.

8 I suggest you call the airline now (at / for) reconfirmation of your flight back to Paris.

9 He asks that he be allowed to speak to the members (for / on) the issue of misuse of club facilities.

10 Jennifer's attempt (at / of) breaking the national record for the 100m sprint was successful.

YOUR SCORE
10

PRACTICE *C* Circle the letters of the correct sentences.

1 A I must get one of those devices for to trap cockroaches.
   B I must get one of those devices for trapping cockroaches.
   C I must get one of those devices trapping cockroaches.

2 A Li Lian informed James about Sue's engagement on Friday.
   B Li Lian informed James on Sue's engagement on Friday.
   C Li Lian informed James of about Sue's engagement on Friday.

3 A Magazines targeted because of teenage audiences are selling well here.
   B Magazines targeted on teenage audiences are selling well here.
   C Magazines targeted at teenage audiences are selling well here.

4 A Mr Grant's complaint about your untidiness is reasonable.
   B Mr Grant's complaint your untidiness is reasonable.
   C Mr Grant's complaint at your untidiness is reasonable.

5 A He was given an award for the originality about his creation.
   B He was given an award for the originality of his creation.
   C He was given an award for originality his creation.

6 A The excellent article on truancy was widely read.
   B The excellent article for truancy was widely read.
   C The excellent article of truancy was widely read.

7 A Let's get an extra sleeping bag about our camping trip.
   B Let's get an extra sleeping bag our camping trip.
   C Let's get an extra sleeping bag for our camping trip.

8 A He doesn't like to talk at the nasty things people have said about him.
   B He doesn't like to talk about the nasty things people have said about him.
   C He doesn't like to talk for the nasty things people have said about him.

9 A Because his diligence, he was highly praised by the supervisor.
   B Because diligent, he was highly praised by the supervisor.
   C Because of his diligence, he was highly praised by the supervisor.

10 A She is remembered about her innovative methods on how to teach young children.
    B She is remembered for her innovative methods on how to teach young children.
    C She is remembered on her innovative methods on how to teach young children.

PRACTICE *D* Rewrite the sentences and replace **because** or the infinitive with **because of** or **for**.

1 He didn't sleep well because it was very noisy outside.
   He didn't sleep well because of the noise outside.

2 The police came to arrest the troublemakers.
   The police came for the troublemakers.

3 They were treated first because their injuries were severe.

4 Jennifer dressed in black to attend a funeral.

_____

_____

5 The little boy ran to his mother to be comforted.

_____

_____

6 We don't want to give Maisie the bad news because she is ill.

_____

_____

7 He worked hard to improve the living conditions of the poor.

_____

_____

PRACTICE _E_ Fill in the blanks with suitable prepositions.

Mabel : Guess who I met when I stopped at the bakery (1) _____ your favourite apple strudel? Anita Lopez.

David : Anita Lopez? The last time we saw her was at our wedding! Where is she now and what's she doing?

Mabel : She's heading an international organisation aimed (2) _____ improving the literacy rate (3) _____ Third World countries. She's now based in Switzerland.

David : Wow! Is she back on holiday?

Mabel : She's here (4) _____ a conference (5) _____ education. She's going to present a paper on computer literacy.

David : I remember in school she often talked (6) _____ her wish to study and work overseas. She worked very hard (7) _____ winning a scholarship and we were all happy when she got a place at Cambridge University. Did you get her phone number?

Mabel : I did more than that. I invited her over (8) _____ dinner on Saturday night.

David : Oh no! Saturday night is out (9) _____ the fund-raising committee's meeting.

Mabel : Can't you miss it? She's leaving on Sunday morning and Saturday's the only time she's free.

David : I know what we can do. Both of you can have dinner here without me and talk (10) _____ old times until I get back from the meeting.

Mabel : That's fine with me.

UNIT 8 SUBJECT AND PREDICATE

Look at the **A** and **B** sentences below. Find out why **B** is correct and **A** is wrong in the **Grammar Points** section.

GRAMMAR POINTS

1A Don't know what to do after I finish my exams.	✗	
1B **I** don't know what to do after I finish my exams.	✓	1
2A The prices of fish and vegetables very high in the market last week.	✗	
2B The prices of fish and vegetables **were** very high in the market last week.	✓	2
3A Kay borrowed **from me fifty dollars** to buy some books.	✗	
3B Kay borrowed **fifty dollars from me** to buy some books.	✓	3

GRAMMAR POINTS

1 A sentence is usually made up of a subject and a predicate. The subject usually comes before the predicate.

EXAMPLE: **SUBJECT**   **PREDICATE**

The company   bought some high-tech machines which are expensive but cost-effective.

2 The predicate must contain at least one verb. It can also have an object, a complement or an adverbial.

EXAMPLES:

Subject	Predicate	
	Verb	**Object**
The whole community	tend	their crops in the fields.
Subject	**Verb**	**Complement**
The group of young men	are	popular singers in their home country.
Subject	**Verb**	**Adverbial**
The bombed parts of the city	were rebuilt	during the post-war period.

(Note that the adverbial can sometimes be placed before the subject, or after the verb, object or complement.)

3 A sentence can contain two objects—an indirect object and a direct object. The direct object is something which receives the action from the subject. The indirect object is usually someone who benefits from the action on the direct object.

The indirect object comes after the direct object if it is in a prepositional phrase.

EXAMPLES:

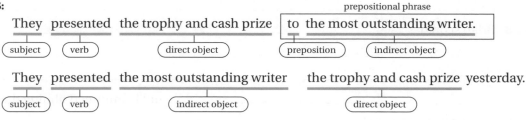

PRACTICE *A* Circle the letters of the correct sentences. There may be more than one answer for each question.

1 A Haven't heard from Sam yet.
　B From Sam we haven't heard yet.
　C We haven't heard from Sam yet.

2 A The dress that Mary's wearing very elegant.
　B The dress that Mary's wearing is very elegant.
　C Mary's wearing a dress that is very elegant.

3 A These two boys are trainee mechanics at Ben's garage.
　B These two boys trainee mechanics at Ben's garage.
　C These two boys trainee mechanics are from Ben's garage.

4 A The names of all who volunteered to help in the campaign I gave them.
　B I gave them the names of all who volunteered to help in the campaign.
　C I gave the names to them of all who volunteered to help in the campaign.

5 A We showed the visitors the Japanese garden which the children had designed and planted.
　B The Japanese garden which the children had designed and planted we showed the visitors.
　C The visitors were shown the Japanese garden which the children had designed and planted.

6 A The police set up road blocks along the highway to check on dangerous drivers.
　B Along the highway the police set up road blocks to check on dangerous drivers.
　C The police set up road blocks to check on dangerous motorists along the highway.

YOUR SCORE
10

PRACTICE *B* Complete the sentences with the expressions in the box.

✎ which contained delicate orchids were placed on each dining table.
✎ huge sums of money to enhance his image.
✎ medical science has provided
✎ four-year-old Nicole motioned
✎ Ryan handed over the video camera
✎ the young thoroughbreds

✎ the conference with a brief survey of recent developments.
✎ the winning goal by heading the ball into the net from the side.
✎ watched the players try to outwit each other at basketball.
✎ left a substantial portion of his estate to animal shelters.

115

1 _____

_____ are trained by experts to become racehorses.

2 The chief minister declared open _____

_____

3 Brian scored _____

_____

4 _____

_____ and I continued filming the whales at play.

5 An enthusiastic crowd _____

_____

6 _____

_____ man with many answers in his quest for health and energy.

7 Little crystal vases _____

_____

8 _____

_____ to everyone in the audience to keep quiet.

9 He paid _____

_____

10 The wealthy recluse _____

_____

YOUR SCORE

/10

PRACTICE **C** Mark with ⋏ where a word is missing in the sentence. Then underline in the brackets the type of word that is missing.

1 Everyone witnessed our bowling champion young Jackie win⋏at the SEA games .
(<u>direct object</u>   indirect object   subject)

2 The motorcyclist snatched and threw it to his accomplice in the black sedan .
(direct object   indirect object   verb)

3 Edmund very busy this morning . He will attend to you later .
(adverbial   subject   verb)

4 The secretary gave to the delivery man from the courier company .
(complement   direct object   verb)

5 The young woman has been standing here since hoping to get a lift to the city centre .
(adverbial   complement   object)

6 Feel like something wonderful is going to happen soon .
(indirect object   subject   verb)

7 Sarah passed her house keys to and then went around absent-mindedly looking for them .
(direct object   indirect object   subject)

116

8 The team studied and concluded that a major quake would occur soon in the eastern sector .

(direct object   indirect object   verb)

9 During we wore pinafore-style uniforms and had our long hair tied back from our faces .

(adverbial   subject   complement)

10 The participants tired after the rally and needed a long period of rest before the awards ceremony .

(direct object   indirect object   verb)

11 Scores of baskets of fruit were loaded by and taken into town for distribution at the markets .

(direct object   indirect object   subject)

YOUR SCORE

10

PRACTICE **D**   Rewrite the sentences correctly.

1 The royal symphony orchestra played at the international music festival two magnificent numbers.

_____

_____

2 The eggs into soft peaks he whipped and gradually folded them into the cake batter.

_____

_____

3 The new president is chosen by the people a man of vision and great courage.

_____

_____

4 Across the room sending us shrieking and running the mouse scuttled in different directions.

_____

_____

5 Didn't realise time had passed so quickly and I had to go.

_____

YOUR SCORE

10

_____

UNIT 9.1 RELATIVE CLAUSES

with **who**

Look at the **A** and **B** sentences below. Find out why **B** is correct and **A** is wrong in the **Grammar Points** section.

CHECKPOINT

GRAMMAR POINTS

1A	The coach rebuked the team members **which** were fighting.	✗	
1B	The coach rebuked the team members **who** were fighting.	✓	1
2A	Fara is one of the students who **excels** in Science.	✗	
2B	Fara is one of the students who **excel** in Science.	✓	2
3A	He is the surgeon who my doctor recommended **him**.	✗	
3B	He is the surgeon who my doctor recommended.	✓	3
4A	I like your **mother who** makes me feel welcome.	✗	
4B	I like your **mother, who** makes me feel welcome.	✓	4

GRAMMAR POINTS

1   A relative clause describes **a noun** in the main clause. We use a relative clause beginning with **who** to describe **a person** or **people**.

EXAMPLE:

> main clause   relative clause
> He likes **girls** ⟨ **who** speak their minds.
> noun described (people)

REMEMBER!

■ A complex sentence is formed when two simple sentences are joined to form **a main clause** and **a subordinate clause**. One type of subordinate clause is **a relative clause**.

EXAMPLES: We have a new colleague. He is our manager's nephew.   (simple sentences)

We have a new colleague **and** he is our manager's nephew.   (compound sentence)

> main clause   relative clause
> We have a new colleague ⟨ who is our manager's nephew.   (complex sentence)

---

2   Like other clauses, a relative clause must have a **subject** and a **finite verb**. The finite verb **must agree** with the subject.

118

EXAMPLES:

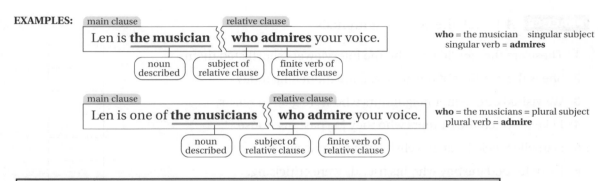

who = the musician   singular subject
singular verb = **admires**

who = the musicians = plural subject
plural verb = **admire**

REMEMBER!

■ Most relative clauses begin with a relative pronoun (**that**, **which**, **who** or **whom**).
The relative pronoun is usually the subject or object of the verb in the relative clause.

---

3 Sometimes, instead of being the **subject** of a relative clause, **who** is the **object** of the finite verb in the clause. We must not add another object to the relative clause.

EXAMPLE:

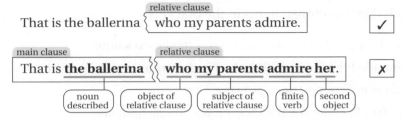

REMEMBER!

■ Traditionally, **who** is used as the **subject** while **whom** is used as the **object** of the relative clause. But nowadays, it is more common to use **who** as **both** the subject and object.

EXAMPLE:

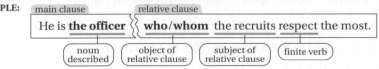

When **who** is the **object** of the relative clause, the subject of the relative clause comes after it.

---

4 A relative clause can be **defining** or **non-defining**. A **defining relative clause** with **who** identifies the **person** or **people** we are referring to.

EXAMPLE:

(identifies the cousin we ran into: that particular cousin who got married last week, not any other cousin)

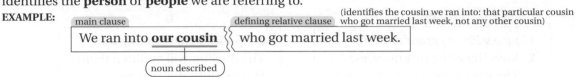

A **non-defining relative clause** with **who** does not identify the **person** or **people** we are referring to but only gives more information. We always put a comma before a non-defining relative clause.

EXAMPLE:

(does not identify the cousin we ran into; only gives more information)

PRACTICE *A* Tick the correct sentences.

1 These are the candidates who the interviewers shortlisted them.
2 She is the prettiest of the girls who are modelling today.
3 We visited our former neighbours who were glad to see us.
4 I like to watch the runners who they jog past my house.
5 Danielle Steele is the novelist who wrote 'Accident'.
6 He defended the boy who his friends were criticising.
7 Sharon is one of the students who taken the test.
8 We waved at our favourite comedian, who waved back at us.
9 Those are the babies who everyone adore.
10 Mr Turner is the one who has done the most for the college.

YOUR SCORE
10

PRACTICE *B* Underline the correct items in the brackets.

1 The guards saluted the general (who / , who) returned their salute.
2 The police commended the boy (who / , who) had reported the drug dealers.
3 She avoids people who (gossip / gossips) about her.
4 This shelter is for families who the fire (has / have) made homeless.
5 I reassured the child who (awakened / had been awakened) by the storm.
6 He rescued his mother, who some hawkers (was / were) pestering.
7 We must consider the person who the news (affects / affects him) most.
8 The call was for Mr Lim (who / , who) must leave at once.
9 Here is a list of the composers who the freshmen (are to / to) study.
10 They are weak men, who politics (are / is) likely to corrupt.

YOUR SCORE
10

PRACTICE *C* Join the sentences. Make those under **A** the main clauses and those under **B** relative clauses beginning with **who**.

A	B
1 I jog with my grandmother.	My patient is consulting him.
2 Miss Hill is the headmistress.	The director will audition them.
3 The story is about Julius Caesar.	He was born this morning.
4 He is the psychiatrist.	The board has appointed her.
5 We have e-mailed the actors.	She is a robust old lady.
6 She is holding her baby boy.	He was a Roman emperor.

1 *I jog with my grandmother, who is a robust old lady.*

2 _____

3 _____

120

4 _____

5 _____

6 _____

PRACTICE [**D**] Rearrange the words to form correct sentences.

1 are — enthralled — performers — the — these — us — who .

_____

2 abandoned — children — have — helps — people — she — who .

_____

3 by — deceived — had — he — he — Lucia — trusted — was — who , .

_____

4 famous — fans — made — the — we — were — who — you .

_____

5 beat — by — Dad — defeated — I — I — usually — was — who , .

_____

PRACTICE [**E**] Rewrite the sentences correctly using relative clauses beginning with **who**.

1 I rushed to hug my parents who cried with joy.
   I rushed to hug my parents, who cried with joy.

2 They are arresting the ship captain which is involved in smuggling.

_____

_____

3 We enjoy spending time with Grandpa who tells marvellous stories.

_____

_____

4 She went to see the commander, who she implored him to spare her son.

_____

_____

5 He is one of the people who has helped me arrange this carnival.

_____

_____

6 A woman claimed the child who the Lims had adopted.

_____

UNIT 9.2 RELATIVE CLAUSES

with **which**

Look at the **A** and **B** sentences below. Find out why **B** is correct and **A** is wrong in the **Grammar Points** section.

			GRAMMAR POINTS
1A	She felt bad about the animals **who** had lost their habitat.	✗	
1B	She felt bad about the animals **which** had lost their habitat.	✓	1
2A	Everyone is speculating about the jewellery which **were** stolen.	✗	
2B	Everyone is speculating about the jewellery which **was** stolen.	✓	2
3A	I respect the values which you **uphold them**.	✗	
3B	I respect the values which you **uphold**.	✓	3
4A	They lived in **Calcutta which** was then under British rule.	✗	
4B	They lived in **Calcutta, which** was then under British rule.	✓	4

GRAMMAR POINTS

1   We use a relative clause beginning with **which** to describe **all nouns except people**.
EXAMPLES:

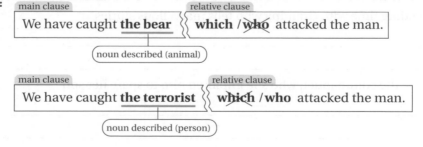

main clause   relative clause
We have caught **the bear** which / ~~who~~ attacked the man.
noun described (animal)

main clause   relative clause
We have caught **the terrorist** ~~which~~ / **who** attacked the man.
noun described (person)

2   Like other clauses, a relative clause with **which** must have a **subject** and a **finite verb**. The finite verb **must agree** with the subject.
EXAMPLES:

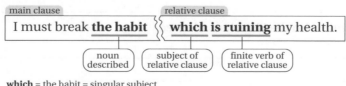

main clause   relative clause
I must break **the habit** **which is ruining** my health.
noun described   subject of relative clause   finite verb of relative clause

which = the habit = singular subject
∴ singular verb = **is ruining**

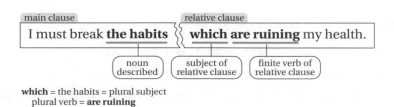

which = the habits = plural subject
plural verb = **are ruining**

3 Sometimes, instead of being the **subject** of a relative clause, **which** is the **object** of the finite verb in the clause. We must not add another object to the relative clause.
EXAMPLE:

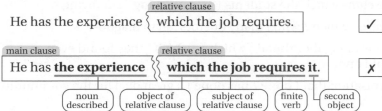

4 A relative clause with **which** can be **defining** or **non-defining**. A **defining relative clause** with **which** identifies the **things** we are referring to.
EXAMPLE:

A **non-defining relative clause** with **which** does not identify the **things** we are referring to but only gives more information. We always put a comma before a non-defining relative clause.
EXAMPLE:

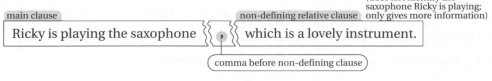

REMEMBER!

- A relative clause beginning with **that** can describe **all nouns including people**.
  EXAMPLES:

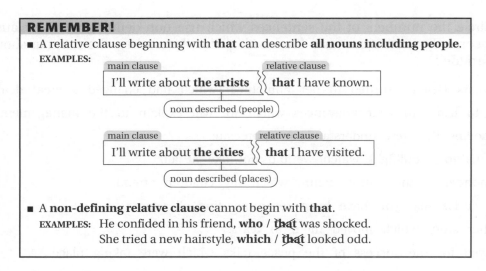

- A **non-defining relative clause** cannot begin with **that**.
  EXAMPLES: He confided in his friend, **who** / ~~that~~ was shocked.
  She tried a new hairstyle, **which** / ~~that~~ looked odd.

123

PRACTICE **A** Underline the correct items in the brackets.

1 We have driven round your campus (that / , which) is impressive.
2 He was carrying the kind of gun (that / , that) hunters use.
3 The soldiers were grateful for the foodstuff which (was / were) dropped by helicopter.
4 The forecasts have been made by economists that the world (respect / respects).
5 I tried your aerobic exercises (which / , which) I found too strenuous.
6 You and I need work that (are / is) both exciting and lucrative.
7 Ours is one of the clubs which the students (are surveying / surveying).
8 This is a rare disease (which / who) many doctors fail to diagnose.
9 They moved to a new neighbourhood (which / , which) they found even noisier than the old one.
10 I know of an organisation that (done / has done) a great deal for the community.

YOUR SCORE
10

PRACTICE **B** Tick the correct sentences.

1 Sally is on a strict diet, that makes her irritable.
2 Jimmy knows the name of the planet which is nearest the sun.
3 The movie will bring back the sad incidents that you forgotten.
4 She worked at Laura's Boutique, which was close to her flat.
5 The shop sells used machinery that looks brand-new.
6 This is the passport which to be renewed by tomorrow.
7 Ben is the most thoughtful boy that I have ever met.
8 These men have the gentleness that come from strength.
9 I hired a donkey, which I struggled to ride.
10 We represent the tenants which you are trying to evict.

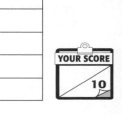
YOUR SCORE
10

PRACTICE **C** Circle the numbers of the sentences which use non-defining relative clauses incorrectly, without commas. Mark with ⟨ the places where the commas should be added.

1 After many years Helen returned to her hometown ⟨ which had changed a great deal.
2 We are here to listen to your grievances which we will explain to the management.
3 Ravi writes poems that few understand or appreciate.
4 Friends took us to a bullfight which we did not like at all.
5 She is the founder of the tuition centre which my children attend.
6 We'll try the cruise that you have been recommending all year.
7 They heard her story which moved them to tears.
8 Everyone prayed for the success of the peace talks which were taking place.
9 Women are protesting against advertisements that make them look undignified.

124

10 I gazed at the Pacific Ocean which looked really peaceful.

11 Shaun went to your concert which he enjoyed immensely.

PRACTICE *D* Rearrange the words in the boxes to complete the sentences.

1 He cancelled all the appointments   for — had — he — made — that — week — which.
He cancelled all the appointments which he had made for that week.

2 They amassed wealth,   bring — failed — happiness — them — to — which.

_____

_____

3 She is one of the great sopranos   entranced — have — that — audiences.

_____

_____

4 You must send us a copy   certified — has — principal — which — your.

_____

_____

5 This is one of the projects   company — financing — is — our — that.

_____

_____

6 I sent a report to a newspaper,   front — it — on — page — published — the — which.

_____

_____

PRACTICE *E* Cross out the incorrect items in the boxes to complete the passage.

I am amused by the generation gap **1** | , that | which | yawns between my parents and me.
I am not interested in their favourite old tunes **2** | which | , which | usually send me to sleep. I like
the sort of music **3** | that | , which | my parents call 'sheer noise'. I do like some of the old
crooners **4** | that | which | they find so enchanting but they cannot stand any of the singers
that **5** | has | have | made it to the top in the past decade.

My parents deplore my hairstyle **6** | that | , which | seems 'ridiculous' to them. They want me
to return to the clean-cut look which I **7** | had to have | to have | in school. Yet that was not the
look **8** | that | , that | they had at my age. I know this from their old photographs **9** | which | , which |
show their weird hairstyles at that time. I love those pictures for showing me
something **10** | that | , that | the two generations have in common.

UNIT 9.3 RELATIVE CLAUSES

with **whose**

Look at the **A** and **B** sentences below. Find out why **B** is correct and **A** is wrong in the **Grammar Points** section.

GRAMMAR POINTS

1A	I am on a ship **that its** crew comprises old men.	✗	
1B	I am on a ship **whose** crew comprises old men.	✓	1
2A	Germs infect people whose resistance **are** low.	✗	
2B	Germs infect people whose resistance **is** low.	✓	2
3A	They dined at a restaurant whose owner **they knew him**.	✗	
3B	They dined at a restaurant whose owner **they knew**.	✓	3
4A	We are touring **Africa whose** wildlife is wonderful.	✗	
4B	We are touring **Africa, whose** wildlife is wonderful.	✓	4

GRAMMAR POINTS

1 We use a relative clause beginning with **whose** to show that the noun after **whose** is related to or belongs to the noun before it.

EXAMPLE:

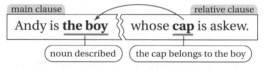

main clause   relative clause

Andy is **the boy** { whose **cap** is askew.

(noun described) (the cap belongs to the boy)

main clause   relative clause

I stared at **the tower** { whose **fame** had brought me to Pisa.

(noun described) (the fame belongs to the tower)

REMEMBER!

- A relative clause beginning with **whose** shows ownership or connection. (**Whose** usually takes the place of **his**, **her**, **its** or **their**.)
- **Whose** at the beginning of a relative clause must always be followed by a noun.
- **Whose** and the noun immediately after it (**whose** + noun) are the subject or object of the verb in the relative clause.
  EXAMPLES: They robbed the motorist. **His** car had broken down.
  They robbed the motorist **whose** car had broken down.
  whose = **his** = the motorist's (showing ownership)

  These are the countries. We have to study **their** exports.
  These are the countries **whose** exports we have to study.
  whose = **their** = the countries' (showing connection)

126

2 Like other clauses, a relative clause with **whose** must have a **subject** and a **finite verb**. The finite verb **must agree** with the subject.

EXAMPLES:

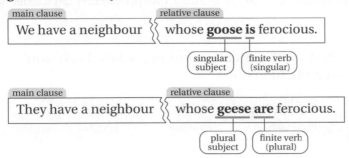

3 Sometimes, **whose** and the noun immediately after it (**whose** + noun) are the **object** of the **finite verb** in the relative clause. We must not add another object to the relative clause.

EXAMPLE:

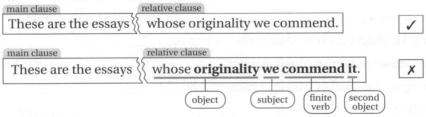

4 A relative clause with **whose** can be **defining** or **non-defining**. A **defining relative clause** with **whose** identifies the **people** or **things** we are referring to.

EXAMPLE:

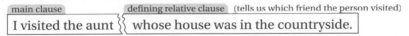

A **non-defining relative clause** with **whose** does not identify the **people** or **things** we are referring to but only gives more information. We always put a comma before a non-defining relative clause.

EXAMPLE:

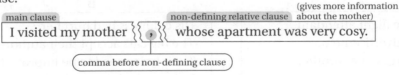

PRACTICE **A** Underline the correct items in the brackets.

1 James smiled at his aunt (whose / , whose) face lit up.

2 The vet recognised the bird whose injuries he had (healed / healed them).

3 They have noticed a tree whose branches (need / needs) trimming.

4 She was tactful to Pete, whose temper (known / was known) to be bad.

5 We will soon catch the burglar whose accomplice we have (questioned / questioned him).

6 I feel comfortable with Dr Spencer, whose bedside manner (are / is) perfect.

7 He praised the artist (whose / whose work) was on display at the gallery.

8 They are surrounding the house (whose / , whose) occupants they suspect of drug dealing.

9 The art treasures are kept in a building whose walls (are crumbling / crumbling).

10 Sue has gone off to the mountains, whose peaceful atmosphere she (need / needs).

 B Fill in the blanks with suitable words in the box. Each word may be used more than once.

are	are ruining	build	build it	is
famous	knows her	ruining	whose	, whose

1 We remember Professor Wang _____ criticism we feared.

2 I live in an area whose streets _____ unsafe.

3 She has many fans, whose adulation _____ nothing to her.

4 John wants a room _____ furnishings are simple.

5 Liz married a politician, whose career she helped to _____ .

6 Tim made a mistake, whose consequences _____ his life.

7 She is glaring at the speaker whose arguments she _____ rebutting.

8 Our footballers were in the aeroplane _____ wings caught fire.

9 Bob hates being a child whose mother is _____ .

10 We'll revisit Bangladesh _____ people we've come to love.

PRACTICE **C** Join the sentences. Make those under **A** the main clauses and those under **B** relative clauses beginning with **whose**.

A
1 She is the flight attendant.
2 It is an advertisement.
3 Laura forgave her brother.
4 Lion-tamers are special people.
5 We grieved for our favourite river.
6 I've heard many songs.

B
His coldness had hurt her.
The big cats accept their authority.
Their lyrics need to be improved.
Its water had grown murky.
Children love its jokes.
I'll never forget her calmness.

1 *She is the flight attendant whose calmness I'll never forget.*

2 _____

3 _____

4 _____

5 _____

6 _____

Rewrite the sentences correctly using relative clauses beginning with **whose**.

1 Tourists are drawn to India whose many, cultures they find fascinating.
Tourists are drawn to India, whose many cultures they find fascinating.
_____

2 He reminds me of a snake whose eyes hypnotises its prey.
_____
_____

3 I have always been the family member, whose plans work best.
_____
_____

4 They were terrified of the man whose son they had bullied him.
_____
_____

5 Ricky is the mischievous boy whose virtuous twin often mistaken for him.
_____
_____

6 We make different types of bread whose quality are guaranteed.
_____

YOUR SCORE
10

_____

PRACTICE *E* Cross out the incorrect items in the boxes to complete the passage.

The tiger is an animal **1** | whose | , whose | majestic looks **2** | has | have |
earned it the title of 'Jungle King'. However, it is seen as a terrorist king by farmers whose
livestock it **3** | threaten | threatens | . They disapprove of environmentalists whose concerns
4 | include | includes | saving the tiger from extinction. To the farmers, the environmentalists
are dreamers, whose message no practical person can **5** | understand | understand it | .

A more receptive audience is made up of young people, whose minds **6** | are | is | still open.
They can be led to view the tiger as a fellow creature whose survival **7** | are | is | their responsibility.
They will think of their country **8** | whose | , whose | flora and fauna they must
9 | cherish | cherish them | . The tiger will become a beloved jungle ruler whose
safety young Asians **10** | has | have | undertaken to guard.

YOUR SCORE
10

UNIT 9.4 RELATIVE CLAUSES

after subjects of main clauses

Look at the **A** and **B** sentences below. Find out why **B** is correct and **A** is wrong in the **Grammar Points** section.

			GRAMMAR POINTS
1A	The girl **drove recklessly who gave me a lift**.	✗	
1B	The girl **who gave me a lift drove recklessly**.	✓	1
2A	The anxiety that tortured our minds **are** over.	✗	
2B	The anxiety that tortured our minds **is** over.	✓	2
3A	The proverbs which you **quoted them** make me think.	✗	
3B	The proverbs which you **quoted** make me think.	✓	3
4A	My **father whose** passion is **fishing wrote** a book on it.	✗	
4B	My father**,** whose passion is **fishing, wrote** a book on it.	✓	4

GRAMMAR POINTS

1 When we use a relative clause to describe the **subject** of the main clause, we insert the relative clause **after** the subject and **before** the finite verb of the main clause.

EXAMPLE:

1st part of main clause	relative clause	2nd part of main clause
The tonic	which strengthened her	is out of stock.

subject of main clause (noun described)   finite verb of main clause

2 Like other clauses, the **main clause** must have a **subject** and a **finite verb**. The finite verb of the main clause **must agree** with its subject.

EXAMPLES:

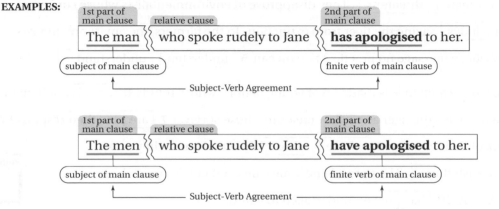

3 When **who**, **which**, **that** or (**whose** + noun) is the **object** of the **finite verb** in a relative clause, we must not add another object.
EXAMPLE:

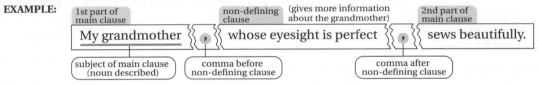

4 A relative clause describing the **subject** of the main clause can be **defining** or **non-defining**. A **defining relative clause** identifies the **people** or **things** we are referring to.
EXAMPLE:

A **non-defining relative clause** does not identify the **people** or **things** we are referring to but only gives more information. We always put a comma **before** and **after** this type of non-defining relative clause.
EXAMPLE:

REMEMBER!

- A **non-defining relative clause** cannot begin with **that**.
  EXAMPLES: Television, ~~that~~ / **which** entertains, can also educate.
  Mr Hill, ~~that~~ / **who** taught us science, was very patient.

PRACTICE *A*   Underline the relative clauses in the sentences.

1 The figures that the commercial artist drew look rather stiff.

2 She knitted him a sweater, which fitted him snugly.

3 Such movies are not for people whose hearts are weak.

4 Elvis Presley, who was a famous singer, led a hectic life.

5 The drapes which the decorator has selected do not appeal to me.

6 He was the greatest tragic actor that ever performed on stage.

7 My truck, whose tyres I had just changed, moved steadily on the wet road.

8 This is the lady who designs exquisite rock gardens.

9 We are heading for the Himalayas, whose lower peaks we plan to climb.

10 Our planet Earth, which man has polluted, will take centuries to clean.

PRACTICE **B** Cross out the incorrect items in the boxes to complete the sentences.

1 The family whose house we are renting │ are │ is │ going abroad.

2 Tokyo │ which │ , which │ is the capital of Japan, is a busy city.

3 Teenagers who like adventure often │ hitchhike │ hitchhikes │ around the world.

4 The cooking utensils that Mum uses │ seem │ seems │ to last forever.

5 The man whose daughter you are │ tutoring │ tutoring her │ was my hockey coach.

6 My partner, who is very shrewd │ protects │ , protects │ my interests.

7 The goods │ which │ , which │ our country exports are of high quality.

8 All able-bodied men │ were accepted who applied │ who applied were accepted │ .

9 His theories, │ that │ which │ are fascinating, may change your thinking.

10 The bravest man that I have ever │ met │ met him │ is your father.

PRACTICE **C** Underline the finite verbs which do not agree with their subjects in the main clauses of the sentences below. Write the correct finite verbs in the boxes.

1 One of the employees who were not appreciated <u>have applied</u> elsewhere for a job.

has applied

2 The latest news, which we never expected, is wonderful.

3 A lot of houses whose owners are away just decays.

4 Julia and Maggie, who are close friends, differs in personality.

5 The chest of drawers that she owns were her grandmother's.

6 The remarks which he makes worry his parents.

7 Miss Gomez, who we all admire, dresses impeccably.

8 Her favourite stars, whose hairstyles she copies, looks silly to me.

9 The army officers who planned the mutiny was arrested.

10 Things that astonish me do not surprise her at all.

11 His kindness, which is genuine, endears him to us.

PRACTICE **D** Rearrange the words in the boxes to form relative clauses. Rewrite the sentences and insert the relative clauses.

1 The mousedeer feeds on leaves.   a — animal — is — little — lively — which , , .
   The mousedeer, which is a lively little animal, feeds on leaves.

2 The boy has green fingers.   brought — gardener — help — him — the — to — who .

132

3 The Tans' bungalow is very old.   have — I — just — repaired — roof — whose , , .

_____

_____

4 Celebrities sometimes disappoint us.   on — see — shows — talk — television — that — we .

_____

_____

5 King Mongkut loved his country.   a — ruler — Thai — was — wise — who , , .

_____

_____

6 Many diseases are related to stress.   afflict — in — modern — people — times — which .

_____

_____

PRACTICE *E*   Rewrite the passage and change the sentences in brackets into relative clauses beginning with **who**, **which** or **whose**.

Vitamin supplements **1** (They are sometimes neither necessary nor beneficial.) are easily available nowadays. People **2** (They take them zealously.) should be warned of certain dangers. A man **3** (His intake of natural food is already rich in vitamins.) can damage his health by taking too many supplements. For instance, the Vitamin C supplement **4** (He takes it in high doses to prevent infection.) may bring him heart problems. Vitamin A **5** (No one can deny its importance to health.) is toxic when taken in much larger quantities than needed. Health writers **6** (Readers tend to trust them.) have a serious responsibility in this matter.

_____

_____

_____

_____

_____

_____

_____

_____

_____

_____

UNIT 10.1 ADVERBIAL CLAUSES

with **because**, **as**, **since**

Look at the **A** and **B** sentences below. Find out why **B** is correct and **A** is wrong in the **Grammar Points** section.

				GRAMMAR POINTS
1A	She had a fall **because she is in a coma**.	✗		
1B	She is in a coma **because she had a fall**.	✓	1	
2A	He is nervous because **this his** first flight.	✗		
2B	He is nervous because **this is his** first flight.	✓	2	

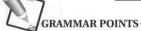

GRAMMAR POINTS

1 We use an adverbial clause beginning with **because** to give the reason for what is happening or what is stated in the main clause.

EXAMPLES:

(main clause)　　　　　　　　　　　　　　(adverbial clause)

| They are short of money now | **because** they were extravagant in the past. |

(main clause)　　　　　　　　　　　　　　(adverbial clause)

| She is smiling with pride | **because** she has just been praised by the instructor. |

2 Like other clauses, an adverbial clause must have a subject and a finite verb.

EXAMPLE:

(main clause)　　　　　　　　　　　(adverbial clause)

| We must leave the building | **because** it is going to collapse. | ✓

(subject)　(finite verb)

We must leave the building **because** is going to collapse.　✗
(missing subject)

We must leave the building **because** it going to collapse.　✗
(missing finite verb)

134

PRACTICE *A*   Circle the letters of the correct sentences. There may be more than one answer for each question.

1 **A**   They liked the play because of it was true to life.
   B   They liked the play because it was true to life.
   C   They liked the play as it was true to life.

2 **A**   He worked long hours because he was ambitious.
   B   He worked long hours since he ambitious.
   C   He worked long hours as he was ambitious.

3 **A**   I love the rainbow as it symbolises hope.
   B   The rainbow symbolises hope because I love it.
   C   I love the rainbow since it symbolises hope.

4 **A**   You have an eye for colour because you should try interior decorating.
   B   You should try interior decorating since you have an eye for colour.
   C   You should try interior decorating because you have an eye for colour.

5 **A**   These stamps are valuable because they are rare.
   B   These stamps are valuable as they are rare.
   C   These stamps are valuable it's because they are rare.

YOUR SCORE

10

PRACTICE *B*   Cross out the incorrect words in the boxes to complete the sentences.

1 He can't keep the tiger cub because it | grown | has grown | too big.

2 Rose wasn't allowed into the clubhouse | because | it's because | she was wearing sandals.

3 They looked for a big jungle tree as they | had to | to | build a boat.

4 The flags were flown at half-mast | because | because of | the governor had passed away.

5 Some areas ☐ under ☐ were under ☐ water as it had rained incessantly.

6 I won't take him with me since he always ☐ behaves ☐ misbehaves ☐ .

7 She didn't buy the house as ☐ they wouldn't ☐ wouldn't ☐ lower the price.

8 The people ☐ feel more ☐ more ☐ neighbourly there because the gardens have no fences.

9 We won't accept the goods since ☐ they ☐ they are ☐ substandard.

10 I found the task ☐ difficult ☐ simple ☐ as I was guided step by step.

PRACTICE _C_   Rearrange the words in the boxes to complete the sentences.

1 Festivals are important to me   back — because — bring — childhood — memories — of — they.
   Festivals are important to me because they bring back memories of childhood.

2 You should install a house alarm   as — burglaries — is — number — of — rising — the.

_____

3 We can propose her name   be — committee — eager — is — on — since — she — the — to.

_____

4 Everyone was subdued   a — because — been — bomb — had — scare — there.

_____

5 The magazine will be launched soon   are — market — positive — results — since — survey — the.

_____

6 My aunt plants certain herbs   as — believes — in — medicinal — she — their — value.

_____

PRACTICE _D_   Tick the correct sentences.

1 She felt depressed as the room was tiny and dingy.

2 He left the army because of he could not take the discipline.

3 The show was below par since the group lacked practice.

4 I am not scared because I done nothing wrong.

5 The negotiations went well it's because both sides were honest.

6 He had a black eye as he had been in a fight.

7 The caller was talking nonsense since I hung up.

8 She wore huge dark glasses because didn't want to be recognised.

9 This movie doesn't need subtitles as the acting is powerful.

10 Pandas need special care since they are very sensitive.

PRACTICE *E* Join the sentences using the words in the boxes. Make those under **A** the main clauses and those under **B** adverbial clauses after the main clauses.

A	B	
1 They noticed nothing.	They were intent on their work.	as

They noticed nothing as they were intent on their work.

2 Umbrellas were unfurled.	It had begun to drizzle.	because
3 We'll have to drop everything else.	This is urgent.	since
4 Volcanic eruptions are useful.	They make the soil fertile.	as
5 You shouldn't do that.	You would be jeopardising your future.	since
6 Her eyes seem to have changed colour.	She is wearing blue-tinted contact lenses.	because

YOUR SCORE
10

PRACTICE *F* Rewrite the sentences in the paragraph correctly.

My next vacation will be special because of I have saved enough to go abroad. I may not be able to do this again for some time since I must choose the right destination. I will not opt for Bali as many of my friends been to that lovely Indonesian island. Katmandu in Nepal might prove too taxing for me it's because I have never done any climbing in my life. Granada in Spain might be the answer as would be intriguing but not too challenging. I will go on my own because of I do want adventure.

YOUR SCORE
10

UNIT 10.2 ADVERBIAL CLAUSES

with **although**, **though**, **even though**

Look at the **A** and **B** sentences below. Find out why **B** is correct and **A** is wrong in the **Grammar Points** section.

			GRAMMAR POINTS
1A	He was not tired **because** he had toiled all day.	✗	
1B	He was not tired **although** he had toiled all day.	✓	1
2A	She kept calm although jackals **wailing** nearby.	✗	
2B	She kept calm although jackals **were wailing** nearby.	✓	2

GRAMMAR POINTS

1 We use an adverbial clause beginning with **although** to show that what is happening or stated in the main clause cannot be changed or prevented by what is happening or stated in the adverbial clause.

EXAMPLES:

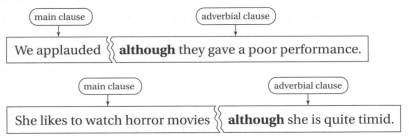

2 Like other clauses, an adverbial clause beginning with **although** has a subject and a finite verb.

EXAMPLE:

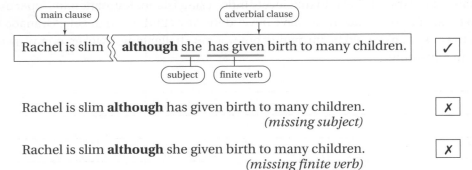

138

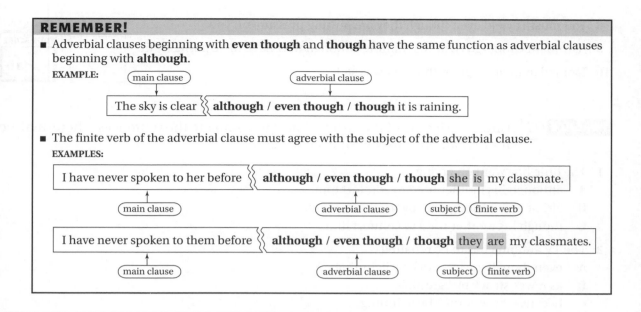

REMEMBER!

- Adverbial clauses beginning with **even though** and **though** have the same function as adverbial clauses beginning with **although**.

  EXAMPLE:

  (main clause)   (adverbial clause)

  The sky is clear ⟨⟨ **although / even though / though** it is raining.

- The finite verb of the adverbial clause must agree with the subject of the adverbial clause.

  EXAMPLES:

  I have never spoken to her before ⟨⟨ **although / even though / though** she is my classmate.

  (main clause)   (adverbial clause)   (subject) (finite verb)

  I have never spoken to them before ⟨⟨ **although / even though / though** they are my classmates.

  (main clause)   (adverbial clause)   (subject) (finite verb)

PRACTICE $\boxed{A}$ Cross out the incorrect words in the boxes to complete the sentences.

1   Our dancer fell ☐ although ☐ because ☐ the floor was slippery.

2   He is still dissatisfied though he ☐ been ☐ has been ☐ made the secretary of the club.

3   I admire her courage even though ☐ don't ☐ I don't ☐ like her manners.

4   The death toll was high ☐ although ☐ because ☐ the rescuers did their best.

5   They ☐ held ☐ postponed ☐ the barbecue though rain had been forecast.

6   We went on marching even though ☐ we were ☐ were ☐ very tired.

7   She is supporting herself though her family ☐ is wealthy ☐ wealthy ☐.

8   The washing machine is still good although it is ☐ ancient ☐ new ☐.

9   The room is stuffy even though the air-conditioner is ☐ not working ☐ working ☐.

10   Your rooster ☐ crowing ☐ is crowing ☐ although it is still dark.

YOUR SCORE

10

PRACTICE $\boxed{B}$ Tick the correct sentences.

1   His mind is clear although he had a sleepless night.

2   They searched us even though they were suspicious.

3   He rejected the offer though it was a chance to make money.

4   It was a pleasant party though the food disappointing.

5   Whales are mammals even though look like fish.

6   Her ski jacket looks new although she bought it second-hand.

7   Our plants are flourishing though we take good care of them.

8 You mustn't yield even though they are putting pressure on you.

9 Astronauts undergo rigorous training although they have to be perfectly fit.

10 I joined in their laughter though I was sad.

PRACTICE *C* Circle the letters of the correct items to complete the sentences. There may be more than one answer for each question.

1 The little boy went on crying
   A although his mother tried to comfort him.
   B although his mother trying to comfort him.
   C though his mother tried to comfort him.

2 The TV antenna has to be repaired
   A even though it was struck by lightning.
   B as it was struck by lightning.
   C because it was struck by lightning.

3 She felt at home
   A although she had never been there before.
   B since she had never been there before.
   C even though she had never been there before.

4 They reached their destination safely
   A though their camels gave them problems.
   B though they lost their way several times.
   C though the journey went smoothly.

5 The moon was still in the sky
   A even though the sun rising.
   B even though the sun was rising.
   C even though the sun had risen.

PRACTICE *D* Fill in the blanks with the correct words in the boxes.

1 She did not get seasick _____ the boat rocked.

| since |
| though |

2 The hotel was filthy although the view was _____ .

| impressive |
| unimpressive |

3 The law was passed even though _____ it.

| opposed |
| we opposed |

4 Rottweilers are dangerous _____ they are aggressive dogs.

| although |
| because |

5 I was punished although I _____ nothing wrong.

| done |
| had done |

6 He is calm though everyone else _____ .

| is screaming |
| screaming |

7 Schools are closed _____ this is a public holiday.

8 Nobody was hurt _____ the car was badly damaged.

9 The class was _____ even though the teacher was away.

10 You can stay though the others _____ go now.

| as |
| even though |

| although |
| since |

| noisy |
| quiet |

| have to |
| to |

YOUR SCORE / 10

PRACTICE **E** Underline the correct words in the brackets.

I often think of careers for myself although most of them are highly **1** (suitable / unsuitable). For instance, I dream of becoming a rock singer even though my voice **2** (is unlikely / unlikely) to impress anybody. I imagine myself as a jet pilot though **3** (am / I am) terrified of flying. I even fantasize about being a scientist although I **4** (have not / not) shown much promise in that field.

Strangely, I have **5** (always / never) wanted to be an artist though **6** (I seem / seem) to have artistic talent. Law **7** (does / does not) interest me although career counsellors **8** (are encouraging / encouraging) me to take it up. Perhaps I am not ready to think seriously about a career even though I will **9** (be leaving / leaving) school next year. It's fun to play with possibilities though **10** (does / it does) not get you anywhere.

YOUR SCORE / 10

PRACTICE **F** Rewrite the extract from the letter correctly.

We have not given up on you even though you been silent for so long. You must be very busy but that is no excuse. All of us here miss you though used to drive us insane with your deafening music.

Mum and Dad are well although Dad is not very energetic now. Joe pulled a muscle even though he had not warmed up sufficiently before jogging at dawn. As for me, I am keeping virtuously to a new diet though I often tempted to be naughty.

_____

_____

_____

_____

_____

_____

_____

_____

YOUR SCORE / 10

UNIT 10.3 ADVERBIAL CLAUSES

with **when** and **while**

Look at the **A** and **B** sentences below. Find out why **B** is correct and **A** is wrong in the **Grammar Points** section.

CHECKPOINT

GRAMMAR
POINTS

1A	We groaned **while** he began reciting his poem.	✗	
1B	We groaned **when** he began reciting his poem.	✓	1
2A	**I daydreamed** when he rapped the table.	✗	
2B	**I was daydreaming** when he rapped the table.	✓	2
3A	They **were enjoying** themselves while we **worked**.	✗	
3B	They **enjoyed** themselves while we **worked**.	✓	3

GRAMMAR POINTS

1 We use an adverbial clause beginning with **when** for a short action that takes place just before another short action in the main clause.

EXAMPLE:

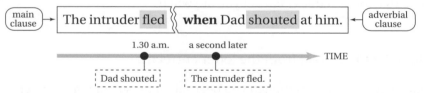

2 We also use an adverbial clause beginning with **when** for a short action that interrupts a long action in the main clause. We use the continuous tense for the main clause.

EXAMPLE:

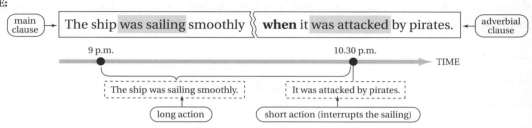

3 We use an adverbial clause beginning with **while** for a long action which takes place at the same time as another action in the main clause. We usually use the same tense for the main clause and the adverbial clause if both actions start and end at the same time.

EXAMPLES:

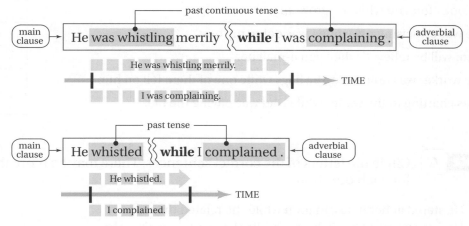

past continuous tense

main clause → He was whistling merrily ⟨⟨ **while** I was complaining . ← adverbial clause

He was whistling merrily.

I was complaining.

TIME

past tense

main clause → He whistled ⟨⟨ **while** I complained . ← adverbial clause

He whistled.

I complained.

TIME

REMEMBER!

■ When an adverbial clause beginning with **when** or **while** refers to a future action or event, the verb is in the present tense, not the future tense.

EXAMPLES: I will explain everything **when** I **see** you.
I will be watching over you **while** you **are sleeping**.

PRACTICE A   Cross out the incorrect words in the boxes to complete the sentences.

1 They gasped in shock | when | while | they saw her hairstyle.

2 She lazed on the beach | when | while | I practised floating.

3 We were flipping through the magazine | when | while | we came across your picture.

4 I was eating all the cakes | when | while | Ivy was sipping tea.

5 You will have a lovely time when you | go | will go | to college.

6 Liza | roasted | was roasting | peanuts when the kerosene stove exploded.

7 Our boss | travelled | was travelling | everywhere while we manned the office.

8 They lowered their voices when they | noticed | were noticing | us.

9 The students are putting up the tents | when | while | the teachers are cooking.

10 The farmers plant other crops while the rice | is ripening | ripens | .

YOUR SCORE

/ 10

PRACTICE B   Tick the correct sentences.

1 We will accept that responsibility when the time will come.

2 He listened unmoved while I pleaded for leniency.

3 They were wading in the shallow part when a huge wave hit them.

4 You are wasting our money while I try to be thrifty.

5 The chair was creaking when the big man sat on it.

6 I'll look after you when I'll grow up.

7 She was criticising me while I was doing my best.

8 Mum will be relieved when you e-mail her.

9 The worker was unloading the bags while one of them fell on him.

10 I was chatting to the waiter while Dad was paying the bill.

PRACTICE **C** Circle the letters of the correct sentences. There may be more than one answer for each question.

1 A He stared at her in fascination while she related the story.
  B He was staring at her in horror while she was telling the story.
  C He gasped in surprise when she confirmed the story.

2 A I was invigilating an exam when one of the candidates was fainting.
  B I was invigilating an exam when one of the candidates fainted.
  C I invigilated an exam when one of the candidates was fainting.

3 A We'll join them when they'll visit the Pyramids.
  B We'll join them when they visit the Pyramids.
  C We'll be photographing them while they're gazing at the Pyramids.

4 A They dragged him out when they spotted him in the bushes.
  B They dragged him out while they spotted him in the bushes.
  C They were looking for him when they spotted him in the bushes.

5 A She smiled serenely while the crowd jeered at her.
  B She was smiling serenely while the crowd was jeering at her.
  C She was smiling serenely while the crowd jeered at her.

PRACTICE **D** Rewrite the sentences correctly.

1 They counted the day's takings when a gunman held them up.
  They were counting the day's takings when a gunman held them up.

2 Jimmy was injured while his motorcycle hit a tree.

3 The vet treated the wounded bird when we watched.

4 We'll be thinking of you while you'll be sitting for the examination.

5 I usually read a novel while I'm waiting for my flight.

6 She was hanging up the balloons when one of them was bursting.

Underline the correct words in the brackets.

My family and I were sleeping in our house near the forest **1** (when / while) a clamour outside jolted me awake. I rushed out of the house when I **2** (recognised / was recognising) the chatter of monkeys. I stared aghast while a troupe of monkeys **3** (plucked / was plucking) bunches of bananas from the trees in our garden. The monkeys scampered away when I **4** (was yelling / yelled) at them furiously. I chased them away with my axe **5** (when / while) my family slept on peacefully.

I **6** (ran / was running) along a forest path when I came to a sudden stop. Two little monkeys were eating bananas **7** (when / while) their mother was cleaning their fur. The mother jumped up to stand in front and defend them **8** (when / while) I approached. I walked away when I **9** (saw / was seeing) the look of loving sacrifice in the mother monkey's eyes. I'll still remember that look when **10** (I'll be / I'm) very old.

YOUR SCORE
10

PRACTICE F Join the sentences using **when** or **while**. Make those under **A** the main clauses and those under **B** adverbial clauses after the main clauses.

A	B
1 Lucy was carrying a suitcase.	She meddled in their affairs.
2 Time is running out.	We will write the story.
3 Jane angered her colleagues.	His foot slipped.
4 We will quote the spokesman.	I saw her outside the bus station.
5 The guard eavesdropped.	You are hesitating.
6 Mr Mason was climbing a hill.	They planned the robbery.

1 *Lucy was carrying a suitcase when I saw her outside the bus station.*

2 _____

   _____

3 _____

   _____

4 _____

   _____

5 _____

   _____

6 _____

YOUR SCORE
10

   _____

145

UNIT 10.4 ADVERBIAL CLAUSES

with **so that** and **so . . . that**

Look at the **A** and **B** sentences below. Find out why **B** is correct and **A** is wrong in the **Grammar Points** section.

			GRAMMAR POINTS
1A	He exercised so that he **will** look trim.	✗	
1B	He exercised so that he **would** look trim.	✓	1
2A	She was **very** persuasive that everyone believed her.	✗	
2B	She was **so** persuasive that everyone believed her.	✓	2

GRAMMAR POINTS

1 We use an adverbial clause beginning with **so that** to show the purpose of the action in the main clause. In the adverbial clause, we usually use a modal which is in the **same tense** (present or past) as the verb in the main clause.

EXAMPLE:

main clause — verb (past tense) — modal (past tense) — adverbial clause (shows purpose for expressing his unhappiness)

He expressed his unhappiness ⟩⟩ **so that** they might reconsider their decision.

REMEMBER!
- An adverbial clause beginning with **so that** can also show the result of an action in the main clause. A comma must be added between the clauses.

EXAMPLE: The disease spread fast, ⟩⟩ **so that** the hospitals were crammed with patients.

main clause — comma between clauses — adverbial clause (shows the result of the disease spreading fast)

---

2 We use **so . . . that** (**so** + adjective / adverb + **that**) to show that something happens because the subject in the main clause has an extreme quality or acts in an extreme way. We do it in this way:
so + adjective / adverb in main clause + adverbial clause beginning with **that**

EXAMPLES:

subject — adjective

main clause → You are **so** efficient ⟩⟩ **that** we know we can rely on you. ← adverbial clause

(We know we can rely on you because you are extremely efficient.)

subject — adverb

main clause → You work **so** efficiently ⟩⟩ **that** we know we can rely on you. ← adverbial clause

(We know we can rely on you because you do things in an extremely efficient way.)

146

REMEMBER!

- Adverbial clauses with **so that** and **so ... that** always come after the main clauses.

EXAMPLES:

(main clause) → I'm tiptoeing around **so that** the baby won't wake up. ← (adverbial clause) ✓

(adverbial clause) → **So that** the baby won't wake up, I'm tiptoeing around. ← (main clause) ✗

PRACTICE *A*   Underline the adverbial clauses that show result.

1 The sketch was so hilarious <u>that the audience was in stitches.</u>

2 The drainage is poor, so that floods are frequent.

3 She suggested a substantial breakfast so that we would have lots of energy.

4 He is used to hardship, so that this setback doesn't worry him.

5 The residents are forming an association so that they will interact more.

6 They live so simply that we almost forget their wealth.

7 I'm explaining everything so that misconceptions may be cleared away.

8 Lynn longed to be free so that she could live her own life.

9 You have guarded your privacy so fiercely that nobody knows anything about you.

10 They want to finance the whole project so that they can have full control.

11 His gaze was so steady that I didn't suspect him of lying.

PRACTICE *B*   Cross out the incorrect words in the boxes to complete the sentences.

1 She had grown | extremely | so | thin that her clothes hung on her.

2 The water was | extremely | so | cold, so that we ran back to the shore.

3 I took slow, deep breaths so that I | will | would | feel calmer.

4 He ended the conversation so abruptly | that | which | she felt hurt.

5 They have agreed to publish the article so that the truth | may | might | be known.

6 The rules are reasonable | , so that | that | we obey them willingly.

7 That cartoon series is | so | very | delightful that even adults watch it.

8 This house is | so quiet | quiet | , so that I find it restful.

9 We bought her a handphone so that we | can | could | contact her easily.

10 Everything happened | quickly | so quickly | that I was in a daze.

Fill in the blanks with suitable words in the box. Each word may be used more than once.

can	everybody	good	have	nobody
so	that	well	would	

1 I was so eager to see the parade _____ I got up at dawn.

2 We separated the two boys so that they _____ not fight.

3 He is known to be unreliable, _____ that I dare not trust him.

4 She has served her constituents so _____ that they are sure to re-elect her.

5 They often play truant, so _____ their grades are poor.

6 My grandparents _____ joined a senior citizens' club so that they may not feel bored.

7 The service at the restaurant is so _____ that we go there frequently.

8 Everybody's views are considered, so that _____ feels frustrated.

9 The authorities are tightening security so that illegal immigration _____ be prevented.

10 The disabled boy is so cheerful that _____ enjoys being with him.

YOUR SCORE
10

Tick the correct sentences.

1 So that the deadline can be met, we are working frantically.

2 The pilot was calm, so that we felt reassured.

3 Her vegetables are so fresh that they are soon sold out.

4 The workers picketed so that the management will give in.

5 That some people have forgotten him, he has been away so long.

6 The room is very stuffy, so that I feel faint.

7 The little girls laughed so heartily that we all joined in.

8 The situation is very delicate that we must be tactful.

9 I wanted to graduate fast so that I could help my family.

10 He was facing a bright light, that his eyes ached.

YOUR SCORE
10

PRACTICE E Rewrite the sentences correctly using **so that** and **so ... that**.

1 I inhaled deeply so that the mountain air will invigorate me.

I inhaled deeply so that the mountain air would invigorate me.

2 He evicted his tenants at very short notice, that they had nowhere to go.

_____

_____

3 Their wedding was expensive that they were in debt for some time.

_____

_____

4 So that she could spend more time with her family, she wanted flexible hours.

_____

_____

5 I worked steadily so that I might panic just before the exam.

_____

_____

6 The view was truly wonderful that we were speechless.

_____

YOUR SCORE
10

_____

PRACTICE F Underline the correct words in the brackets.

For the first time our family has a house with a garden where we **1** (can / cannot) grow our own flowers and vegetables. We are **2** (so / very) happy about this that we all do some work in the garden every weekend.

When we first moved to this house, I was afraid that the family would suddenly become bored with gardening **3** (so as / so that) projects **4** (will / would) be left half finish. So far this has not happened.

We are lucky to have a neighbour who is a **5** (so / very) enthusiastic gardener. He has given useful advice **6** (so that /that) we choose the right plants. My favourite flower is the rose, but he told me it **7** (will / would) not be wise to plant rose bushes in this soil.

I am **8** (very / so that) pleased that we can plant fruit trees. Our neighbour's trees give so much fruit **9** (so / that) he always has extra to give us and other friends. We will be **10** (and that / very) proud when we can give him some of our fruit

YOUR SCORE
10

149

UNIT 10.5 ADVERBIAL CLAUSES

with **if**

Look at the **A** and **B** sentences below. Find out why **B** is correct and **A** is wrong in the **Grammar Points** section.

			GRAMMAR POINTS
1A	They may attack him if he **will go** there tomorrow.	✗	
1B	They may attack him if he **goes** there tomorrow.	✓	1a
2A	She would faint if a lizard **falls** on her head.	✗	
2B	She would faint if a lizard **fell** on her head.	✓	1b
3A	We could have rescued them if they **called** us.	✗	
3B	We could have rescued them if they **had called** us.	✓	2

GRAMMAR POINTS

1 We use an adverbial clause beginning with **if** to show the condition for the action or event in the main clause.

(a) When the condition is fairly likely, we use the simple present tense or the present perfect tense in the adverbial clause beginning with **if**. We often use a modal + the base form of the verb in the main clause.

EXAMPLE:

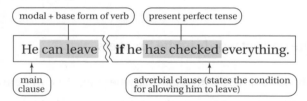

(b) When the condition is unlikely or impossible, we use the simple past tense in the adverbial clause beginning with **if**. We use **would**, **should**, **could** or **might** + the base form of the verb in the main clause.

EXAMPLE:

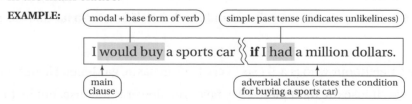

2 When the condition could have happened but did not happen, we use the past perfect tense in the adverbial clause beginning with **if**. We use **would have**, **should have**, **could have** or **might have** + the past participle in the main clause.

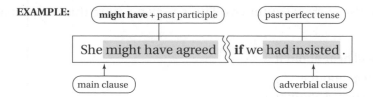

might have + past participle   past perfect tense

She might have agreed **if** we had insisted .

main clause   adverbial clause

> **REMEMBER!**
> - To show a condition which is unlikely or impossible, **were** is used instead of **was** in an adverbial clause beginning with **if** when the subject is **I**.
>
>   EXAMPLES: I would buy a ski resort in Switzerland, **if** I **were** a millionaire.
>   I would not take the risk, **if** I **were** you.

PRACTICE *A*   Cross out the incorrect words in the boxes to complete the sentences.

1 I will respect your decision if you considered | have considered all options.

2 We would defend | would have defended him if he had been accused.

3 She might still reject him if he offered | offers her the moon.

4 You may use my computer if you like | liked .

5 The tonic would have invigorated her if she had taken | took it.

6 I cannot | could not bring myself to do that, if I were you.

7 They'll regret it if they | they'll betray us.

8 I would write a sonnet to her, if I is | were Shakespeare.

9 The plants would have grew | grown well if you had tended them.

10 Certainly you can | could do well if you use your brains.

YOUR SCORE
10

PRACTICE *B*   Tick the correct sentences.

1 I would live differently if I can turn back the clock.

2 He must be Tim's twin if he looks exactly like Tim.

3 We would invest in your company if we had known about it.

4 My mother will make a great general if she is a man.

5 She might not notice any difference if the sun rose in the west.

6 They would have cheated us if they had had a chance.

7 You ought to be more considerate if you wish to keep friends.

8 Brian may still admire you if you turned into a monster.

9 You can sleep in our spare room if you had nowhere else to stay.

10 Her talent might have blossomed if someone had nurtured it.

YOUR SCORE
10

PRACTICE C Circle the letters of the correct sentences. There may be more than one answer for each question.

1 A They will disapprove if they will hear about it.
  B They will disapprove if they hear about it.
  C They would disapprove if they heard about it.

2 A His behaviour would have been cute if he had been a child.
  B His behaviour would be cute, if he was a child.
  C His behaviour would be cute if he is a child.

3 A You can stop coming if you have learnt enough.
  B You can stop coming if you are bored.
  C You can stop coming if you have a good excuse.

4 A Joe could keep going if we had supported him.
  B Joe could have kept going if we had supported him.
  C Joe can keep going if we support him.

5 A Life might be dull if every wish was fulfilled.
  B Life might be dull if every wish had been fulfilled.
  C Life might be dull if every wish is fulfilled.

PRACTICE D Fill in the blanks with suitable words in the box. Each word may be used more than once.

passes	are	can't	had	hang	stands	will
abated	were	couldn't	have	stayed	stood	would

1 I could have introduced you to her if you _____ come.

2 They would not notice him if he _____ on his head.

3 We shall leave tonight if the storm _____ .

4 He might have _____ around indefinitely if you had let him.

5 The noise may keep you awake if you _____ not used to it.

6 He would _____ basked in the limelight if he had been here.

7 They _____ forget her if they tried for a thousand years.

8 We can't do anything if you _____ made up your mind.

9 You would have _____ tremendous success if you had entered for that race.

10 Everyone _____ be pleased if Ken accepts the nomination.

Join the main clauses under **A** with the adverbial clauses under **B** to form sentences. Place the adverbial clauses after the main clauses.

A
1 They will sue you . . .
2 I wouldn't emigrate . . .
3 We'll tell you the latest news . . .
4 We could have climbed the hill . . .
5 This house would stand firm . . .
6 I might have stayed . . .

B
if I had had job satisfaction.
if you like.
if the fog had cleared.
if a herd of elephants charged at it.
if I were you.
if you don't pay.

1 *They will sue you if you don't pay.*

2 _____

_____

3 _____

_____

4 _____

_____

5 _____

_____

6 _____

_____

YOUR SCORE
10

PRACTICE *F* Underline the correct words in the brackets.

Dearest Fara,

I'll graduate in May if all **1** (go / goes) well. I couldn't **2** (has / have) come this far if you **3** (had / have) not urged me to keep trying. Indeed, my life **4** (will / would) have **5** (been / being) much less happy if you had **6** (given / giving) up on me.

Yes, you can come over here anytime if you **7** (are / were) able to get away. You couldn't be an 'inconvenience' if you **8** (tried / try)! You might be a delightful distraction if you **9** (are / were) less bent on making me work. Don't worry. **10** (I / I'll) be more motivated than ever if you pamper me a little.

Love,
Kim

YOUR SCORE
10

UNIT 10.6 ADVERBIAL CLAUSES

with **as**

Look at the **A** and **B** sentences below. Find out why **B** is correct and **A** is wrong in the **Grammar Points** section.

GRAMMAR
POINTS

1A	She treats people **as how** her parents do.	✗	
1B	She treats people **as** her parents do.	✓	1a
2A	They are joking **as what** they did in the old days.	✗	
2B	They are joking **as** they did in the old days.	✓	1b

GRAMMAR POINTS

1 We use an adverbial clause beginning with **as** to describe how the subject in the main clause acts or feels.

(a) We do not add **how** after **as** in the adverbial clause.

EXAMPLE:
David doesn't care about convenience and comfort.

main clause → He lives {{ **as how** most rural people do. ← adverbial clause   ✗

David doesn't care about convenience and comfort.

main clause → He lives {{ **as** most rural people do.   adverbial clause (describes how David lives)   ✓

subject = David   verb = action

Meaning: How does David live? He lives in the way that most rural people do.

(b) We do not add **what** after **as** in the adverbial clause.

EXAMPLE:
The tiger cubs like to play **as what** other young animals do.   ✗

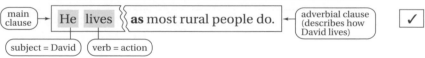

main clause → The tiger cubs like to play {{ **as** other young animals do.   ✓

subject = The tiger cubs   verb = action

adverbial clause (describes how the tiger cubs like to play)

Meaning: How do the tiger cubs like to play? The tiger cubs like to play in the way that other young animals do.

REMEMBER!

■ Sometimes, **like** or **the way** can be used instead of **as** to begin the adverbial clause.

EXAMPLES: It is happening **the way** I planned it. ✓   She enjoys painting **like** her father did. ✓

It is happening **as** I planned it. ✓   She enjoys painting **as** her father did. ✓

- Traditionally, **as** is used before a clause and **like** before a noun. Nowadays, it is common to begin an adverbial clause with **like.**

- The verb 'to do', 'to be' or 'to have' is often used in the adverbial clause to avoid repeating the verb in the main clause.

    EXAMPLES: I'll stay up tonight as I **stayed up** last night.   ✗

    I'll stay up tonight as I **did** last night.   ✓

    They were deceived by flattery like most of us **are deceived**.   ✗

    They were deceived by flattery like most of us **are**.   ✓

    He has succeeded the way his brothers **have succeeded**.   ✗

    He has succeeded the way his brothers **have**.   ✓

PRACTICE *A*   Circle the correct adverbial clauses to complete the sentences. There may be more than one answer for each question.

1 In this matter you may do
  A as you like.
  B as how you like.
  C as what you like.

2 The epidemic was beyond control
  A the way how we had feared.
  B as we had feared.
  C like we had feared.

3 He is facing bankruptcy
  A as his friend did.
  B like his friend did.
  C like his friend faced.

4 This is an affluent society
  A as you can see.
  B as it has been for decades.
  C as everyone knows.

5 The rivers will be clean and sparkling again
  A as they were once.
  B like they did once.
  C the way they were once.

YOUR SCORE

10

PRACTICE *B*   Tick the correct sentences.

1 Our home is near an industrial area as we were warned.

2 The new manager does not shout like his predecessor was.

3 We mustn't gloat over their problems the way they did over ours.

4 She has graduated with honours as what she promised to do.

5 The firemen put out the flames fast as the bystanders will testify.

6 The institution doesn't inspire confidence like it used to do.

7 My son is enthusiastic about everything like how I was.

8 Other nations have followed our progress the way we have theirs.

9 They pride themselves on their wealth like their ancestors prided.

10 He is full of energy the way how very healthy people often are.

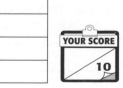

YOUR SCORE

10

PRACTICE *C* Fill in the blanks with suitable words in the boxes.

1 I sent my car for servicing _____ you had suggested. | as | as how |

2 She prefers imported furniture like her mother _____ . | did | was |

3 The villagers are kind _____ they've always been. | the way | the way how |

4 The secretary handles aggressive people like her boss _____ . | does | handles |

5 The jokes broke the ice as they were meant to _____ . | be | do |

6 The zoo animals are no longer sickly the way they _____ last year. | are | were |

7 I am not a slave to fashion _____ some people are. | as what | like |

8 They have not experienced hardship _____ we have. | like what | the way |

9 He is rather sensitive as elderly people often _____ . | are | do |

10 Julie has not helped us like the others _____ . | helped | have |

YOUR SCORE

/10

PRACTICE *D* Rearrange the words in the boxes to complete the sentences.

1 I will reconsider   as — do — have — me — to — urged — you.

_____

_____

2 He is not boastful   be — men — tend — the — to — way — some.

_____

_____

3 She won a gold for us   as — had — our — predicted — reporters — sports.

_____

_____

4 They are helping us move house   did — for — like — son — their — we.

_____

_____

5 The city is serene again   before — it — raid — the — the — was — way.

_____

YOUR SCORE

/10

_____

156

Underline the correct words in the brackets.

At the age of three, my brother Jeff walked and talked like Dad **1** (did / was). He insisted on having his hair cut short the way Dad's hair **2** (has / was). He looked and behaved **3** (like / like how) Dad did at three. He was Dad Junior **4** (as / as what) family and friends said.

Now, at 13, Jeff struts around tossing his wild locks like his favourite singer **5** (acts / does). His speech is a nasal drawl as his idol's **6** (does / is). He has become a total fan the way his friends **7** (be / have).

However, these are just phases in Jeff's life **8** (as / like what) people assure me. He will grow up in due course **9** (like / the way how) everyone does. Then Jeff will be Jeff **10** (as how / the way) a mature person is truly himself.

YOUR SCORE
10

PRACTICE *F* Rewrite the sentences correctly.

1 She is considerate as she was brought up to do.
She is considerate as she was brought up to be.

2 The parade was magnificent like how I had imagined it to be.

3 I am enchanted with this place the way you did last year.

4 We are narrating the incident as what it was told to us.

5 Nobody else has understood my situation the way you have understood.

6 They often dance till dawn like what we used to do.

YOUR SCORE
10

UNIT 11.1 REPORTED CLAUSES

with **that**, **whether**, **if**

Look at the **A** and **B** sentences below. Find out why **B** is correct and **A** is wrong in the **Grammar Points** section.

			GRAMMAR POINTS
1A	We learnt that oxygen **was** essential for our survival.	✗	
1B	We learnt that oxygen **is** essential for our survival.	✓	1
2A	She suggested that we **gave** the new restaurant a try.	✗	
2B	She suggested that we **give** the new restaurant a try.	✓	2
3A	He wondered if / whether **should he resign** at once.	✗	
3B	He wondered if / whether **he should resign** at once.	✓	3
4A	The policeman asked **if** the purse snatcher was tall or short.	✗	
4B	The policeman asked **whether** the purse snatcher was tall or short.	✓	4

GRAMMAR POINTS

1   We use a clause beginning with **that** to report a statement or someone's opinion. We often use the past tense for the main clause and the reported clause. However, to stress that the statement is still true at the time of reporting, we use the simple present tense in the reported clause.

EXAMPLES:

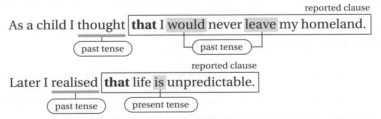

(The simple present tense in the reported clause stresses that the statement is still true at the time of reporting.)

REMEMBER!

- The reported clause is very useful, especially in writing. It is often used to present information that we have read or heard about somewhere else.
- These are some verbs that are commonly used with reported clauses beginning with **that**:

  announce, claim, discover, explain, feel, hope, learn, mention, reveal, say, think

- The word **that** can often be omitted from its reported clause.

  EXAMPLE: I thought **that** Jane was with you.   ✓

            I thought Jane was with you.   ✓

158

2 When a reported clause beginning with **that** is used with a verb like **advise**, **demand**, **insist**, **propose**, **recommend**, **request**, **suggest**, etc, we use the base form of the verb or modal + verb in the reported clause.

EXAMPLES: They recommended | **that** he restructure the firm. ✓

past tense — base form of verb

reported clause

They recommended | **that** he should restructure the firm. ✓

past tense — modal + verb

reported clause

3 We use a clause beginning with **if** or **whether** to report someone's query or a question that has **yes** or **no** as its answer. But we use the word order for a statement, not a question, in the reported clause.

EXAMPLE: We'll check | **if / whether** the session has begun . ✓

subject + verb

reported clause

We'll check | **if / whether** has the session begun . ✗

verb + subject

reported clause

In such cases, the word **whether** can be followed by **or not**.
EXAMPLE:

We'll check | **whether or not** the session has begun . ✓

subject + verb

reported clause

REMEMBER!
■ These are some verbs that are commonly used with reported clauses beginning with **if / whether**:

ask
enquire
wonder

4 We use a reported clause beginning with **whether** when the question offers a choice of two or more possibilities as the answer.

EXAMPLE:

I asked | **whether** horror films thrilled or repelled them. ✓

reported clause

I asked | **if** horror films thrilled or repelled them. ✗

reported clause

PRACTICE | *A* | Fill in the blanks with the correct words in the boxes.

1 The man complained that I _____ insulted him.

| had | have |

2 A science teacher told us that the sun _____ a star.

| is | was |

3 We enquired if _____ finance our venture.

| he would | would he |

4 He's asking _____ you'll stay here or at a motel.

| if | whether |

5 They're demanding that the two workers _____ promoted.

| are | be |

6 Napoleon vowed that he _____ conquer Europe.

| will | would |

7 They want to see if _____ handle this crisis.

| can I | I can |

8 He suggested that the company _____ public.

| should go | went |

9 She remembered that wild animals _____ fire.

| fear | feared |

10 I want to know _____ or not you are guilty.

| if |
| whether |

YOUR SCORE

/10

Cross out the incorrect words in the boxes to complete the sentences.

1 Last night she admitted that she | is | was | terrified.

2 I propose that nominations | are | be | closed.

3 She couldn't tell | if | whether | he was serious or teasing.

4 We were taught that sound pollution | is | was | bad for the nerves.

5 He enquired if | it was | was it | safe to scuba dive there.

6 They prayed that the hostages | were | would be | released.

7 Wendy learnt to accept that dreams | didn't | don't | always come true.

8 I'll ask whether | I may | may I | observe the proceedings.

9 They refused to believe that the Earth | goes | went | round the Sun.

10 You must find out if the venue is | suitable | suitable or not | .

YOUR SCORE 10

PRACTICE *C* Tick the correct sentences.

1 Seeing your car there, I assumed that you were around.

2 He explained that every language had its own peculiarities.

3 They will find out if he is a citizen or a permanent resident.

4 We requested that the meeting be held next weekend.

5 You must tell us whether have you found everything satisfactory.

6 The club secretary reminded us that rules are meant to be obeyed.

7 We couldn't decide whether he was a genius or a lunatic.

8 He is pleading that she gave him a second chance.

9 They asked if I would chair their forum on drug abuse.

10 Elaine suspected that she has been tricked by the salesman.

YOUR SCORE 10

PRACTICE *D* Rearrange the words to form correct sentences.

1 foolproof — guaranteed — method — that — their — they — was.

_____

2 if — she — she — surveillance — under — was — wondered.

_____

3 be — begged — he — his — life — mother's — spared — that.

_____

4 experiment — is — maintained — successful — that — their — they.

_____

5 are — check — must — rumours — the — true — we — whether.

_____

YOUR SCORE 10

PRACTICE *E* Underline the correct words in the brackets.

Dear Jan,

You must be wondering **1** (if / whether) my job interview was promising or disastrous. Well, one of the two interviewers enquired if **2** (had I / I had) been rebellious in my teens. I replied honestly that my parents **3** (had / have) found me quite difficult. The interviewer smiled and remarked that honesty **4** (is / was) not always the best policy. The other interviewer suggested that I **5** (tried / try) to convince them of my maturity. He added that they **6** (did / will) not want an employee who might give them problems.

I said that my testimonials from school, college and former employers **7** (shall / should) carry some weight. They both smiled and I wondered whether I **8** (had said / say) the wrong thing. Then the first interviewer asked whether **9** (could I / I could) give them my views on how to improve their company. I recommended that they **10** (change / changed) some of their methods, and the two interviewers kept nodding and chuckling.

What do you think of my chances?

Ken

YOUR SCORE
10

PRACTICE *F* Rewrite the sentences correctly.

1 I told them that Mount Kinabalu was the highest mountain in Malaysia.
I told them that Mount Kinabalu is the highest mountain in Malaysia.

2 He wondered if could he unify his people.

3 She proposed that they held an inquiry immediately.

4 We were warned that Aedes mosquitoes were dangerous.

5 They're asking whether do you suffer from insomnia.

6 Julie wants to know if you're fluent in French or not.

YOUR SCORE
10

UNIT 11.2 REPORTED CLAUSES

with wh-words

Look at the **A** and **B** sentences below. Find out why **B** is correct and **A** is wrong in the **Grammar Points** section.

			GRAMMAR POINTS
1A	I wonder **what did she say** to surprise them.	✗	
1B	I wonder **what she said** to surprise them.	✓	1
2A	I know **what** you admire and I'll introduce you to her.	✗	
2B	I know **who** you admire and I'll introduce you to her.	✓	2
3A	He tells everyone **who** his position is in the department.	✗	
3B	He tells everyone **what** his position is in the department.	✓	3

GRAMMAR POINTS

1 We use a clause beginning with a wh-word to report a wh-question. But we use the word order for a statement, not a question, in the reported clause.

EXAMPLE:

He asked | **who** we would elect. | ✓
            (subject) (verb)

He asked | **who** would we elect. | ✗
            (verb) (subject)

2 We must use the appropriate wh-word to begin the reported clause. We use a reported clause beginning with **who** to refer to a person.

EXAMPLE:

The report reveals | **who** started the rebellion.
(verb in main clause) (the person that started the rebellion)

3 We use a reported clause beginning with **what** to refer to a thing.

EXAMPLE:

The report reveals | **what** the rebels did.
(verb in main clause) (the things that the rebels did)

PRACTICE | *A* | Underline the reported clauses in the sentences and write in the brackets what they refer to: person, thing, time, place, reason or manner.

1 She explained <u>why she had declined the offer</u>.   (*reason*   )

2 I can't imagine what you see in those people.   (   )

3 We understand how they feel about us.   (   )

4 He remembers who found him the job.   (   )

5 Everyone is wondering where you are hiding.   (   )

6 They asked when the interview would be held.   (   )

YOUR SCORE 10

PRACTICE | *B* | Fill in the blanks with the correct words in the boxes.

1 We will recommend _____ should be appointed. | what | who |

2 I don't know _____ I dislike maths. | when | why |

3 You've taught me _____ dedication is. | what | why |

4 He'll never forget _____ they helped him. | how | who |

5 They'll tell you _____ the jewels are kept. | where | who |

6 I've been informed _____ the results are expected. | what | when |

7 The urban children will see _____ rural people live. | how | what |

8 I can guess _____ you couldn't concentrate. | who | why |

9 Grandpa keeps forgetting _____ he puts his spectacles. | when | where |

10 The principal announced _____ would succeed him. | who | why |

YOUR SCORE 10

163

PRACTICE *C* Cross out the incorrect words in the boxes to complete the sentences.

1 You mustn't repeat ⟦ what | who ⟧ I've told you in confidence.

2 We should keep in mind who ⟦ are we | we are ⟧ addressing.

3 I've studied ⟦ how | where ⟧ she puts people at ease.

4 Julia can understand ⟦ what | why ⟧ I'm behaving oddly.

5 From her accent I can tell where ⟦ did she grow | she grew ⟧ up.

6 They can't figure out ⟦ when | where ⟧ he came to this country.

7 Suddenly she recalled ⟦ who | why ⟧ he really was.

8 I wonder what ⟦ would you | you would ⟧ do in my place.

9 She knows ⟦ what | who ⟧ makes a party successful.

10 Tim often enquires ⟦ how | when ⟧ you are these days.

YOUR SCORE

10

PRACTICE *D* Circle the letters of the correct reported clauses to complete the sentences. There may be more than one correct answer for each question.

1 He had foreseen
   A what would take place centuries later.
   B who would they kill centuries later.
   C who they would kill centuries later.

2 I understand
   A what you became disenchanted with politics.
   B why you became disenchanted with politics.
   C how you became disenchanted with politics.

3 We daren't suggest
   A who should you choose.
   B what you ought to do.
   C when you should leave.

4 They are checking
   A where he was born.
   B why he emigrated.
   C how he made his fortune.

5 The museum authorities can't discover
   A how the security system was breached.
   B when the artefacts they were stolen.
   C why did the thieves take certain artefacts.

YOUR SCORE

10

164

PRACTICE *E* Underline the correct words in the brackets.

When Lisa regained consciousness, someone asked her **1** (what / who) her name was. She just could not remember who **2** (she was / was she)! Yet she could tell **3** (when / where) she was: on a hospital bed. She knew **4** (what / who) had asked her the question: a doctor. She understood **5** (what / when) was spoken to her. But who **6** (she was / was she)? She begged the doctor to tell her **7** (how / why) she could not recall her name. He realised **8** (what / why) had happened. He wondered **9** (when / where) she would recover from this loss of memory. He asked himself how **10** (could he / he could) help her cope with it.

YOUR SCORE

10

PRACTICE *F* Rewrite the sentences correctly.

1 The captain calmly asked what did the hijackers want.
The captain calmly asked what the hijackers wanted.

2 He found out what I liked and invited them to the party this weekend.

_____

_____

3 The little boy wants to know when can he ride in a spaceship and fly to Mars.

_____

_____

4 Step by step I learnt what an earthenware pot is made.

_____

_____

5 The old lady who is lost won't tell me where does she live.

_____

_____

6 I don't see how we must follow fashion blindly.

_____

_____

YOUR SCORE

10

UNIT 11.3 REPORTED CLAUSES

with **which** and **whose**

Look at the **A** and **B** sentences below. Find out why **B** is correct and **A** is wrong in the **Grammar Points** section.

			GRAMMAR POINTS
1A	He's asking himself **what** course he should take, law or medicine.	✗	
1B	He's asking himself **which** course he should take, law or medicine.	✓	1
2A	I forget **who's** suggestion was accepted at the meeting.	✗	
2B	I forget **whose** suggestion was accepted at the meeting.	✓	2
3A	She can't decide which chain **should she wear**, the gold or the silver one.	✗	
3B	She can't decide which chain **she should wear**, the gold or the silver one.	✓	3

GRAMMAR POINTS

1 We use a reported clause beginning with **which + noun** to refer to a person or thing to be chosen from a group or list.

reported clause

EXAMPLE: We're discussing | **which** name we should give the baby—Dan, Paul or Carl. |

which + noun

2 We use a reported clause beginning with **whose + noun** to refer to a relationship such as ownership, or a connection between the noun and the subject of the reported clause.

EXAMPLE:

reported clause

Nobody knows | **whose** child she is. |

referring to relationship

We must not confuse **whose** with **who's**. Who's is the short form of **who is** or **who has**.

EXAMPLE: Nobody knows **who's** (who is) coming tonight.   ✓

Nobody knows **who's** child she is.   ✗

3 We use the word order for a statement, not a question, in the reported clause.

EXAMPLE:

reported clause

I wonder | whose house **they will burgle** next. | ✓

subject   verb

reported clause

I wonder | whose house **will they burgle** next. | ✗

verb   subject

166

REMEMBER!

- To avoid repetition, the noun after **which** or **whose** at the beginning of a reported clause is dropped.

  EXAMPLES: Of the two options, I can see **which** ~~option~~ you prefer.

  That's a strange hut. We'll find out **whose** ~~hut~~ it is.

- **One** can be used to replace the noun after **which** but not the noun after **whose**.

  EXAMPLES: Of the two options, I can see which **one** you prefer. ☑

  That's a strange hut. We'll find out whose **one** it is. ☒

PRACTICE $\boxed{A}$ Fill in the blanks with the correct words in the boxes.

1 He realised too late whose laboratory _____ entered.

| had he | he had |

2 I can imagine _____ of the cars she'll like.

| which | which car |

3 They found an earring and guessed _____ it was.

| whose | whose one |

4 She asked _____ type of music he wanted, classical or rock.

| what | which |

5 Jim tried on many ties but couldn't decide _____ looked the least conventional.

| which one | which the |

6 Sally could estimate _____ time it was.

| what | which |

7 We mustn't ask whose fault _____ .

| is it | it is |

8 You must remember _____ money this is.

| who's | whose |

9 I guessed which of the two applicants _____ choose.

| would you | you would |

10 She has discovered _____ arranging the celebration lunch.

| who's | whose |

YOUR SCORE
10

PRACTICE $\boxed{B}$ Tick the correct sentences.

1 We enquired which test should we take, the first or the second.

2 I can't make out who's photograph this is.

3 She wanted the land. She didn't care whose it was.

4 Of the two travel packages, she knew which one would be more fun.

5 He can predict whose career will the boss advance.

6 They'll recommend to us what flat we should buy, this one or the one in the city.

7 This handwriting is familiar but I can't recall whose one it is.

8 The latest evidence will show which of the suspects is guilty.

9 I am trying to work out what sort of person he is.

10 We're calling to ask which day is better for you, Saturday or Sunday.

YOUR SCORE
10

PRACTICE **C**   Underline the correct words in the brackets.

1   She refused to say (which / which painting) of the paintings was hers.

2   We could guess (who's / whose) life story you were narrating.

3   Bobby's wondering (what / which) planet is nearer the sun, Mars or Venus.

4   Each of us has a problem. They'll judge (whose one / whose problem) is the most pressing.

5   Everyone has heard (who's / whose) challenging the heavyweight champion.

6   You've shown us what heights (can you / you can) reach.

7   Of all your fans, you know (which fan / which one) is the most devoted.

8   I forget whose wedding (are we / we are) supposed to attend.

9   She picked up a wig. She couldn't imagine (whose / whose one) it might be.

10   The interior designer asked me which colour (I would / would I) prefer, beige or white.

YOUR SCORE
10

PRACTICE **D**   Rearrange the words in the boxes to complete the sentences.

1   We must ascertain   contraband — is — items — of — the — which.

We must ascertain which of the items is contraband.

2   They will note   disbelief — expression — of — shows — signs — whose.

3   Of the three contenders, she could tell   most — one — resolute — the — was — which.

4   The shopkeepers daren't disclose   been — extorting — from — money — them — who's.

5   I saw the pistol and tried to think   be — could — it — possibly — whose.

6   We've studied the projects and will decide   benefit — country — most — the — this — which — would.

YOUR SCORE
10

168

PRACTICE *E* Cross out the incorrect words in the boxes to complete the passage.

My friend and I are writing a history of our village. We have talked to people **1** | who's | whose | families have lived here for a long time and we have found **2** | which | what | books we should read.

There are many aspects of village history to consider and we have to decide **3** | which | which aspect | to stress. We could focus on political history and show how our village has been governed and **4** | who's | whose | ideas were considered important. We could also choose social history and describe how people lived their daily lives and **5** | which | which special days | they celebrated. We are all interested in agriculture and we could write about the different farms and **6** | which | which farms | were most successful.

Everybody wants their family to be mentioned and we are not sure **7** | who's | whose | family history **8** | we should | should we | emphasise . We have been given so much advice that we are rather confused and not sure **9** | whose | whose advice | to follow. Tomorrow, we will climb the hill, sit quietly and look down at our village. I think we will be able to decide then **10** | which | whose | are the things we want to write about.

YOUR SCORE
/ 10

PRACTICE *F* Rewrite the sentences correctly.

1 Everyone's trying to find out whose is that amazing vintage car.
   Everyone's trying to find out whose that amazing vintage car is.

2 Journalists are speculating who's work will win the Nobel Prize.
   _____
   _____

3 After living in two countries, I can't tell which country I prefer.
   _____
   _____

4 He enquired what cuisine she preferred, Chinese or Japanese.
   _____
   _____

5 She told me whose biography was she writing.
   _____
   _____

6 We saw a huge footprint and could only guess whose one it was.
   _____
   _____

YOUR SCORE
/ 10

UNIT 12.1 ADJECTIVAL PHRASES

with prepositions

Look at the **A** and **B** sentences below. Find out why **B** is correct and **A** is wrong in the **Grammar Points** section.

			GRAMMAR POINTS
1A	She is the most important person **is in** my life.	✗	
1B	She is the most important person **in** my life.	✓	1
2A	We rented a chalet **that by** a lake.	✗	
2B	We rented a chalet **by** a lake.	✓	2

GRAMMAR POINTS

1 An adjectival clause has a finite verb. An adjectival phrase does not have a finite verb.

EXAMPLE:

He brings happiness to people | who **are** around him. |

- noun described
- finite verb
- adjectival clause
- adjectival phrase

He brings happiness to people | around him. |

2 An adjectival phrase does not begin with **who, which** or **that**. It can begin with a preposition.

EXAMPLE:

He brings happiness to people | around him. | ✓
— adjectival phrase

He brings happiness to people **who** around him. ✗

These are some other examples of adjectival phrases beginning with prepositions:

against the law	down the lane	in front of me
next to the station	opposite the gallery	over the mountains
under surveillance	up the street	within our capacity
beyond the hills	on my mind	under his rule

REMEMBER!

■ An adjectival phrase beginning with a preposition is used after a noun to give more information about the noun.

EXAMPLE: The warehouse | across the bridge | is owned by that company. ✓

- noun described
- adjectival phrase describing **the warehouse**

- adjectival phrase describing **the warehouse**

The warehouse is owned by that company | across the bridge. | ✗

Take note that the adjectival phrase must come immediately after the noun it describes.

PRACTICE *A*   Some of the sentences contain adjectival phrases. Underline the adjectival phrases and circle the nouns they describe.

1   He is a (man) of great wisdom and foresight.
2   Theirs is a family that has faced many problems.
3   Teens are the years between childhood and adulthood.
4   All of us loved the stream behind our house.
5   She composes music which is touched with melancholy.
6   This is a planet that has been badly abused.
7   The cameraman photographed the girl in blue.
8   We spoke to the students who were in the hall.
9   They want to interview people over 80.
10   She has a manner which is disarming.
11   You are speaking of something beyond my understanding.

YOUR SCORE
10

PRACTICE *B*   Fill in the blanks with suitable words in the boxes.

1   We enjoyed watching boats _____ the river.
2   He owns one of the houses _____ that road.
3   I'm looking for an apartment _____ my budget.
4   Those are things _____ your notice.
5   The museum is the building _____ the library.
6   He is the person _____ the uprising.
7   This is an issue _____ our scope.
8   They seem to enjoy gossip _____ the rich and famous.
9   You seem to like temperatures _____ zero.
10   He was in a state _____ collapse.

on	were on
along	which along
in	within
below	beneath
against	opposite
behind	who behind
is outside	outside
about	that about

are below	below
almost	near

YOUR SCORE
10

PRACTICE *C*   Tick the correct sentences.

1   Grandma remembers the years before the last World War.
2   The noise comes from the floor that above mine.
3   I treasure those quiet moments between projects.
4   We'd like to try the new road to the capital.
5   She has found a place is off the beaten track.
6   He has achieved success which beyond his wildest dreams.
7   You seem to be a person without ambition.

8 They gave me a window seat towards the rear of the plane.

9 Teenagers liked the cybercafé was around the corner.

10 The manager has to evaluate the employees who on probation.

PRACTICE *D* Circle the letters of the correct adjectival phrases to complete the sentences. There may be more than one answer for each question.

1 You'll be meeting people
  A without scruples of any sort.
  B with vibrant personalities.
  C who without a sense of responsibility.

2 He's renting a room
  A close to his place of work.
  B is in an elderly couple's house.
  C on the top floor of this building.

3 I admire the shady trees
  A are by the riverside.
  B by the riverside.
  C beside the river.

4 Theirs was a fight
  A for freedom and equality.
  B against injustice and corruption.
  C over some family property.

5 The police detective was observing the man
  A who in black.
  B is behind a grey van.
  C with an iron rod.

PRACTICE *E* Join the sentences under **A** with the sentences under **B**. Change the sentences under **B** into adjectival phrases beginning with prepositions.

A	B
1 We saw a magnificent horse.	The horse had a splendid mane.
2 Carl is reading a novel.	This novel is about a brilliant boy.
3 He worked out at a gymnasium.	The gymnasium was near his college.
4 The main character is a girl.	The girl has tremendous courage.
5 I was received by a secretary.	The secretary was in a bad mood.
6 These are delicious oranges.	The oranges come from China.

172

1 *We saw a magnificent horse with a splendid mane.*

2 _____

3 _____

4 _____

5 _____

6 _____

PRACTICE F Rewrite the sentences correctly using adjectival phrases beginning with prepositions.

1 He often helps friends who in trouble.
He often helps friends in trouble.

2 We held a barbecue one evening was around mid-term.

_____

_____

3 She resented the constant comparison which is with her sister.

_____

_____

4 I resigned myself to a life that without security.

_____

_____

5 Joan has a cottage is within walking distance of the beach.

_____

_____

6 That was a moving tribute which is to our forefathers.

_____

_____

UNIT 12.2 ADJECTIVAL PHRASES

with present participles

Look at the **A** and **B** sentences below. Find out why **B** is correct and **A** is wrong in the **Grammar Points** section.

			GRAMMAR POINTS
1A	My aunt is the lady **is weaving** a mat.	✗	
1B	My aunt is the lady **weaving** a mat.	✓	1
2A	She thought of the days **that passing** so quickly.	✗	
2B	She thought of the days **passing** so quickly.	✓	2

GRAMMAR POINTS

1 Unlike an adjectival clause, an adjectival phrase does not have a finite verb. It can have a non-finite verb, for instance a present participle.
EXAMPLE:

adjectival clause

We gazed at the river which **was shimmering** in the sun.

noun described — finite verb

adjectival phrase

We gazed at the river **shimmering** in the sun.

non-finite verb (present participle)

2 An adjectival phrase does not begin with **who**, **which** or **that**. It can begin with a present participle.
EXAMPLE:

adjectival phrase

We gazed at the river shimmering in the sun.   ✓

We gazed at the river **that** shimmering in the sun.   ✗

REMEMBER!

- An adjectival phrase beginning with a present participle is used after people or things to describe or identify them by saying what they are doing or what happens to them.
  EXAMPLE: adjectival phrase describing **the girl**

  The girl dancing gracefully on the stage can also swim well.   ✓

  noun described

  adjectival phrase describing **the girl**

  The girl can also swim well dancing gracefully on the stage.   ✗

Take note that the adjectival phrase must come immediately after the noun it describes.

PRACTICE *A*   Some of the sentences contain adjectival phrases. Underline the adjectival phrases and circle the nouns they describe.

1 My brother is the boy wearing a leather jacket.

2 I sat beside the man who was steering the boat.

3 We learnt how to treat a patient suffering from typhoid.

4 She's studying the factors unifying her people.

5 He was kind to the prisoner quaking before him.

6 Joe listened to his own voice which was echoing in the empty house.

7 The couple felt sorry for the child that was sobbing at the street corner.

8 You mustn't disturb the birds that are nesting in those trees.

9 The director wants shots of the coconut palms swaying in the breeze.

10 The lecturer glared at the students who were giggling in the corner of the lecture hall.

YOUR SCORE

10

PRACTICE *B*   Cross out the incorrect words in the boxes to complete the sentences.

1 They rounded up the people | smuggling | who smuggling | arms.

2 We met a young girl | travelling | was travelling | by herself.

3 He waved at the detective | is tailing | tailing | him.

4 It's a painting of three ladies | are sipping | sipping | tea.

5 I watched those agile fingers | threading | were threading | a needle.

6 We were entranced by the scene | that unfolding | unfolding | before us.

7 They spoke to a girl | voting | would be voting | for the first time.

8 I'll throw out the food | has been rotting | rotting | in there.

9 Jan joined a group | sunbathing | that sunbathing | on the beach.

10 We were scared of the lightning | which zigzagging | zigzagging | across the sky.

YOUR SCORE

10

PRACTICE *C*   Rearrange the words to form sentences with adjectival phrases.

1 decisions — he — is — making — man — the — the.

_____

_____

2 a — Alaska — friend — have — I — in — living.

_____

_____

175

3 are — enjoying — students — their — they — vacation.

_____

_____

4 a — an — building — ex-addict — life — new — she's.

_____

_____

5 fighting — garden — growing — in — our — the — weeds — we're.

_____

_____

YOUR SCORE
10

Circle the letters of the correct adjectival phrases to complete the sentences. There may be more than one answer for each question.

1 I'm going to give up some of the activities
   A cluttering up my life.
   B that cluttering up my life.
   C are cluttering up my life.

2 She is a fresh graduate
   A exploring job options.
   B joining the job market.
   C hunting for a job.

3 We saw a lot of graffiti
   A making the walls unsightly.
   B which expressing political dissatisfaction.
   C marring the splendour of the old castle.

4 He is a young artist
   A has been leading a hermit's life.
   B experimenting with new techniques.
   C trying to make a name for himself.

5 Ours is a city
   A losing its identity.
   B bursting at the seams.
   C is humming with activity.

YOUR SCORE
10

PRACTICE *E* Tick the correct sentences.

1 She couldn't sort out the thoughts crowding into her mind.

2 We must deal with the bullies who terrorising the younger students.

3 The school has a mural showing different careers.

4 This is a task that demanding concentration.

5 He has joined the climbers are climbing Mount Everest.

6 She's a member of the panel judging the art competition.

7 We are from the company sponsoring your trip.

8 He was one of the boys were loitering near the bank.

9 He's scrutinising each passenger alighting from the plane.

10 They resolved to fight the pollution which destroying the lake.

YOUR SCORE

10

PRACTICE *F* Underline the incorrect sentences. Rewrite them correctly using adjectival phrases beginning with present participles.

At a children's exhibition, I was intrigued by works revealing the young artists' impressions of the world around them. 'My City' was a charcoal piece which showing vehicles perched one on top of another. There were even a few cars floating in the air. A watercolour entitled 'Family' fascinated many people who viewing the exhibits. It depicted a pink mum was comforting two blue, bawling children and a scowling dad in a grey suit. 'Teacher' was a colour-pencil creation showing just the brown legs of a kindergarten teacher surrounded by smiling, multi-coloured little faces.

'Friends', a pencil sketch, portrayed a little boy and a television cartoon character were sticking their tongues out at each other. A charcoal drawing entitled 'Be good!' showed Dad's hand waving from the window of an aeroplane. 'Holiday' was a watercolour of a blue sky, a blue sea and golden children flying like birds between the two. An abstract masterpiece by a three-year-old was a riot of daubs and blobs that bearing the legend 'Me'.

1 _____

2 _____

3 _____

4 _____

5 _____

YOUR SCORE

10

UNIT 12.3 ADJECTIVAL PHRASES

with past participles

Look at the **A** and **B** sentences below. Find out why **B** is correct and **A** is wrong in the **Grammar Points** section.

GRAMMAR
POINTS

1A	I have read two novels **were written** by Ken Falcon.	✗	
1B	I have read two novels **written** by Ken Falcon.	✓	1
2A	We liked the proverbs **which quoted** in your magazine.	✗	
2B	We liked the proverbs **quoted** in your magazine.	✓	2

GRAMMAR POINTS

1 Unlike an adjectival clause, an adjectival phrase does not have a finite verb. It can have a non-finite verb, for instance a past participle.
EXAMPLE:

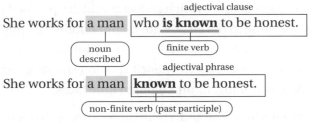

adjectival clause

She works for a man | who **is known** to be honest.

noun described

finite verb

adjectival phrase

She works for a man | **known** to be honest.

non-finite verb (past participle)

2 An adjectival phrase does not begin with **who**, **which** or **that**. It can begin with a past participle.
EXAMPLE:

adjectival phrase

She works for a man | known to be honest. | ✓

She works for a man **who** known to be honest. | ✗

REMEMBER!

■ An adjectival phrase beginning with a past participle is used after people or things to describe or identify them by saying what they are doing or what happens to them.
EXAMPLE:

adjectival phrase describing **the man**

The man | chosen to be the new director | has many years' experience. | ✓

noun described

adjectival phrase describing **the man**

The man has many years' experience | chosen to be the new director. | ✗

Take note that the adjectival phrase must come immediately after the noun it describes.

■ An adjectival phrase beginning with a present participle has an active meaning.
EXAMPLE:

We marvelled at the child | painting the picture. | ✓

We marvelled at the child | painted the picture. | ✗

178

- An adjectival phrase beginning with a past participle has a passive meaning.

EXAMPLE:
We marvelled at the picture painted by the child. ✓

We marvelled at the picture painting by the child. ✗

PRACTICE **A** Some of the sentences contain adjectival phrases. Underline the adjectival phrases and circle the nouns they describe.

1 They've bought expensive furniture that was imported from Italy.

2 She has natural beauty enhanced by subtle make-up.

3 We are eating vegetables which were grown by my grandmother.

4 I love that snapshot of Miss Lim caught in a frivolous mood.

5 Some people have personalities eaten up by ambition.

6 The doctor's treating a man who was bitten by a dog.

7 I admired the table set by the little girl.

8 That was a remark meant to cheer you up.

9 They sensed the kindness that was hidden behind his gruff manner.

10 Lara has some secret documents which are kept under lock and key.

YOUR SCORE
10

PRACTICE **B** Rearrange the words to form sentences with adjectival phrases.

1 at — he — jeans — knees — the — torn — wears.

_____

_____

2 by — is — she — tormented — eczema.

_____

_____

3 donkeys — by — carts — drawn — in — rode — we.

_____

_____

4 exciting — conducted — experiments — heard — here — of — the — we've.

_____

_____

5 board — can't — I — message — on — scribbled — the — the — understand.

_____

_____

YOUR SCORE
10

PRACTICE C Tick the correct sentences.

1 They spoke in voices filled with sadness.
2 I stared at a wall this morning riddled with bullets.
3 This is the team made our country famous.
4 These are safety rules broken at your own risk.
5 They employ people skilled in various fields.
6 He was a man who driven beyond endurance.
7 She showed us pictures were taken on the trip.
8 We saw young children traumatised by war.
9 Lillian gave me a smile tinged with mockery.
10 The police arrested the gang stolen the diamonds.

YOUR SCORE

10

PRACTICE D Fill in the blanks with suitable words in the box.

| borne | centred | concocted | cut | marred |
| recommended | famous | edged | thrown | worn |

1 We go to a dentist _____ by a friend.
2 You've got a story _____ by an over-imaginative mind.
3 I saw terrible pain _____ with dignity.
4 They lead lives _____ on the community.
5 The drain is blocked by the garbage _____ into it.
6 She walked along a path _____ with flowers.
7 He's living on a budget _____ down to the bare essentials.
8 Steve chose the gown _____ by his bride.
9 We had a vacation _____ by a minor crisis.
10 They went to a restaurant _____ for its steaks.

YOUR SCORE

10

PRACTICE E Rewrite the sentences correctly using adjectival phrases beginning with past participles.

1 They lived in a castle which surrounded by a moat.
   They lived in a castle surrounded by a moat.

2 Next came the school song was sung with gusto.

   _____

   _____

3 I had to smooth an awkward situation was created by my boss.

_____

_____

4 She felt for the children who abandoned by their families.

_____

_____

5 We'll meet the artist tomorrow commissioned to do a mural for us.

_____

_____

6 You're looking at a man that forgotten by the world.

_____

_____

PRACTICE **F** Fill in the blanks with suitable words in the boxes to complete the poem entitled 'Classmates'.

Lee is a scholar (1) _____ to a book,

glued
who glued

Fay is a loner (2) _____ in her nook,

ensconce
ensconced

Kit is a clown (3) _____ to amuse,

born
was born

Tina's a tabloid (4) _____ with news,

fill
filled

Raz is a sportsman (5) _____ with soccer,

besotted
has besotted

Mike's a guitarist (6) _____ 'The Rocker',

had nicknamed
nicknamed

Jan's a cyber surfer (7) _____ 'The Whiz',

called
that called

Linda's a performer (8) _____ for showbiz,

is destined
destined

Jill's a debater (9) _____ to quibbling,

addicted
which addicted

And I'm a dreamer (10) _____ with scribbling.

am obsessed
obsessed

UNIT 13.1 ADVERBIAL PHRASES

with **because of**

Look at the **A** and **B** sentences below. Find out why **B** is correct and **A** is wrong in the **Grammar Points** section.

			GRAMMAR POINTS
1A	People avoid her because of **she is thoughtless**.	✗	
1B	People avoid her because of **her thoughtlessness**.	✓	1
2A	You are liked because of **you are warm and friendly**.	✗	
2B	You are liked because of **your warmth and friendliness**.	✓	2

GRAMMAR POINTS

1 Unlike an adverbial clause, an adverbial phrase does not have a finite verb. The adverbial phrase contains either a noun alone or a noun phrase.

EXAMPLE:

We always feel tired | **because** we work long hours. |

adverbial clause

(finite verb)

We always feel tired | **because of** our long working hours . |

adverbial phrase

(noun phrase)

2 An adverbial phrase beginning with **because of** often contains:

(a) a noun

EXAMPLE: They became tough **because of** hardship .

noun

(b) adjective + noun

EXAMPLE: They became tough **because of** severe hardship .

adjective noun

(c) article + noun

EXAMPLE: We fled to the hills **because of** the heat .

article noun

(d) article + adjective + noun

EXAMPLE: We fled to the hills **because of** the terrible heat .

article adjective noun

(e) possessive pronoun + noun

EXAMPLE:
She succeeded **because of** her determination .

possessive pronoun noun

(f) possessive pronoun + adjective + noun

EXAMPLE:
She succeeded **because of** her unshakeable determination .

possessive pronoun adjective noun

(g) article / possessive pronoun + adjective + noun with 'ing'

EXAMPLE:
They fled from the war-torn city **because of** the fierce fighting .

article adjective noun with 'ing'

PRACTICE | **A** | Tick the correct sentences.

1 She treasured the ring because of her sentimental value.

2 Crime was rife because of crushing poverty.

3 He is trusted because of his good character.

4 Her case has been given priority because of it's urgent.

5 Many accidents take place because of carelessness.

6 I was refused entry because of didn't bring my pass.

7 Many couples have broken up because of jealous.

8 We liked her because of the common sense of her approach.

9 I'm sorry I can't do that because of have no time.

10 Shopkeepers sometimes fail because of overzealous selling.

YOUR SCORE

10

PRACTICE | **B** | Rearrange the words in the boxes to complete the sentences.

1 He felt depressed   because — incessant — of — rain — the.

   He felt depressed because of the incessant rain.

2 They got into trouble   because — behaviour — bad — of — their.

3 She was appointed   because — expertise — field — her — in — of — the.

4 We lost   a — because – fall — in — money — of — prices — share — sudden.

5 You weathered the storm   because — faith — of — of — strength — the — your.

6 People get lost   because — completely — of— maps — inaccurate.

_____

_____

PRACTICE _C_ Circle the letters of the correct sentences. There may be more than one correct answer for each question.

1 A We love this place because of it's restful.
  B We love this place because of its restfulness.
  C We love this place because it's restful.

2 A They've chosen him because of their originality.
  B They've chosen him because of the originality of his thinking.
  C They've chosen him because of his original ideas.

3 A Man is ruining the Earth because of greed.
  B Man is ruining the Earth because of his greedy.
  C Man is ruining the Earth because of his greediness.

4 A We postponed our fishing trip because of the storm.
  B We postponed our fishing trip because of the stormy weather.
  C We postponed our fishing trip because of stormy.

5 A Her novels are memorable because of their realism.
  B Her novels are memorable because of realistic.
  C Her novels are memorable because they are realistic.

PRACTICE _D_ Fill in the blanks with the correct words in the boxes.

1 They had to pawn their jewellery because of pressing _____ . | need | needy |

2 He lost his friend because of _____ . | a pride | pride |

3 She'll be successful _____ she's gifted. | because | because of |

4 I lost faith in them because of _____ unreliability. | my | their |

5 We failed because of _____ of our arguments. | the weakness | weakness |

6 The child grew tired because of prolonged _____ . | travel | travelling |

7 She likes pearls _____ their soft glow. | because | because of |

8 They gave away the book because of _____ boring content. | its | their |

9 The meeting broke up early because of _____ exchange of words. | a bitter | bitter |

10 We hated the King in the folk tale because of _____ evil deeds. | he | his |

Rewrite the sentences correctly using adverbal phrases with **because of**.

1 He didn't climb with us because of he afraid of heights.
 He didn't climb with us because of his fear of heights.

2 She's rather spoilt because her doting parents.

_____

_____

3 You don't feel the strain because of you tremendously energetic.

_____

_____

4 My little brother is lazy because of I'm unable to motivate him.

_____

_____

5 I did badly because of I had a foolish goal.

_____

_____

6 We must stop it because of its potentially destructive.

_____

_____

YOUR SCORE
10

Rewrite the paragraph, changing the adverbial clauses into adverbial phrases.

My trip to your country was wonderful because you carefully chose the places to take me. The jungle is my all-time favourite because it is unique. I'll always remember its night sounds because they are mysterious. I'm sorry the deer that came to our tent ran off because I gasped in wonder at seeing it. I also remember the folk dances because they are enchantingly graceful. Last but not least, I'll come again soon because I long for the delicious food.

 My trip to your country was wonderful because of your careful choice of the places to

take me to.

_____

_____

_____

_____

_____

_____

_____

_____

YOUR SCORE
10

UNIT 13.2 ADVERBIAL PHRASES

with **although**, **though**, **despite**, **in spite of**

Look at the **A** and **B** sentences below. Find out why **B** is correct and **A** is wrong in the **Grammar Points** section.

				GRAMMAR POINTS
1A	They've accepted the plan in spite of its **absurd**.	✗		
1B	They've accepted the plan in spite of its **absurdity**.	✓		1
2A	He is modest despite **he is** a renowned surgeon.	✗		
2B	He is modest despite **being** a renowned surgeon.	✓		2
3A	She was still cheerful although **was burdened** by many problems.	✗		
3B	She was still cheerful although **burdened** by many problems.	✓		3

GRAMMAR POINTS

1 An adverbial phrase beginning with **despite** or **in spite of** does not have a finite verb. In an adverbial phrase, **despite** or **in spite of** is usually followed by a noun. Before the noun, we can add an article, a possessive pronoun, an adjective or a combination of some of these.

EXAMPLES:

They sailed **despite** article the noun storm.

They sailed **despite** article the adjective raging noun storm.

She smiled **in spite of** possessive pronoun her noun dejection.

She smiled **in spite of** possessive pronoun her adjective deep noun dejection.

2 An adverbial phrase beginning with **despite** can also have the base form of a verb + 'ing' (or the present participle form of a verb).

EXAMPLES:

She stayed calm **despite** base form + 'ing' realising her plight.

We loved the country we visited **despite** base form + 'ing' hating its climate.

3 Both an adverbial clause and an adverbial phrase can begin with **although** or **though**. The clause has a finite verb but the phrase does not.

In an adverbial phrase, **although** or **though** can be followed by:

(a) a past participle
   EXAMPLE: He was persuaded to stay **although** / **though** past participle shaken by the incident.

(b) an adjective
   EXAMPLE: He was persuaded to stay **although** / **though** adjective fearful of the consequences.

186

PRACTICE $\boxed{A}$ Underline the adverbial phrases in the sentences.

1 He was not offended though mistaken for a burglar.

2 The film was well reviewed despite the director's lack of experience.

3 They've decided to employ him in spite of his brashness.

4 He made up his mind to punish the child although amused by her excuse.

5 She managed to work despite the unreliability of her computer.

6 The weather is still fine despite threatening to rain since morning.

7 The harvest was satisfactory in spite of the drought.

8 The room is cosy although cluttered with books and tapes.

9 He looked presentable in spite of his unusual hairstyle.

10 The hero was timid in behaviour though bold in words.

YOUR SCORE

10

PRACTICE $\boxed{B}$ Rearrange the words in the boxes to complete the sentences.

1 The team remained mediocre   attempts — despite — several — win — to.

The team remained mediocre despite several attempts to win.

2 The anthem is rousing   of — out — sung — though — tune.

3 He is still agile   arthritis — his — in — of — problem — spite.

187

4 This issue is often neglected although — economic — for — growth — our — vital.

_____

_____

5 She will be promoted despite — her — high — indifference — position — to.

_____

_____

6 Pollution is still not taken seriously all — although — forms — hazardous — life — of — to.

_____

_____

PRACTICE *C* Tick the correct sentences.

1 She daren't make decisions in spite of given a free hand.

2 He was able to appear cool despite shivering with fear.

3 They live frugally despite of their enormous wealth.

4 I am interested in all four subjects although plan to major in Physics.

5 You are not extravagant though sometimes too generous.

6 Dad was careful not to gloat despite being proven right.

7 Celia is under stress though maintains her composure.

8 They enjoyed the party in spite of the coldness of their reception.

9 The panel likes our ideas despite critical of our approach.

10 The full moon was lovely though half-hidden by a cloud.

PRACTICE *D* Cross out the incorrect words in the boxes to complete the sentences.

1 They are happy on the beach | although | despite | forbidden to swim.

2 Ken is not athletic | though | though is | strong and healthy.

3 The task does not daunt us in spite of its | complex | complexity | .

4 She is not widely admired despite | being beautiful | beautiful | to look at.

5 You look cool | despite of | in spite of | the sweltering heat.

6 The guests are smiling though | fill | filled | with dismay.

7 He made foolish mistakes in spite of | his | its | intelligence.

8 Nadya is likely to stay here despite | pines | pining | for home.

9 I still feel guilty despite | forgiven | having been forgiven | by everybody.

10 She is actually a confident person though | diffident | is diffident | in manner.

PRACTICE *E*   Rewrite the sentences correctly using adverbial phrases beginning with the words in the brackets.

1   Our athletes are in high spirits although are exhausted after the games. (although)
    Our athletes are in high spirits although exhausted after the games.

2   She could concentrate on her work despite of the noise around her. (despite)

3   We tried to look optimistic despite disheartened by the news. (despite)

4   He held his ground in spite of they persisted. (in spite of)

5   They were bored after a while although were enthusiastic at first. (although)

6   I was prepared for the worst though hope of a last-minute rescue. (though)

YOUR SCORE
10

PRACTICE *F*   Rewrite the paragraph, changing the underlined clauses into phrases beginning with the words in the brackets.

I'm enjoying university life though I miss home badly (despite). The lecturers have turned out to be approachable although they were initially aloof (despite). The famous Patrick de Jong's lectures are inspiring though they are incomprehensible at times (although). The 'orientation' of new students by seniors was fun although it was marred by one case of rather wild ragging (though). I've made some good friends though I lack social confidence (in spite of). We are a fairly quiet group though we dream of changing the world (despite).

    I'm enjoying university life despite missing home badly.

YOUR SCORE
10

UNIT 13.3 ADVERBIAL PHRASES

with **in order to, so as to, to**

Look at the **A** and **B** sentences below. Find out why **B** is correct and **A** is wrong in the **Grammar Points** section.

GRAMMAR POINTS

1A	They whistled in order to **irritated** me.	✗	
1B	They whistled in order to **irritate** me.	✓	1
2A	We tiptoed in **so as to not** awaken him.	✗	
2B	We tiptoed in **so as not to** awaken him.	✓	2
3A	She fled **not to** face his anger.	✗	
3B	She fled **in order not to** face his anger. / She fled **so as not to** face his anger.	✓	3

GRAMMAR POINTS

1   In an adverbial phrase, **in order to**, **so as to** or **to** must be followed by the base form of a verb.

EXAMPLE:

He showered her with gifts | in order to / so as to / to **please** her. | ✓

         adverbial phrase

(base form of verb)

He showered her with gifts | in order to / so as to / to **pleased** her. | ✗

         adverbial phrase

(past tense or past participle)

2   We cannot add **not** immediately after **in order to** or **so as to**. For a negative phrase, we must use **in order not to** or **so as not to**.

EXAMPLE: I spoke softly **in order not to** / **so as not to** frighten the child.   ✓

I spoke softly **in order to not** / **so as to not** frighten the child.   ✗

3   We do not normally begin a negative phrase with **not to**.

EXAMPLES: He used simple words **in order not to** / **so as not to** confuse us.   ✓

He used simple words **not to** confuse us.   ✗

We can begin a negative phrase with **not to** when it is accompanied by a positive phrase.

EXAMPLE:

Lucy dresses well | not to show off | but | to feel confident. | ✓

     negative phrase   positive phrase

Lucy dresses well | to feel confident | and | not to show off. | ✓

     positive phrase   negative phrase

PRACTICE A   Underline the adverbial phrases showing purpose.

1 Jake attended vacation classes so as to graduate fast.

2 Meg entered a bookshop in order not to be soaked by the rain.

3 Father worked hard to make everyone's life easier.

4 She moved away so as not to inhale his cigarette smoke.

5 They always sit in front in order to catch every word.

6 Some people use long words to appear learned.

7 Ken has kept away in order not to be asked awkward questions.

8 He plans to reform so as to set a good example for his children.

9 The team will practise hard in order not to lose a third time.

10 I've been avoiding the subject so as not to have a confrontation with him.

PRACTICE B   Circle the letters of the correct sentences. There may be more than one answer
for each question.

1 A   They tightened logging laws so as not to destroy their forests.
   B   They tightened logging laws so as to not destroy their forests.
   C   They tightened logging laws to preserve their forests.

2 A   He's doing this in order to helping us build good work habits.
   B   He's doing this not to encourage laziness but to build good work habits.
   C   He's doing this not to impose external discipline on us.

3 A   They're studying their education system in order not to be left behind.
   B   They're modernising their education system in order not to be left behind.
   C   They're modifying their education system to make it more job-oriented.

4 A   She remained silent in order to not be thought aggressive.
   B   She remained silent in order not to be thought aggressive.
   C   She remained silent to avoid being thought aggressive.

5 A   I'm suggesting this to improve your work and not to belittle it.
   B   I'm suggesting this not to belittle your work but to improve it.
   C   I'm suggesting this so as to improve your fine work.

191

PRACTICE *C*   Rearrange the words in the boxes to complete the sentences.

1 They are taking firm steps   another — cholera — of — outbreak — prevent — to.

_____

_____

2 I'll do some of those duties   as — not — overburden — so — to — you.

_____

_____

3 We're here to help them and   exploit — not — plight — sad — their — to.

_____

_____

4 This is done   in — order — punish — the — to — criminals.

_____

_____

5 She's writing a book   as — certain — dispel — misconceptions — so — to.

_____

_____

YOUR SCORE
10

PRACTICE *D*   Cross out the incorrect words in the boxes to complete the sentences.

1 The gangsters called him day and night to   break | broke   down his resistance.

2 Maria checked the report again in order   not to | to not   miss any errors.

3 We must practise tact   not to | so as not to   worsen the situation.

4 He wrote it not to intimidate   and | but   to persuade.

5 I'm sending you these lovely pictures so as to   attract | attracting   you here.

6 They go to great lengths in order to be   deem | deemed   fashionable.

7 She has closed her eyes so as not to   see | seen   the ugly view.

8 Ted has changed his job in order to   has | have   more leisure.

9 You are employed to run the company and   not to | to   line your own pockets.

YOUR SCORE
10

10 He was sent there to be   bringing | brought   to his senses.

Join the sentences. Change those under **B** into adverbial phrases beginning with the words in the brackets.

A	B	
1 He is counselling them.	He wants to effect a reconciliation.	(to)
2 They have to tread carefully.	They don't want to upset anyone.	(so as)
3 She learnt to use the loom.	She wanted to weave silk shawls.	(in order)
4 We must practise singing.	We want to have a good choir.	(so as)
5 I turned my face away.	I didn't want to show my distress.	(in order)
6 You are being unreasonable.	You want to try my patience.	(to)

1 *He is counselling them to effect a reconciliation.*

2 _____

3 _____

4 _____

5 _____

YOUR SCORE

6 _____

10

Rewrite the paragraph correctly using adverbial phrases showing purpose.

I read not to improving my mind but to enjoy myself. As far as possible, I plan each day so as to spent at least two hours with a good book. I take careful measures in order to not be disturbed. Sometimes I put on soft music to given myself a double treat. The music has to be without words not to compete with my book. I need these quiet pleasures in order to feels complete.

I read not to improve my mind but to enjoy myself.

_____

_____

_____

_____

_____

YOUR SCORE

_____

10

UNIT 13.4 ADVERBIAL PHRASES

with present participles

Look at the **A** and **B** sentences below. Find out why **B** is correct and **A** is wrong in the **Grammar Points** section.

GRAMMAR POINTS

1A	She threw a tantrum, **upset** the other children.	✗	
1B	She threw a tantrum, **upsetting** the other children.	✓	1
2A	**Making them proud**, their son won a medal for bravery.	✗	
2B	Their son won a medal for bravery, **making them proud**.	✓	2

GRAMMAR POINTS

1 We can use an adverbial phrase beginning with the 'ing' (present participle) form when describing an action done by or an event caused by the same subject in the main clause.

EXAMPLE:

adverbial phrase showing result

A minor accident occurred, **causing** a major traffic jam.

present participle

2 We put the adverbial phrase after the main clause if the action or event is the result of the action in the main clause.

EXAMPLE:

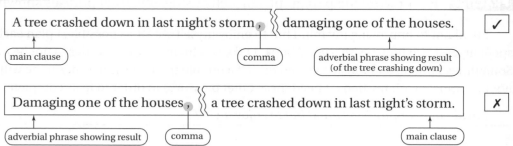

A tree crashed down in last night's storm, damaging one of the houses. ✓

main clause — comma — adverbial phrase showing result (of the tree crashing down)

Damaging one of the houses, a tree crashed down in last night's storm. ✗

adverbial phrase showing result — comma — main clause

REMEMBER!

■ A comma is usually placed between the main clause and the adverbial phrase beginning with an 'ing' form.

EXAMPLE:

He often makes thoughtless remarks, hurting other people's feelings.

comma

Fill in the blanks with suitable words in the boxes.

1 He dieted sensibly, _____ a kilo a month.

2 The tiger roared, _____ all of us.

3 She recovered completely, _____ the doctors.

4 We _____ about politics, disturbing other people.

5 Joel grinned at us, _____ our hopes.

6 Lydia ran fast, _____ her friends far behind.

7 I did something _____ , embarrassing my friends.

8 You overprotected them, stunting _____ growth.

9 Share prices _____ , enriching some people.

10 They did well, bringing _____ to their country.

shed	shedding
terrified	terrifying
amazing	ignoring
argued	read
raise	raising
leaving	left
useful	stupid
their	your
plunged	soared
honour	sorrow

YOUR SCORE
10

PRACTICE **B** Tick the correct sentences.

1 He resigned suddenly, caused surprise.

2 She brought the plane down safely, winning our gratitude.

3 Gripping young readers, the novel is well-written.

4 Their predicament was terrible, filling us with compassion.

5 The hero then makes a tragic mistake, nullifying his past achievements.

6 This city is magical, draws people from all over the world.

7 The girl just vanished, breaking her family's heart.

8 Tourists flocked to the little town, disrupting its peace.

9 He was charged with murder, devastated his admirers.

10 Changing their lives, she counselled unhappy young people.

YOUR SCORE
10

PRACTICE **C** Rearrange the words to form sentences containing adverbial phrases showing result.

1 burst — delighting — into — she — song — us , .
   She burst into song, delighting us.

2 acted — applause — getting — he — tremendous — well , .

_____

_____

3 a — arrived — bouquet — creating — the — quite — stir , .

_____

_____

4 cancelled — disappointing — fans — her — her — show — they've , .

_____

_____

5 critics — our — proving — succeeded — we — wrong , .

_____

_____

6 expectations — goals — I — scored — surpassing — their — three , .

_____

YOUR SCORE

10

_____

PRACTICE *D*   Match the main clauses with the correct adverbial phrases showing result.

A	B
1 He has behaved rather badly,	astonishing the adults.
2 It rained heavily for a week,	delaying everyone else.
3 They held riotous parties,	annoying their neighbours.
4 The reunion dinner was a success,	moving the audience to tears.
5 You brought in irrelevant points,	resulting in serious floods.
6 She took a long time to get ready,	reviving old friendships.
7 Francis gave a wonderful speech,	ruining the evening.
8 Dad came in a dinosaur costume,	saving ourselves a tiresome journey.
9 We took a short cut,	thrilling the children.
10 The little boy solved the problem,	weakening your case.

1 He has behaved rather badly, _____

2 It rained heavily for a week, _____

3 They held riotous parties, _____

4 The reunion dinner was a success, _____

5 You brought in irrelevant points, _____

6 She took a long time to get ready, _____

7 Francis gave a wonderful speech, _____

8 Dad came in a dinosaur costume, _____

9 We took a short cut, _____

10 The little boy solved the problem, _____

YOUR SCORE

10

Join the sentences. Change those under **B** into adverbial phrases showing result.

A	B
1 The campaign was effective.	It opened the eyes of the people.
2 He treated them with contempt.	He undermined their confidence.
3 Her books are brilliant.	They introduce the reader to an exciting world.
4 They rejected his thesis.	They cured him of intellectual vanity.
5 This music is nostalgic.	It torments me with memories.
6 You challenged us.	You impelled us to develop our potential.

1 *The campaign was effective, opening the eyes of the people.*

2 _____

3 _____

4 _____

5 _____

6 _____

Rewrite the paragraph correctly using adverbial phrases of result.

You decide it is time to decorate the house, make everything look clean and fresh. You read magazines and discuss with friends, develop many ideas. Then you realise that the ideas conflict, prevented you from making a final design. You want a house that is modern and efficient, create an ideal living space. You also want a place that is comfortable and traditional, encouraged relaxation. Finally, you make your decision, understand compromise is necessary.

You decide it is time to decorate the house, making everything look clean and fresh.

_____

_____

_____

_____

_____

_____

UNIT 13.5 ADVERBIAL PHRASES

with **after**, **before**, **when**, **while**

Look at the **A** and **B** sentences below. Find out why **B** is correct and **A** is wrong in the **Grammar Points** section.

1A	They take off their shoes before **enter** the temple.	✗	
1B	They take off their shoes before **entering** the temple.	✓	1
2A	He regained consciousness while **taken** to the hospital.	✗	
2b	He regained consciousness while **being taken** to the hospital.	✓	2

GRAMMAR POINTS

1 We can begin an adverbial phrase with **after**, **before**, **when** or **while** followed by a present participle but not a finite verb.

EXAMPLE:

adverbial phrase

She felt rejuvenated after **going** for a holiday. ✓

present participle

adverbial phrase

She felt rejuvenated after **went** for a holiday. ✗

finite verb

2 We can begin an adverbial phrase with **when** followed by a past participle. **After**, **before** or **while** cannot be followed by a past participle.

EXAMPLES:

The child cried **when bitten** by mosquitoes. ✓

The child was crying **while bitten** by mosquitoes. ✗

The child was crying **while being bitten** by mosquitoes. ✓

The child cried **after bitten** by mosquitoes. ✗

The child cried **after being bitten** by mosquitoes. ✓

The child was already crying **before bitten** by mosquitoes. ✗

The child was already crying **before being bitten** by mosquitoes. ✓

- An adverbial phrase beginning with **after**, **before**, **when** or **while** usually indicates time.

    EXAMPLE: She felt nervous after / before / when / while making the announcement.

    adverbial phrase

    When did she feel nervous? After / Before / When / While making the announcement.

- **When** at the beginning of an adverbial phrase can be followed by a **past participle** only in a passive structure.

    EXAMPLES: Plants thrive when **grown** by loving hands.   ✓
    (= they **are grown** – passive)

    I went away when **grown** tired of waiting.   ✗
    (= I **had grown** – active)

PRACTICE *A*   Underline the adverbial phrases showing time.

1   He is quite calm when placed in a difficult situation.

2   They went into hiding after inciting the people to rebel.

3   The reports must be checked before being handed in.

4   She was humming softly while cooking in her new kitchen.

5   He began to counsel me after listening to my problems.

6   You must be careful when dealing with strangers.

7   I checked my bank balance before writing the cheque.

8   She kept smiling into the camera while being interviewed.

9   The gentlest creature can be vicious when cornered.

10   He was very healthy after having his tonsils removed.

PRACTICE *B*   Circle the letters of the correct sentences. There may be more than one answer for each question.

1   A   The child was moaning softly while untied by his rescuers.
    B   The child tried to stand up when untied by his rescuers.
    C   The child was moaning softly while being untied by his rescuers.

2   A   We counted the crates before unloading them.
    B   We counted the crates after unloading them.
    C   We counted the crates after unloaded them.

3   A   The picture looked too big when hung in her room.
    B   She didn't like the picture when hung it in her room.
    C   She didn't like the picture after hanging it in her room.

4   A   I hesitated for some time before knock on the door.
    B   I hesitated for some time before knocking on the door.
    C   I looked around fearfully while knocking on the door.

5   A   A trumpet sounds terrible when blown by a beginner.
    B   He smiled at us before blown the trumpet.
    C   He smiled at us before blowing the trumpet.

PRACTICE `C` Rearrange the words in the boxes to form adverbial phrases showing time and complete the sentences.

1 She read the passage twice `attempting — before — it — summarise — to.`

She read the passage twice before attempting to summarise it.

2 A present is precious `given — affection — real — when — with.`

_____

_____

3 He sighed contentedly `having — his — massaged — neck — while.`

_____

_____

4 I was exhausted `after — boys — little — lively — playing — three — with.`

_____

_____

5 You must take care `a — buying — car — used — when.`

_____

_____

6 We need to think `agreeing — before — responsibilities — accept — these — to.`

_____

_____

YOUR SCORE 10

PRACTICE `D` Fill in the blanks with suitable words in the box.

approved	being approved	are torn	torn	being X-rayed	X-rayed
call	calling	hearing	were hearing	identify	identifying
learning	learnt	seen	sees		
skating	was skating	worry	worrying		

1 He administered first aid to the victim before _____ an ambulance.

2 I was trembling with anxiety while _____ .

3 Hardship is bearable when _____ as a challenge.

4 We worked out a strategy after _____ our goals.

5 Linda always feels happy while _____ on ice.

6 Dad is grouchy when _____ about something.

7 Mark toured the world after _____ several languages

8 Films are classified before _____ for public viewing.

9 People often do nothing when _____ between two obligations.

10 They were convinced after _____ eye-witness accounts.

YOUR SCORE 10

Rewrite the sentences correctly using adverbial phrases showing time.

1 We rested after put up our tents in a clearing.
   We rested after putting up our tents in a clearing.

2 We can all relax after did a good job.

3 They attended a special course before sent abroad.

4 An injury is hurtful when inflicting by a trusted animal.

5 I was imagining all sorts of disasters while was waiting for your call.

6 People often reveal the truth when take by surprise.

YOUR SCORE
/10

PRACTICE *F*   Rewrite the paragraph. Change each underlined sentence into an adverbial phrase beginning with the word in brackets. Then join the adverbial phrase to the sentence before it.

I spoke only a few words of English. I attended an English-speaking school (before). I began to fear English Language. I got low marks in the subject throughout the first term (after). Then, I discovered a new world. I was visiting an uncle during the holidays (while). I got to know and like the English language. I was introduced to 'Grimm's Fairy Tales' in my uncle's library (when). English became my friend. It had been my dreaded enemy (after). Moreover, since then I've been able to turn to books. I need relaxation or knowledge (when).

   I spoke only a few words of English before attending an English-speaking school.

YOUR SCORE
/10

UNIT 14.1 NOUN PHRASES

with infinitives and present participles

Look at the **A** and **B** sentences below. Find out why **B** is correct and **A** is wrong in the **Grammar Points** section.

			GRAMMAR POINTS
1A	He is beginning **likes** Picasso's paintings.	✗	
1B	He is beginning **to like** Picasso's paintings.	✓	1
2A	Hardly anyone enjoys **to go** to the dentist.	✗	
2B	Hardly anyone enjoys **going** to the dentist.	✓	2

GRAMMAR POINTS

1 A noun phrase does not have a finite verb. It can have a non-finite verb, for instance, an infinitive (the 'to' form) or a present participle (the 'ing' form).

EXAMPLE:

He began | **to take** / **taking** piano lessons last month. | ← noun phrase

non-finite verb (infinitive) — non-finite verb (present participle)

REMEMBER!

■ A noun phrase answers the question "What?". When it is used as the object of the main clause, it occurs after the verb in the main clause.

EXAMPLE: He **promised** | to join them on a safari. |

subject — verb — object (noun phrase)

What did he promise? To join them on a safari.

The noun phrase is said to be the object of the verb **promised**.

---

2 Some verbs can have as objects

(a) noun phrases beginning with **infinitives** and **present participles**, for instance:

| begin | continue | hate | like | love | prefer | remember | start | try |

EXAMPLE: He **remembered** | **to call** / **calling** her. |
noun phrase

(b) noun phrases beginning with **infinitives** but not **present participles**, for instance:

| choose | decide | hope | manage | need | offer |
| plan | promise | refuse | seek | want | wish |

EXAMPLE: He **refused** | **to call** her. |
noun phrase

(c) noun phrases beginning with **present participles** but not **infinitives**, for instance:

admit	avoid	consider	deny	detest	endure	enjoy
finish	imagine	mention	miss	postpone	practise	recall
resent	resume	stop	suggest	take		

EXAMPLE: He **admitted** | **calling** her. |
                                 noun phrase

PRACTICE *A*   Underline the noun phrases in the sentences.

1 He has failed to impress them.

2 We'll miss having fun with you.

3 After a while, I managed to run the programme myself.

4 They did not even attempt to regain credibility.

5 Frankly, I enjoy watching silly comedies.

6 As children we hated reciting rhymes in front of the class.

7 Rita plans to spend August up in the mountains.

8 You really must stop blaming yourself.

9 They did offer to compensate us for our losses.

10 She regrets selling that old sofa.

PRACTICE *B*   Fill in the blanks with suitable words in the boxes.

1 He demanded _____ the contract.

see	to see

2 I can't tolerate _____ this way.

being treated	treated

3 They sought _____ the major problems first.

solving	to solve

4 We _____ postponing the merger to next year.

decided	suggested

5 You _____ to settle down in this area.

chose	enjoyed

6 Grandpa started _____ for his old home.

to yearn	yearned

7 She'll continue _____ driving lessons.

taking	takes

8 Bobby imagined _____ a jumbo jet.

fly	flying

9 The firm is trying _____ your interests.

safeguard	to safeguard

10 We'll now resume _____ the first proposition.

discussing	to discuss

Rearrange the words in the boxes to form noun phrases and complete the sentences.

1 I want | director — managing — now — right — see — the — to. |

I want to see the managing director right now.

2 She resented | baby — being — hold — left — the — to. |

_____

_____

3 They have promised | efficient — provide — staff — to — us — with. |

_____

_____

4 Dad can't afford | abroad — send — to — to — universities — us. |

_____

_____

5 He didn't mind | a — future — give — good — hard — working — to — them. |

_____

_____

6 Every day she practises | ball — into — net — shooting — the — the. |

_____

YOUR SCORE
10

_____

PRACTICE **D** Underline the correct words in the brackets.

1 She can't stand (being ridiculed / ridiculed) by the group.

2 As far as possible, we'll avoid (confront / confronting) him.

3 I don't recall (seeing / to see) you at that meeting.

4 He has always tried (act / to act) according to our club rules.

5 Lydia must have forgotten (locks / to lock) up before leaving.

6 Ben would never accept (being passed / pass) over without protesting.

7 The students suggested (have / having) the whole college linked to the Internet.

8 My uncle (loves / enjoys) to have young people around him.

9 After school, Kim (decided / took) to work rather than go to college.

10 Each of them denied (have / having) met him.

YOUR SCORE
10

Circle the letters of the correct sentences. There may be more than one answer for each question.

1 A I intended decline the offer but somehow accepted it.
   B I intended declining the offer but somehow accepted it.
   C I intended to decline the offer but somehow accepted it.

2 A They will continue fighting for freedom.
   B They will continue to fight for freedom.
   C They will continue fight for freedom.

3 A He likes to think about the fun we had last summer.
   B He likes thinking about the fun we had last summer.
   C He loves to think about the fun we had last summer.

4 A The tension in the room began to affect us.
   B The tension in the room began affecting us.
   C The tension in the room is starting affecting us.

5 A She admitted to lose the records in that file.
   B She admitted lost the records in that file.
   C She admitted losing the records in that file.

PRACTICE F Rewrite the interview correctly using noun phrases.

Reporter : Why did you decide to became a comedian?

Comedian : Actually, I planned being an actor. At school, I practised lines from Shakespeare's tragedies. I attended an audition once, trying get the leading role in 'King Lear'. As I strutted and spouted, everyone present began laughed uncontrollably. I wanted playing the tragic hero. Instead, I got the role of the Falstaff in 'The Merry Wives of Windsor'.

Reporter : _Why did you decide to become a comedian?_

Comedian : _____

_____

_____

_____

_____

_____

_____

_____

_____

_____

UNIT 14.2 NOUN PHRASES

as complements

Look at the **A** and **B** sentences below. Find out why **B** is correct and **A** is wrong in the **Grammar Points** section.

GRAMMAR POINTS

1A	The decision **proved being** a wise one.	✗	
1B	The decision **proved to be** a wise one.	✓	1
2A	My greatest pleasure **surfing** the Internet.	✗	
2B	My greatest pleasure **is surfing** the Internet.	✓	2

GRAMMAR POINTS

1 A noun phrase can be the complement of the verb before it. Verbs that take complements are called link verbs. They include the verbs: **become**, **appear**, **grow**, **prove**, **seem** and **turn out**. The link verb before a noun phrase must not be dropped.

EXAMPLE:

The child **appears** to be happy there.

link verb — noun phrase (complement of **appears**)

2 A noun phrase beginning with a **present participle** can be the complement of the verb 'to be' but not of other link verbs.

EXAMPLES:

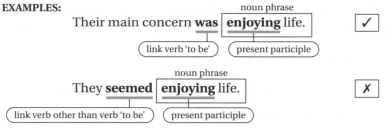

A noun phrase beginning with an **infinitive** can be the complement of the verb 'to be' and other link verbs.

EXAMPLES:

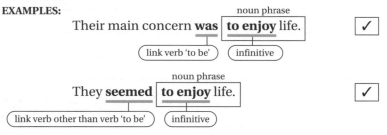

206

REMEMBER!

■ A noun phrase does not have a finite verb. It can have a non-finite verb, for instance, an infinitive or a present participle.

EXAMPLES:

noun phrase

Those tourists seem to like our hill resorts.

infinitive

noun phrase

He does his work without wasting any time.

present participle

PRACTICE *A* Some of the sentences contain noun phrases that are complements. Underline them.

1 His dream is to go back to the Philippines one day.

2 She has always detested hearing talk of that sort.

3 Their favourite occupation was hanging around malls.

4 My suspicions about the new hospital plans proved to be correct.

5 We don't expect you to make great changes overnight.

6 Their favourite pastime is playing chess against their children.

7 The students observed the surgeon operating on a cancer patient.

8 After a while, we became enthusiastic members of the group.

9 A prize will be given to the noisiest person at the party.

10 We plan to move to a quiet suburb next year.

11 For me the major problem has been dealing with difficult customers.

YOUR SCORE
10

PRACTICE *B* Tick the correct sentences.

1 I have grown to appreciate her devastating frankness.

2 To us he seems be out of touch with reality.

3 The idea is lets each student learn at his own pace.

4 The amazing news report turned out to be true.

5 One of the functions of protein building muscles.

6 We saw the vacant plot grow into a fine garden.

7 The spectators appeared to have gone berserk.

8 Your intuition has proven being amazingly accurate.

9 His top priority was reunited his divided people.

10 One of their tactics is feigning exhaustion in the second half.

YOUR SCORE
10

207

PRACTICE *C* Rearrange the words in the boxes to form noun phrases and complete the sentences.

1 The timid girl came | as — be — 'Dynamite' — known — to. |

The timid girl came to be known as 'Dynamite'.

2 His speciality was | art — fakes — identifying — in — of — the — world. |

_____

_____

3 The new schedule appears | everyone — firm — in — suit — the — to. |

_____

_____

4 My role is | needed — everyone — giving — when — help. |

_____

_____

5 The experience seems | a — done — good — have — her — of — to — world. |

_____

_____

6 His contribution should be | counselling — couples — problems —with — young. |

_____

_____

PRACTICE *D* Underline the correct words in the brackets.

1 Your approach has proved (being / to be) the right one.

2 Bobby's idea of fun is (draws / drawing) murals with his mother's lipstick.

3 The atmosphere seemed (to vibrate / vibrating) with excitement.

4 Her obsession has long been (stay / staying) at the top of the list.

5 In time they'll come (understanding / to understand) our feelings.

6 Rose's dearest wish was (to win / win) back the cup.

7 Their players appear (having / to have) improved vastly.

8 Her chief entertainment (is making / making) him laugh.

9 My vocation may be (teach / teaching) the disabled.

10 The puppy (was whining / whining) to arouse our sympathy.

Change the sentences in **B** into noun phrases to complete **A**. Use the verb forms in the brackets.

A	B
1 The once magnificent mansions seem . . .	They have been left to rot. (infinitive)
2 Her weakness has always been . . .	She makes unrealistic plans. (present participle)
3 His seemingly absurd idea proved . . .	It was perfectly sound. (infinitive)
4 The troubled people have come . . .	They trust and respect you. (infinitive)
5 What infuriates us is . . .	We are treated like idiots. (present participle)
6 For me the difficult part would be . . .	I ignore the sound of traffic. (present participle)

1 *The once magnificent mansions seem to have been left to rot.*

2 _____

3 _____

4 _____

5 _____

6 _____

YOUR SCORE
10

Rewrite the paragraph correctly using noun phrases as complements.

Our lecturer on Shakespeare appeared lived in a world of his own. Our faces seemed being just a blur to him. When we greeted him, his notion of a friendly response muttering something with a vague smile. One of our joys was took advantage of his absentmindedness. Sometimes, his melodious voice proved been soporific and some of us slept happily right in front of him. One day, we were jolted awake by his calling out our names and saying, "Shakespeare's Hamlet says: to die, to sleep . . . I say: A sure way to die to sleep through lectures."

Our lecturer on Shakespeare appeared to live in a world of his own.

_____

_____

_____

_____

_____

_____

YOUR SCORE
10

UNIT 14.3 NOUN PHRASES

as objects of prepositions

Look at the **A** and **B** sentences below. Find out why **B** is correct and **A** is wrong in the **Grammar Points** section.

1A	He checked my blood pressure **after took** my temperature.	✗	
1B	He checked my blood pressure **after taking** my temperature.	✓	1
2A	She wants to be useful **besides to be** liked.	✗	
2B	She wants to be useful **besides being** liked.	✓	2

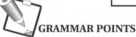

GRAMMAR POINTS

1 A noun phrase beginning with a present participle can be the object of the preposition before it.

EXAMPLE:

noun phrase
(object of the preposition **on**)

I insisted **on** | **seeing** the managing director.

preposition · present participle

2 A noun phrase beginning with an infinitive cannot be the object of a preposition.

EXAMPLE:

noun phrase
(object of the preposition **of**)

He is fond **of** | **making** childish jokes. ✓

preposition · present participle

noun phrase
(object of the preposition **of**)

He is fond **of** | **to make** childish jokes. ✗

preposition · infinitive

REMEMBER!

- When a noun phrase is used as a complement, it occurs after a link verb. When it is used as the object of a preposition, it occurs after the preposition.

EXAMPLES: Her aim **was** | to master the trumpet.

link verb 'to be' · noun phrase (complement)

What was her aim? To master the trumpet.

John is adept **at** | repairing electrical appliances.

preposition · noun phrase (object of preposition)

What is John adept at? Repairing electrical appliances.

PRACTICE **A** Underline the noun phrases that are objects of prepositions.

1 We've spoken seriously about offering her a partnership.
2 Ella is satisfied with being a full-time housewife.
3 He persisted in doing things his own way.
4 She was sternly rebuked for crossing the border.
5 I pride myself on keeping all my promises.
6 They coaxed me into changing my plans.
7 Everyone must work towards making this nation strong and peaceful.
8 Sally felt remorse after breaking the rule.
9 The artist wants more time before holding a solo exhibition.
10 You can't attain lasting success by bluffing your way around.

YOUR SCORE | 10

PRACTICE **B** Fill in the blanks with suitable words in the box.

| besides | caring | of | on | restoring |
| seeing | starting | telling | through | without |

1 That angelic-looking witness is not above _____ a lie.
2 Lisa slowly learnt tact _____ handling difficult situations.
3 I was in agony and past _____ about dignity.
4 Most of us were against _____ afresh elsewhere.
5 She typed out the report _____ making a single mistake.
6 They love the thrill _____ meeting challenges in life.
7 We cheered uproariously upon _____ our soccer hero.
8 Travel is exciting _____ broadening the mind.
9 Entry depends _____ obtaining excellent results.
10 He specialises in _____ faces disfigured by accidents.

YOUR SCORE | 10

PRACTICE **C** Rearrange the words in the boxes to form noun phrases and complete the sentences.

1 By that time I was beyond | feeling — of — slightest — sorrow — the — twinge.

By that time I was beyond feeling the slightest twinge of sorrow.

2 I was given the task of | family — cooking — entire — for — the.

_____

_____

211

3 She drew the line at | a — choose — for — her — career — letting — them. |

_____

_____

4 He has problems stemming from | a — as — been — child — having — ill. |

_____

_____

5 They quarrelled over | ancestral — dividing — land — the. |

_____

_____

6 Sometimes, ragging is practised under the pretext of | at — feel — home — making — new — students. |

_____

_____

PRACTICE *D*   Circle the letters of the correct sentences. There may be more than one answer for each question.

1 A   I rebelled against given up my room to her.
  B   I balked at giving up my room to her.
  C   I protested against giving up my room to her.

2 A   He was given a medal as well as being made captain.
  B   He was given a medal as well as to be made captain.
  C   He was given a medal as well as was made captain.

3 A   You are used to having your orders obeyed.
  B   You are accustomed to being obeyed.
  C   You are used to be obeyed.

4 A   We banked on to be warmly welcomed.
  B   We were confident of getting a warm welcome.
  C   We banked on receiving a warm welcome.

5 A   The hero thought dying was preferable to being disgraced.
  B   The hero thought dying was preferable than being disgraced.
  C   The hero thought drying was better than being disgraced.

6 A   Ken is doubtful about signing up for French classes.
  B   Ken is doubtful about sign up for French classes.
  C   Ken is doubtful to sign up for French classes.

PRACTICE E Rewrite the sentences correctly using noun phrases that are objects of prepositions.

1   You have saved me from become a drug addict.
    You have saved me from becoming a drug addict.

2   She is totally justified on making that statement.

_____

_____

3   He impressed us by to repair both the cars.

_____

_____

4   I look forward to see you next week.

_____

_____

5   We're having second thoughts about promote him.

_____

_____

6   There's no solution short off changing the whole system.

_____

YOUR SCORE

10

_____

PRACTICE F Underline the correct words in the brackets.

I had long set my heart on **1** (learn / learning) to drive. I took driving lessons immediately after **2** (sitting / was sitting) for my school certificate exam. Somehow I had no difficulty **3** (at / in) backing into a parking lot. My instructor praised me warmly **4** (for / on) doing this perfectly the very first time.

I was less successful, however, when it came to **5** (stop / stopping) on a slope. I could not restart the car **6** (not / without) letting it slide backwards. Once, I frightened another learner behind me **7** (into / to) backing right to the bottom of a hill. My instructor nearly despaired of **8** (getting / to get) me ready for the test. I failed it twice before **9** (obtained / obtaining) my licence. Even then, the examiner could not refrain **10** (from / with) making this remark: "If cars were built to go backwards, you'd make a fine driver."

YOUR SCORE

10

UNIT 15 SENTENCE STRUCTURE

joining two simple sentences with **either . . . or** and **neither . . . nor**

Look at the **A** and **B** sentences below. Find out why **B** is correct and **A** is wrong in the **Grammar Points** section.

GRAMMAR POINTS

1A	He was **neither** rich **or** famous but he had many friends.	✗	
1B	He was **neither** rich **nor** famous but he had many friends.	✓	1
2A	**Neither** the spectators cheered **nor** jeered.	✗	
2B	The spectators **neither** cheered **nor** jeered.	✓	2
3A	You **either should** stay **or** leave for good.	✗	
3B	You **should either** stay **or** leave for good.	✓	3

GRAMMAR POINTS

1 (a) We join two simple sentences with **either ... or** to indicate that one out of the two choices or events is possible.

EXAMPLE: Janice wants to buy the white sneakers. She wants to buy the black boots.
Janice wants to buy **either** the white sneakers **or** the black boots.

(b) We join two simple sentences with **neither ... nor** to indicate that both choices or events are not possible.

EXAMPLE: They are not my schoolmates. They are not my friends. I don't know them.
They are **neither** my schoolmates **nor** my friends. I don't know them.

The two simple sentences should have subjects referring to the same person or thing, and they should have the same tense.

2 We can use **either ... or** / **neither ... nor** to join two simple sentences if the words after **either** and **or** / **neither** and **nor** have the same grammatical structure.

EXAMPLES: His poems tease the mind. They touch the heart.

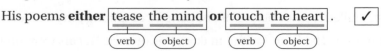

214

She was not sad when I broke the news to her.
She was not shocked when I broke the news to her.

She was **neither** sad **nor** shocked when I broke the news to her.   ☑

complement (adjective)

She does not cook. She does not clean. So she hired a maid.

She **neither** cooks **nor** cleans . So she hired a maid.   ☑

verb

3 We can use **either … or / neither … nor** to join two simple sentences that have the same modals but different main verbs. We usually put the modal before **either / neither**.

EXAMPLES: Lin **may** learn tennis. She **may** pick up golf.

Lin **may either** learn tennis **or** pick up golf .

modal   verb   object   verb   object

My uncle has a weak heart. He **cannot** smoke. He **cannot** drink.

My uncle has a weak heart. He **can neither** smoke **nor** drink .

modal   verb

PRACTICE *A*   Fill in the blanks with suitable words in the boxes.

1 She _____ _____ walk nor talk coherently.

could	couldn't
either	neither

2 You _____ behave _____ leave.

either	neither
nor	or

3 We _____ neither doubt nor _____ his loyalty to the group.

question	questioned
should	shouldn't

4 He _____ pushed her _____ frightened her.

either	neither
nor	or

5 I _____ worry _____ care about anything.

either	neither
nor	or

YOUR SCORE

10

PRACTICE **B** Cross out the incorrect words in the boxes to complete the sentences.

1 We either | neither control the disease now or face an epidemic later.

2 The girl neither admitted the charge nor | nor she denied it.

3 You may either go home now or finish | finished the job first.

4 Hardship either | neither broke them nor made them bitter.

5 Babies either awaken you at dawn nor | or keep you up all night.

6 Either you help us or | or you leave us alone to complete our work.

7 They neither would | would neither betray their leader nor deny him.

8 He neither missed his high position nor he thought | thought about it.

9 Either admit the monks | The monks either admit their wrongdoing to the discipline master or face the abbot.

10 Neither the rescuers | The rescuers neither rested nor felt tired.

YOUR SCORE
10

PRACTICE **C** Join the sentences using **either ... or** or **neither ... nor**.

1 The rebels might surrender. They might fight to the end.

_____

_____

2 They are caught in a traffic jam. They left late.

_____

_____

3 The medicine could not heal her. It could not relieve her pain.

_____

_____

4 John doesn't want to work. John doesn't want to study.

_____

_____

5 They didn't understand the boy. They didn't approve of him.

_____

YOUR SCORE
10

_____

Underline the correct words in the brackets to complete the conversation.

Celia : Usually, interview results **1** (either / neither) delight or disappoint. You look very calm.

Russ : **2** (Either / Neither) you are joking **3** (nor / or) you can't read body language. I could **4** (either / neither) feel **5** (nor / or) look calm at this moment.

Celia : Come on! You must either tell me the news or **6** (gave / give) me a broad hint.

Russ : Would a big grin do?

Celia : Congratulations! Now you either tell me everything or **7** (hit / I'll hit) you on that brilliant head of yours!

Russ : I **8** (can neither / neither can) believe the results nor **9** (bring / brought) myself to say it to anyone, not even you.

Celia : Okay, you either nod **10** (nor / or) shake your head. Did you get a definite acceptance? A nod! That's awesome!

YOUR SCORE

/ 10

PRACTICE $\boxed{E}$ Rewrite the sentences correctly.

1 Unfortunately, they neither reached an agreement or parted amicably.
   Unfortunately, they neither reached an agreement nor parted amicably.

2 You neither should belittle people nor gossip about them.

_____

_____

3 Neither the receptionist looked up nor responded to our greeting.

_____

_____

4 The machine either would make a horrid noise or break down.

_____

_____

5 Some reporters neither respect privacy nor they care about accuracy.

_____

_____

6 Next vacation, Ken will either work on a farm or hitchhikes around the country.

_____

_____

YOUR SCORE

/ 10

UNIT 16.1 REFERENCE

pronouns and nouns

Look at the **A** and **B** sentences below. Find out why **B** is correct and **A** is wrong in the **Grammar Points** section.

			GRAMMAR POINTS
1A	There were many vehicles on the road. **It** caused a traffic jam.	✗	
1B	There were many vehicles on the road. **They** caused a traffic jam.	✓	1
2A	Computer users were warned about a new virus. **A new virus** is programmed to wipe out the data stored in all drives.	✗	
2B	Computer users were warned about a new virus. **The (new) virus** is programmed to wipe out the data stored in all drives.	✓	2
3A	Mr Lee informed the city council that **a snake** was in his garden. By the time the council workers arrived, **the cobra** had disappeared.	✗	
3B	Mr Lee informed the city council that **a cobra** was in his garden. By the time the council workers arrived, **the snake** had disappeared.	✓	3

GRAMMAR POINTS

1 When we write an essay, a letter, a report, etc, we often refer back to someone or something we mentioned earlier in the sentence or in an earlier part of the text. When we use a pronoun to refer back to a noun, we must make sure it agrees with the noun in person, gender and number.

EXAMPLES:

— refers back to —
— refers back to —

Julie can't come because **she** injured **her** wrist while moving the furniture. ☑

- noun – **female**, 3rd person, singular
- pronoun – **female**, 3rd person, singular
- pronoun – **female**, 3rd person, singular

— refers back to —

The children in my neighbourhood are enterprising. **They** want to start

- noun – 3rd person, plural
- pronoun – 3rd person, plural

a recycling programme. ☑

218

— does not refer back to —

The children in my neighbourhood are enterprising. **We** want to start

> noun –
> 3rd person, plural

> pronoun –
> 1st person, plural

a recycling programme.   ✗

*(**The children** in the first sentence does not include the writer. **We** in the second sentence includes the writer. Therefore the two sentences are not connected.)*

2   We can also repeat the head word in a noun phrase when we refer back to someone or something mentioned earlier. We must use the definite article **the** with the repeated word to show that we are pointing back to an earlier part of the sentence or text.

EXAMPLE:

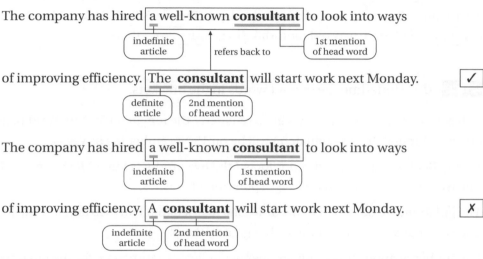

The company has hired | a well-known **consultant** | to look into ways

> indefinite article
> refers back to
> 1st mention of head word

of improving efficiency. | The **consultant** | will start work next Monday.   ✓

> definite article
> 2nd mention of head word

The company has hired | a well-known **consultant** | to look into ways

> indefinite article
> 1st mention of head word

of improving efficiency. | A **consultant** | will start work next Monday.   ✗

> indefinite article
> 2nd mention of head word

When the indefinite article **a** is used in the second sentence, it signals that there are two consultants, not one, that the writer is talking about.

3   We can use a different noun in the second sentence to point to a noun in the first sentence if the second noun is general and can include the first noun in meaning or category. We must also use **the** to show that we are referring to the same person or thing already mentioned.

EXAMPLE:

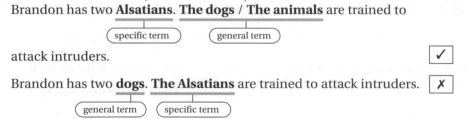

— refers back to —

Brandon has two **Alsatians**. **The dogs** / **The animals** are trained to

> specific term
> general term

attack intruders.   ✓

Brandon has two **dogs**. **The Alsatians** are trained to attack intruders.   ✗

> general term
> specific term

REMEMBER!

- Words that are general in meaning often refer to a class of things. Words that are specific come under the words that are general in meaning.

EXAMPLES:

General	→ More specific	→ Most specific
furniture	→ cupboard (type of furniture)	→ wardrobe (type of cupboard)
hotel	→ four-star hotel	→ Richmond Hotel

PRACTICE *A* Cross out the incorrect words in the boxes to complete the sentences.

1 Gail has been having horrible nightmares lately. | It is | They are | all about | her | their | falling off a cliff.

2 Mum plans to invite our new neighbours over for dinner because | he | she | thinks they need help in adjusting to | our | their | new environment.

3 Olive oil is often used by people in Italy and the Middle East in | our | their | cooking. | It is | They are | said to help prevent heart disease.

4 My favourite pastime is writing poems. Dad thinks | it is | they are | time wasted but he was proud of | it | me | when I won 1st prize in a poetry-writing competition.

5 My friend, Mike, and I plan to spend the day at Templer's Park. Mike will use | his | her | father's trusty old motorbike to get | us | we | there.

YOUR SCORE
10

PRACTICE *B* Underline the correct words in the brackets.

1 Bob Nelson will meet Max Lewis in (a rematch / the rematch) for the World Boxing Council crown. (A rematch / The rematch) will be on 15 November in Las Vegas.

2 Beauty Bar has launched (five products / the five products) for older women. (The products / The women) are to help reduce age spots and blemishes.

3 The girl found an old violin in the attic. She realised that (an instrument / the instrument) had once belonged to (a grandfather / her grandfather).

4 (A number of applicants / The number of applicants) turned up for the job interview. (A number of applicants / The applicants) ranged in age from 20 to 40.

5 Mandy's bulldog and Persian cat went missing yesterday. (Animals / The animals) were last seen running into the park. Mandy and her family searched everywhere for (they / them) but they were nowhere to be found.

YOUR SCORE
10

PRACTICE *C* Tick the sentences in column **B** that should come after the sentences in column **A**.

A	B
1 Care for the environment. Care for your children.	A ☐ Your future depends on it. B ☐ Their future depends on it.
2 Millennium Art Institute is holding an art exhibition from 15th August to 28th August.	A ☐ The institute will showcase the talents and skills of its students at the exhibition. B ☐ An institute will showcase the talents and skills of its students at the exhibition.
3 Mobile phones and computers are becoming smaller every year.	A ☐ There may come a time when it will be reduced to the size of a matchbox! B ☐ There may come a time when they will be reduced to the size of matchboxes!

4 It was time to head out to sea but our captain, a Mexican called Santos, was missing. We sat down on the beach and waited for him.

A ☐ It was another hour before a Mexican arrived, dragging behind him two sacks of coconuts.

B ☐ It was another hour before the Mexican arrived, dragging behind him two sacks of coconuts.

5 Music and dance play an important role in the life of this community.

A ☐ They mark the beginning of the harvesting season and express the people's joy and sorrow.

B ☐ It marks the beginning of the harvesting season and expresses the people's joy and sorrow.

YOUR SCORE
10

PRACTICE *D* Read the passage and state what nouns or noun phrases the underlined words refer back to. State the number of the sentences where the nouns or noun phrases are located.

(1) My brother David has one household chore he hates — cleaning the refrigerator every Saturday. (2) He asked whether I would like to exchange duties with <u>him</u> but I refused. (3) Dad says <u>he</u> has got the easiest job in the house but David disagrees. (4) He hates having to remove all the food and drink from the fridge in order to clean <u>it</u>. (5) He gets irritated when he sees juice or milk spilt in the fridge and complains that whoever caused <u>it</u> is totally inconsiderate. (6) He makes such a fuss that Dad, Mum and I make sure <u>we</u> are never in the kitchen when he is at work.

(7) David dreams of inventing a fridge that can take good care of <u>itself</u>. (8) He says his fridge will have a touch screen and a hatch. (9) <u>The screen</u> will display many icons. (10) All he will have to do is press an icon for 'Clean' on <u>it</u> and the fridge will self-clean. (11) Another icon will tell him which food items will run out in a day or two. (12) Then he can buy <u>them</u> just a day ahead. (13) A third icon will indicate which foodstuff has gone stale. (14) He will then need to press a red button and <u>it</u> will come through <u>the hatch</u> for disposal.

1 Sentence (2) : him – *'My brother David' in Sentence (1).*

2 Sentence (3) : he – _____

3 Sentence (4) : it – _____

4 Sentence (5) : it – _____

5 Sentence (6) : we – _____

6 Sentence (7) : itself – _____

7 Sentence (9) : The screen – _____

8 Sentence (10): it – _____

9 Sentence (12): them – _____

YOUR SCORE
10

10 Sentence (14): it – _____

11 Sentence (14): the hatch – _____

221

UNIT 16.2 REFERENCE

demonstrative adjectives, demonstrative pronouns, nouns

Look at the **A** and **B** sentences below. Find out why **B** is correct and **A** is wrong in the **Grammar Points** section.

CHECKPOINT

1A	**The Taj Mahal** is one of the most beautiful buildings in the world. **The Taj Mahal** was built by Mughal emperor Shah Jahan in memory of his wife Mumtaz Mahal.	✗	
1B	**The Taj Mahal** is one of the most beautiful buildings in the world. **The white marble mausoleum** was built by Mughal emperor Shah Jahan in memory of his wife Mumtaz Mahal.	✓	1
2A	The competition results will be announced on **12th June** at Grand Hotel. The hotel will be full of people on **12th June**.	✗	
2B	The competition results will be announced on **12th June** at Grand Hotel. The hotel will be full of people on **that day**.	✓	2
3A	You read the instructions in your exam papers carefully **is why** you do well in your exams.	✗	
3B	You read the instructions in your exam papers carefully. **This is why** you do well in your exams.	✓	3

GRAMMAR POINTS

1 Sometimes, we need to avoid using the same pronoun, noun or noun phrase again and again in our writing. We can make our writing more interesting by using other words to refer back to what was mentioned earlier. We must use **the** before the new words.

EXAMPLE: Mrs Barnes' **husband** walked slowly down the stairs. **He** leaned heavily on her arm.

(1st mention of Mr Barnes)   (2nd mention of Mr Barnes)

He was breathing heavily. It was obvious that **the retired banker** was quite ill.

(3rd mention of Mr Barnes)   (4th mention of Mr Barnes)

The reader knows the words **retired banker** refer back to Mr Barnes because we signalled this fact with the definite article **the**.

2 We can use **this**, **that**, **these** and **those** with a noun or noun phrase to refer back to the person or thing mentioned earlier. **This** and **these** are used to indicate closeness to the speaker in time and space, and **that** and **those** are used to indicate distance.

EXAMPLES:

Space:

refers back to

I can't find **my notes** which I left on the table just now. **Those** notes are crucial to my finishing my report.

(the notes are not with the speaker)

refers back to

I found **my notes** which I had lost just now. **These** notes are crucial to my finishing my report.

(the notes are with the speaker)

refers back to

Time:

We are going to attend **my elder brother's convocation** on Friday. **This** occasion will be very special for our family.

(the convocation will take place soon)

I still remember **my 21st birthday party** years ago. Many of my friends and

refers back to

relatives came to celebrate **that** memorable event with me.

(the birthday was a long time ago)

REMEMBER!

■ **This** or **that** can be used to refer back to time expressions like this:

on 1st May – on this / that day
in January – in this / that month
in 2004 – in this / that year

---

3 We can also use **this**, **that**, **these** and **those** without a noun or noun phrase to point back to a noun, noun phrase, clause or sentence mentioned earlier.

EXAMPLES:

refers back to

Janice bought two cowboy outfits for her twin nephews. **These** were for their birthday on 4th September.

Mr Hicks complained about his secretary every time something went wrong at the office.

refers back to

That was why she left her job.

The word **That** refers back to the whole of the previous sentence. Mr Hicks' complaining about his secretary every time something went wrong at the office caused her to leave her job.

PRACTICE *A* Underline the correct words in the brackets to replace the words in bold print in the conversation.

Tony : Mr Hayes, have you ever played Scrabble before?

Mr Hayes : Of course! **1 Scrabble** (The game / That) was a game I used to be crazy about in college. There were many other students who loved **2 Scrabble** (this habit / this wonderful form of relaxation) too. We played in the students' lounge whenever we needed a break from our studies. **3 The students' lounge** (The place / The studies) was very conducive because we always drew a crowd of onlookers and before we

223

knew it, **4 the crowd of onlookers** (we / the spectators) themselves wanted to play **5 Scrabble** (the game / them).

Tony : Were you very good at it?

Mr Hayes : Well, I used to be called Speedo-Dicto.

Tony : What a funny name! Why were you called **6 Speedo-Dicto** (that / the funny name)?

Mr Hayes : Because I played a very fast game and I memorised all sorts of words in the dictionary. Very often, I would play an odd word and my opponent would cry out 'Challenge!' He would then check the dictionary, very sure that **7 the odd word** (the challenge / the word in question) was a figment of my imagination. I would sit there smiling smugly, waiting for **8 him** (my challenge / my opponent) to scowl at me and admit that he was wrong and I was right.

Tony : Did you have Scrabble competitions in college?

Mr Hayes : Oh, yes! The competitions were exciting because we had to play so many rounds. **9 The rounds** (It / These) lasted 50 minutes. **10 The 50 minutes** (They / The time limit) was tough for many but . . .

Tony : But not for Speedo-Dicto!

YOUR SCORE
10

PRACTICE *B* Fill in the blanks with the correct words in the box. Each word may only be used once.

that	this talent	the building	the dishes	the four-star hotel
these	those	the prized possession	the procedure	this service

1 Mum and I cooked mushroom soup, chicken macaroni and caramel custard for our Sunday lunch. Dad smacked his lips at the end of the meal and said that _____ were excellent.

2 My teacher says I have a flair for languages. I hope _____ will come in useful when I go abroad to study.

3 He paid a large sum of money for a painting at an auction. _____ now hangs in his bedroom.

4 Astoria Inn was our first choice because it was away from the bustle of the city. _____ _____ was affordable too.

5 You can browse through the books on the table but you can't touch _____ _____ in the cupboard over there because they are old and in need of new binding.

6 Batik-making involves many steps that include repeated waxing of the textile. _____ _____ may be laborious but the finished work is stunning.

7 Suzie is allergic to animals' fur. _____ is why her parents do not allow her to have a pet.

8 When I went back to my hometown, I wanted very much to see my old school again. I was

sad to find _____ was gone and a supermarket in its place.

9 The airline provides hotel accommodation for passengers travelling long distances. _____

_____ applies only for passengers that make overnight stops before heading on to
their final destinations.

10 We sing songs and listen to stories of bygone days every New Year's Eve. _____

_____ have been part of our family tradition for more than five generations.

YOUR SCORE

10

PRACTICE **C** Read the passage and state what the underlined words refer back to.

I used to judge people on the basis of their outward appearance. (1) <u>Those</u> who dressed well and
used refined language impressed me. I did not realise (2) <u>this</u> was such a shallow way of looking at
people until I met Mary.

Mary was by society's standards a failure. She was not born with good looks. She had no sense of
style in dressing. Her speech was coarse and her ways were rough. Yet there was something about (3)
<u>this unpretentious woman</u> that made me like her. At first I could not put a finger to (4) <u>it</u>. One day,
after several visits to the orphanage where she served as a cook, I realised what it was.

Jimmy, one of the orphans, had slipped and fallen down a flight of steps. His knees began to bleed
and he began to scream. The matron, the supervisor and I tried to attend to him but he would not let
any of (5) <u>us</u> touch him. He called out for Mary and she came running from the kitchen, anxiety
written all over her face. (6) <u>The tearful little boy</u> held out his hands to her and she scooped him up in
her arms. As she washed the wounds and applied dressing to them, he sat quietly watching her,
complete trust in his eyes. (7) <u>That look</u> came as a complete surprise to me.

I looked at Mary and for the first time I saw her for what she was – a person with a heart full of
love and compassion. Jimmy knew (8) <u>this</u>. I was glad I had come to know it too.

1 Those – *people* _____
2 this – *judging people on the basis of their outward appearance* _____
3 this unpretentious woman – _____ [1 *mark*]
4 it – what _____ [2 *marks*]
5 us – _____ [2 *marks*]
6 The tearful little boy – _____ [1 *mark*]
7 That look – _____ [2 *marks*]
8 this – that _____ [2 *marks*]

YOUR SCORE

10

TEST 1

A | Ten of the underlined verbs are incorrect. Write the correct verbs in the boxes.

a The staff member <u>assigning</u> the task of organising the company dinner was annoyed about it because she wanted time <u>to finalise</u> the accounts.

1. [ ]
2. [ ]

b Paula <u>arrive</u> on my doorstep with her daughter and <u>asked</u> if Val <u>could staying</u> with me for a few days.

3. [ ]
4. [ ]

c <u>Stirs</u> the batter until you find there are no more lumps in it and then <u>you can</u> start making the pancakes.

5. [ ]
6. [ ]

d My overseas guests know that in our country the custom is <u>taking off</u> our shoes before we <u>enter</u> anyone's house.

7. [ ]
8. [ ]

e Jeff <u>making</u> arrangements for some of his overseas friends to stay with his cousins when they <u>come</u> next month for his wedding.

9. [ ]
10. [ ]

f Though Alan's design <u>surpassed</u> that of the other bidders, the building contract <u>wasn't grant</u> to him.

11. [ ]
12. [ ]

g The public <u>wants</u> the mayor to give an explanation of how the funds raised for the rebuilding of the old library <u>had disappearing</u>.

13. [ ]
14. [ ]

h Eric not only <u>manage</u> his farm but also a small supermarket in town and he never <u>shows</u> any stress or anxiety.

15. [ ]
16. [ ]

i Bob, take some photographs of the filmstars <u>waiting</u> in the foyer for their limousines and <u>making</u> sure you include my favourite actress Mandy Penn.

17. [ ]
18. [ ]

j The witness <u>testified</u> for the defence looked frightened when he <u>was asked</u> by the prosecuting attorney where he had first met the accused.

19. [ ]
20. [ ]

YOUR SCORE

10

B Tick the correct words in the boxes to complete the sentences.

1 All of the cash donated by the public | was given / were given | to the parents of the baby who needed life-saving surgery.

2 Someone in the finance section | has made / have made | a wrong entry in my payment slip and given me extra money.

3 The hotel staff | wasn't told / weren't told | about their possible redundancy at the end of the year.

4 The number of schoolchildren affected by the flu epidemic | has been rising / have been rising | since last week.

5 None of the equipment in this laboratory | was used / were used | effectively during the last eight months.

6 Anyone who | experience / experiences | symptoms of chest pains and breathlessness should seek medical help.

7 Racial prejudice | cause / causes | people to discriminate against ethnic minorities.

8 Economic prosperity | are / is | something developing countries hope for in the years ahead.

9 | Do / Does | the employees know that the profit margins for the end of this month are exceptionally good and therefore we may get a bonus?

10 A number of explanations | was offered / were offered | as to why the final examinations were being postponed.

YOUR SCORE 10

C Underline the correct verb forms in the brackets.

Last Monday evening, Dad **1** (astounded / had astounded) us with a surprise announcement. He **2** (just made / had just made) reservations for the whole family to join a pleasure cruise.

"It **3** (will be / would be) a kind of 'going away' present for Steve before he **4** (leaves / is leaving) for Ireland on the 15th of next month," said Dad. I **5** (deeply touched / was deeply touched) that my parents, who **6** (seldom travels / seldom travelled) to any place far from home, were willing to do this for me.

Hectic preparations **7** (had taken / took) up much of our time before our departure date. Before we **8** (boarded / had boarded) the ship, Sue and I **9** (determined / were determined) to make sure that our parents would have a wonderful holiday.

The first day **10** (flew / has flown) by. The crew **11** (arranged / had arranged) a range of activities to keep us completely occupied. They **12** (persuaded / were persuading) us into taking an active role in games, and song and dance competitions. We even **13** (produce / produced) light comic sketches. We had so much of fun and laughter that Mum said, "I **14** (don't think / didn't think) that it would be so enjoyable." We were so engrossed in what we were doing that no one **15** (realises / realised) it was time for us to return to port.

On the return journey, however, disaster **16** (has struck / struck). Without any warning a storm began and became progressively worse. As the ship **17** (was battering / was being battered), we **18** (prayed / was praying) fervently that it **19** (will manage / would manage) somehow to reach the harbour safely. When we finally caught sight of the port after more than two hours, all of us on board **20** (heaved / were heaving) a sigh of relief.

"That really was a frightening experience," said Mum, sighing. "My sailing days are certainly over."

YOUR SCORE
20

D Complete the sentences in either the active or passive voice.

1 The constituents have elected Dr Perez as their new representative in parliament.
Dr Perez _____
_____

2 The suspect was questioned by the police officer until she broke down and confessed.
The police officer _____
_____

3 They have already frozen all new applications for car loans.
All new applications _____
_____

4 The renovations to the house will have been completed by the end of the month.
They will _____
_____

5 Jane was still finalising the reports for the annual general meeting at 2 p.m. today.
The reports for _____
_____

YOUR SCORE
10

TEST 2

A   Underline the correct words in the brackets.

1   Kim (needn't finish / needn't to finish) the ironing now.

2   They (should launching / should be launching) the spaceship any time now.

3   Catherine (might not have received / might not have been received) your e-mail.

4   Can't the cake mixer (be repaired / will be repaired) by Saturday?

5   Tom (would have given / would have been given) a lift if he had only said he needed one.

YOUR SCORE

5

B   Some of the underlined prepositions are incorrect. Write the correct prepositions in the boxes.

1   His house is located <u>along</u> Leeds Street.

2   This hardy table is made <u>of</u> teak.

3   Shape the dough <u>to</u> balls.

4   That fashion designer's summer collection is very different <u>than</u> his collection last summer.

5   I collided <u>on</u> Mary when I was rushing up the stairs.

6   He drove <u>in</u> 80 kph and ignored his friend's urging to go faster.

7   Alan was <u>in</u> despair when he heard that the company was going to close down.

8   I woke up <u>with</u> a horrible feeling that something bad was going to happen.

9   Please send these documents <u>with</u> express mail.

10   They bought a bungalow <u>with</u> a lovely view of the ocean.

YOUR SCORE

10

C Complete the direct or indirect speech sentences.

1 Anne said to us, "When do you plan to go to Bangkok?"

Anne asked _____

_____

2 Mrs Larsen said proudly to my mother, "My daughter has graduated with first-class honours in law."

Mrs Larsen proudly informed _____

_____

3 "Don't you know that this is a no-parking zone?" the traffic policeman asked Mr Sims.

The traffic policeman asked _____

_____

4 Sam said that my chiffon cake was so good that he wanted another slice.

Sam said _____

_____

5 Bill asked if Debbie was interested in joining the ceramic workshop the following weekend.

Bill said to _____

_____

YOUR SCORE 10

D Tick the correct sentences.

1
A Take a good look at the map so that we don't lose our way again.
B Don't lose our way again so take a good look at the map.

2
A He caused us a great deal of trouble with the senior manager.
B He caused us with the senior manager a great deal of trouble.

3
A The whole school to give support to their football team turned up for the match.
B The whole school turned up for the match to give support to their football team.

4
A Major construction work on the highway will be carried out next month.
B Next month will be carried out major construction work on the highway.

5
A Scientists they are noted on the international scene.
B They are noted scientists on the international scene.

YOUR SCORE 5

E Fill in the blanks with the correct words in the boxes.

1 We remember the pledge that you _____ .

| made | made it |

2 I was skiing down a slope _____ I fell.

| when | while |

3 They sensed _____ he loathed and avoided it.

| what | who |

4 He has met Doris Lessing _____ works he admires.

| whose | , whose |

5 She _____ erase the past if she could.

| will | would |

6 You can find out to which club he _____ .

| belongs | belongs to |

7 The speaker was _____ brilliant that we were entranced.

| so | very |

8 Lynn is revisiting Penang _____ she liked so much.

| , that | , which |

9 Everyone wondered _____ you were serious or joking.

| if | whether |

10 Bob remained courteous _____ he was furious.

| since | though |

YOUR SCORE /10

F Circle the letters of the correct sentences. There may be more than one answer for each question.

1 A The person must be insane who did this.
  B The person who did this must be insane.
  C The person that did this must be insane.

2 A She wondered why they were giving her odd looks.
  B She wondered why were they giving her odd looks.
  C She wondered why they kept giving her odd looks.

3 A We sat still so that the burglars would not notice us.
  B We sat so still that the burglars did not notice us.
  C We sat still so that the burglars will not notice us.

4 A I'll tell you one of the secrets that's making me unhappy.
  B I'll tell you one of the secrets that are making me unhappy.
  C I'll tell you the secret that's making me unhappy.

5 A The villagers welcomed him as they had always done.
  B The villagers welcomed him as how they had always done.
  C The villagers welcomed him the way they had always done.

YOUR SCORE /10

231

TEST 3

A Cross out the incorrect words in the boxes to complete the sentences.

1 Anita was calm though | hurt | is hurt | by their remarks.

2 They can become violent when | are scolded | scolded | in public.

3 We resolved our differences so | as | that | to present a united front.

4 Everybody dislikes you in spite of your | exuberant | exuberance | .

5 They are saying that in order | that | to | confuse us.

6 The noise went on all night, | rob | robbing | me of sleep.

7 The young officer was dismissed | for | for he | insubordination.

8 She worked part-time while | waited | waiting | for the exam results.

9 Jeff is not spoilt | despite | despite of | being an only child.

10 Teak wood was chosen because of its | strength | strong | .

YOUR SCORE
10

B Fill in the blanks with suitable words in the box.

| behind | crawling | hidden | quoted | riding |
| roughened | sparkling | spoken | under | without |

1 We often regret words _____ in anger.

2 Her office-mates eyed the diamond _____ on her finger.

3 He is the person _____ the scheme.

4 The city is full of cars _____ on congested roads.

5 I touched those dear hands _____ by work.

6 She is a woman _____ great stress.

7 We can't guess the secret _____ in his heart.

8 They trusted a man _____ enough training.

9 Andy is the boy _____ on the elephant.

10 I recognise the poem _____ by the speaker.

YOUR SCORE
10

C Underline the mistakes in some of the sentences. Write the correct word or words in the boxes provided.

1 Either we visit them or they came to stay with us during vacations.

2 She neither accepted his proposal nor rejected it.

3 Either you tell me the whole truth or I won't take your case.

4 These comments either shocked nor angered me.

5 We either resolve our differences or risk a breakdown in communications.

6 Neither the youngsters ate nor drank all day.

7 He would either stare silently at me or was very talkative.

8 The principal neither rebuked us nor showed any sign of displeasure.

9 His latest hobby will either amuse or alarm his parents.

10 Colin neither can make friends with his neighbours nor move away.

YOUR SCORE

10

D Circle the letters of the correct sentences. There may be more than one answer for each question.

1 A I love to watch the children dance.
  B I love watch the children dance.
  C I love watching the children dance.

2 A One of his pleasures are chatting on the Internet.
  B One of his pleasures is chatting on the Internet.
  C One of his pleasures is to chat on the Internet.

3 A We managed to save the company from bankruptcy.
  B We tried to save the company from bankruptcy.
  C We managed saving the company from bankruptcy.

4 A My presence here seems to upset you.

   B My presence here seems upsetting you.

   C My presence here seems to be upsetting you.

5 A The assembly voted against demolishing the old buildings.

   B The assembly voted to preserve the old buildings.

   C The assembly voted against to demolish the old buildings.

E Read the passage and state what the underlined words refer back to.

I attended a workshop where the instructor showed participants how to save an old table from being thrown away. (1) He began by cleaning (2) the table with a rag. Then he brushed the top with a coat of white emulsion paint, making sure (3) the paint was dry before he applied another coat of it.

After that, he got (4) us to tear glossy wrapping paper and pages of glossy magazines into odd shapes. (5) These were placed into piles according to their colour. Then he picked up the coloured pieces at random, squeezed glue on (6) their backs and stuck them to the table-top. He arranged them in such a way that each piece was surrounded by a white border. The final step was applying varnish to seal in the pieces. He told us (7) it had to be applied thinly and had to be completely dry before the next two layers were applied. When he finally put down his brush and stepped back, (8) we saw before us a beautiful fake-mosaic table. Everyone wanted to buy (9) the finished product but our instructor had a better idea. "Bring (10) your own table and glossy paper next week," he said.

1 He — _____

2 the table — _____

3 the paint — _____

4 us — _____

5 These — _____

6 their — _____

7 it — _____

8 we — _____

9 the finished product — _____

10 your — _____

TEST 4

When I was in secondary school, my headmistress was a lady called Anne Buchanan. She was a no-nonsense person, always outspoken, always tough with her handling (1) _____ disciplinary problems. We students often said her surname (2) _____ have been 'Cannon'.

One of her favourite projects (3) _____ improving our speaking skills. When she realised we (4) _____ say much beyond fashion and boys, she set (5) _____ a Speakers' Corner. Her rules were clear: no (6) _____ criticism and no foul language.

The first speaker (7) _____ Miss Buchanan herself. Her voice was surprisingly gentle (8) _____ her speech was humorous. Finally, the mask she (9) _____ worn for so long had come off. She (10) _____ human and she was lovely. That day, she revealed to us another part of herself and I am glad to say we treasured that trust and never took advantage of it.

YOUR SCORE

10

B Circle the letters of the correct words to complete the dialogue.

Tom   :   Julie! I (1) _____ you since the time we graduated. Where (2) _____ these past three
            years?

Julie   :   Hello, Tom. It's so good (3) _____ old friends again. You (4) _____ a little older now.
            I guess we (5) _____ . I (6) _____ from Papua New Guinea where I was serving as a
            volunteer with the U.N. medical team in the rural interior. It (7) _____ a remarkable
            experience for me.

Tom   :   Julie, you (8) _____ the life and soul of the party in university! What (9) _____ the
            bright lights of the city for such an isolated place?

Julie   :   I (10) _____ an advertisement in the Melbourne Weekly asking for medical personnel
            in Papua New Guinea. Two of my Australian friends who (11) _____ in a hospital
            near Bougainville persuaded me to join them. They told me the health situation there
            (12) _____ pathetic. People (13) _____ simply because of a lack of qualified doctors
            and medicine. I (14) _____ then that I (15) _____ my bit for mankind. And that is what
            I've been doing now for two years. What about you, Tom? I (16) _____ that you wanted to
            be a heart specialist. (17) _____ your postgraduate studies?

Tom   :   I (18) _____ the course. By this time next year, I (19) _____ a specialist, if everything
            goes well.

Julie   :   That's wonderful, Tom. You (20) _____ an excellent cardiologist. Have you ever thought
            of working in Papua New Guinea?

1   **A**   didn't see
    B   don't see
    C   haven't seen
    D   hasn't seen

2   **A**   were you
    B   have you been
    C   you have been
    D   had you been

3   **A**   to meet
    B   to be meeting
    C   to met
    D   to have met

4   **A**   are looking
    B   look
    C   looking
    D   looked

5   **A**   can all change
    B   are all changing
    C   have all changed
    D   had all changed

6   **A**   just return
    B   was just returning
    C   will return
    D   have just returned

7   **A**   is
    B   were
    C   was
    D   had been

8   **A**   are
    B   was
    C   were
    D   had been

9   **A**   makes you sacrifice
    B   making you sacrifice
    C   made you sacrifice
    D   have made you sacrifice

10 **A**   come across
    B   coming across
    C   had come across
    D   came across

11 **A**   working
    B   were working
    C   have been working
    D   will work

12 **A**   was
    B   has been
    C   were
    D   had been

13 **A**   had died
    B   will be dying
    C   was dying
    D   were dying

14 **A**   resolved
    B   have resolved
    C   has resolved
    D   will resolve

15 **A**   will be doing
    B   would do
    C   will have done
    D   had done

16 **A**   remembers
    B   remember
    C   have remembered
    D   had remembered

17 **A**   Were you doing
    B   You are doing
    C   Have you done
    D   Will you do

18 **A**   wasn't quite complete
    B   haven't quite completed
    C   hadn't completed
    D   won't quite complete

19 **A**   will have became
    B   will become
    C   will have becomes
    D   will have become

20 **A**   would made
    B   will make
    C   would be making
    D   will be making

YOUR SCORE

20

C Join the **B** sentences to the **A** sentences. Change the **B** sentences into phrases beginning with the words in the brackets.

A	B	
1 The police were planning.	They'd raid the gambling den.	(to)
2 We'll photograph that building.	It has a spiral chimney.	(with)
3 They supported him.	He had a bad record.	(despite)
4 You must brief the agent.	She'll take your place.	(taking)
5 He was furious.	He was told of the fiasco.	(when)

1 _____

2 _____

3 _____

4 _____

YOUR SCORE
10

5 _____

D Rewrite the sentences correctly.

1 David reminded us that shouldn't made unkind remarks about others.

_____

2 Jenny, her piano skills are superb, won a scholarship to study at Trinity College.

_____

3 Some important files disappeared when my boss questioned all of us.

_____

4 The packers worked so quickly so in half an hour they had packed and sealed the boxes containing our household items.

_____

5 I will definitely help you if encounter any difficulties during the course.

_____

YOUR SCORE
10

TEST 5

A Fill each blank with the most suitable word.

WHAT'S ON THIS MONTH

▶ The Green Club will hold its third 'Plant and Preserve' Open Day on Saturday, 1st May from 9 a.m. to 6 p.m. All those (1) _____ are interested to attend are requested to bring (2) _____ them a plant, a gardening spade, a bucket (3) _____ lots of energy. For enquiries call Murad at 03-25984567 (4) _____ May at 017-3885401.

▶ The International Club invites all young people wishing (5) _____ develop their leadership skills and those keen to (6) _____ in community services to meet at the Club (7) _____ 14 Raleigh Road on 15th May at 3 p.m.

▶ Members of the public who wish to get rid of unwanted household items (8) _____ make some money can sell those items at (9) _____ flea market held every Sunday in the basement (10) _____ Ocean Mall. Just phone 45987890 and ask for Mandy, the Mall's representative, to book a table for a mere 10 dollars. The flea market is open from 10 a.m. to 5 p.m.

YOUR SCORE
10

B Circle the letters of the correct words to complete the passage.

Mike and Sue Hanna (1) _____ that their children (2) _____ their best at their studies and ultimately (3) _____ the careers of (4) _____ choice. So far, Jon, the older child (5) _____ them down. He (6) _____ prizes both in the academic and in the sports arenas. His gold medals in swimming and tennis (7) _____ in the family room. Currently, he (8) _____ an honours student at a well-known university. Everyone in the family (9) _____ highly of him.

Opinions (10) _____ dramatically, however, when the family mentions Laurie, the younger child. Neither Mike nor his wife (11) _____ to discuss their teenage daughter.

Friends who (12) _____ them well will tell you that Laurie (13) _____ the source of much worry to her parents. At 15, she (14) _____ against the strict code of discipline which her father (15) _____ down. She even (16) _____ away from home at one stage.

In the past two months, however, her mother (17) _____ a change in Laurie and credit must go to Jon for this. He (18) _____ home on vacation and during that time he spent long hours talking to his sister. No one (19) _____ the transformation in Laurie. Her parents (20) _____ that she has taken steps to shed her past ways and become a caring and responsible young woman.

1 A always hope
   B has always hoped
   C always hoping
   D have always hoped

2 A will be doing
   B will do
   C will have done
   D did

3 A pursue
   B pursued
   C are pursuing
   D will be pursued

4 A his
   B her
   C their
   D our

5 A haven't let
   B hasn't let
   C don't let
   D didn't let

6 A wins
   B was winning
   C has won
   D had won

7 A was proudly exhibited
   B are proudly exhibited
   C have proudly exhibited
   D had been proudly exhibited

8 A is
   B are
   C were
   D was

9 A thought
   B is thinking
   C think
   D thinks

10 A are differing
   B differ
   C differs
   D have differ

11 A likes
   B like
   C has liked
   D will like

12 A knows
   B has known
   C had known
   D know

13 A was
   B had been
   C has been
   D will be

14 A rebelled
   B rebels
   C has rebel
   D was rebelling

15 A has laid
   B have laid
   C lays
   D had laid

16 A threaten to run
   B threatening to run
   C threatened to run
   D threatened to ran

17 A had begun to see
   B is beginning to see
   C has begun to see
   D has began to see

18 A had come
   B was coming
   C has been coming
   D will come

19 A have explained
   B is able to explain
   C able to explain
   D will be explaining

20 A is truly delighted
   B was truly delighted
   C has been truly delighted
   D are truly delighted

YOUR SCORE
20

C Rewrite the sentences and change the underlined phrases into clauses using the words in the brackets.

1 The chairman suggested that the money <u>be donated to needy children</u>. (should)

_____

_____

2 The football match was not postponed <u>in spite of the heavy rain</u>. (even though)

_____

_____

3 The Smith family lost a lot of money in the stock exchange <u>because of their foolishness</u>. (because)

_____

_____

4 <u>Despite our warning him of the consequences of his rash plans</u>, Ralph still went ahead. (although)

_____

_____

5 Mary is confident <u>of getting the majority of votes for the post of union president</u>. (that)

_____

_____

YOUR SCORE / 10

D Rewrite the interview correctly.

Interviewer : Why have you set your heart on to study medicine?

Student : It's not a decision involved only my heart. I've considered several other careers carefully so that not to make the wrong choice.

Interviewer : What makes you think you have the abilities and qualities need to succeed in the medical field?

Student : I'd like believing that love of science and my fellowmen will help make me a good doctor.

Interviewer : _____

_____

Student : _____

_____

_____

Interviewer : _____

_____

Student : _____

_____

YOUR SCORE / 10

TEST 6

A   Fill each blank with the most suitable answer.

Dear Editor,

     I have been hit by viruses on the Internet so often that I have begun to develop a fear of opening my mailbox. What kind of minds are these that are bent on (1) _____ havoc and destruction? Don't these heartless people realise (2) _____ amount of frustration and misery we go through (3) _____ our computer systems are crippled?

     I find myself (4) _____ to buy new anti-virus software often because upgrading (5) _____ weekly from the Internet doesn't help. I wonder (6) _____ kind of education these hackers received. What values (7) _____ they learn from family and school? (8) _____ only they would use their clever minds for (9) _____ good of society and the advancement of science, (10) _____ for selfish pleasure and desire for power.

Long-suffering victim

B   Circle the letters of the correct words to complete the passage.

     My plane touched down at the airport on the tiny Caribbean island of Mystique late yesterday evening. "By the time I (1) _____ at the hotel, the sun (2) _____," I thought. My taxi whisked me from the terminal and (3) _____ its way through island streets crowded with busy shoppers.

     My first impression of the Hotel Royale (4) _____ that it looked magnificent. While (5) _____ on the balcony of my hotel room, I (6) _____ a glorious view of the port and harbour. Myriads of colourful lights (7) _____ all along the shoreline. I (8) _____ with awe at the natural beauty of the island. The scene was enough (9) _____ my nerves and temporarily blot out all memories of hectic schedules and office routines.

     You can't imagine how close I am to nature now. The hotel (10) _____ by lush bougainvillea. Ornate fountains and cascading waterfalls help (11) _____ the air. What a contrast (12) _____ to my apartment back home! Nothing (13) _____ me here; neither the continuous ringing of the phone nor the buzz of traffic. There (14) _____ only a few cars on the island and I (15) _____ many calls. My trip to Mystique was a closely-guarded secret, (16) _____ only to my editor and very selected friends.

     The islanders (17) _____ of their way to make you feel at home. Last night, a group of college students (18) _____ that I join them at a beach party. The rhythm of the music (19) _____ . No one (20) _____ that the prim and proper Amanda Sims was able to cast aside her inhibitions and enjoy herself.

1 A will arrive
   B arrived
   C am arriving
   D arrive

2 A will already set
   B will have already set
   C have already set
   D had already set

3 A wound
   B winds
   C is winding
   D has wound

4 A is
   B were
   C was
   D will be

5 A relax
   B was relaxing
   C relaxing
   D relaxed

6 A able to enjoy
   B am able to enjoy
   C was able to enjoy
   D have been able to enjoy

7 A glistening
   B glistened
   C was glistening
   D glisten

8 A have filled
   B filled
   C was filled
   D will be filled

9 A soothing
   B to be soothed
   C soothed
   D to soothe

10 A surrounded
    B is surrounded
    C was surrounded
    D has surrounded

11 A will refresh
    B refreshed
    C to refreshing
    D to refresh

12 A this are
    B this was
    C this is
    D this were

13 A was going to disturb
    B is going to disturb
    C had disturbed
    D is disturbing

14 A was
    B had
    C are
    D have

15 A don't expect
    B won't be expecting
    C can't expect
    D shouldn't expect

16 A knowing
    B is known
    C was known
    D known

17 A go out
    B are go out
    C was going out
    D going out

18 A insist
    B was insisting
    C insisted
    D had insisted

19 A was captivating
    B captivated
    C has captivated
    D were captivating

20 A believe
    B believing
    C will believe
    D has believed

YOUR SCORE
20

242

C Rewrite the underlined phrases in the passage, turning them into clauses. Use the words provided.

I became a serious chess player (1) while trying to find a job. I became good friends with some of the people (2) playing against me at the chess club. Eventually, I decided (3) to talk to them about my problem. I did this (4) despite being embarrassed about being unemployed for so long. In fact, they were all sympathetic and made useful suggestions. I would recommend this sort of networking to anybody(5) looking for employment.

1 while I _____

2 that _____

3 that I _____

4 although I _____

5 who _____

D Rewrite the underlined clauses in the passage, turning them into phrases. Use the words provided.

My playful brother Charlie surprised us (1) when he won a scholarship to study in Texas in the United States. In their letters to him, my parents always reminded him (2) that he should not copy 'wild Western ways'.

The first time he came home on vacation, Charlie appeared at the airport with shaggy green hair, (3) which sent the whole family into shock. Moreover, he spoke with the drawl of someone (4) that had been raised among cowboys. Then, he pulled off his wig and spoke naturally. We were vastly relieved (5) though we were somewhat annoyed with him for fooling us.

1 by _____

2 not _____

3 sending _____

4 raised _____

5 though _____

243

ANSWERS

1.1 VERBS

Practice A

1 –	5 coach	8 go
2 renew	6 explain	9 –
3 Open	7 Telephone, be	10 make, send
4 attend		

Practice B

2 <u>to compensates</u> → to compensate

3 <u>enjoys</u> → enjoy

6 <u>Gets</u> → Get

7 <u>needs</u> → need

9 <u>should informs</u> → should inform

Practice C

1 to like	5 want	8 broadcast
2 apologise	6 be	9 to enquire
3 give	7 Hang	10 exchange
4 Try		

Practice D

2 <u>We aims to please.</u> → We aim to please.

3 <u>Please to ring for service.</u> → Please ring for service.

4 <u>In less than 15 minutes, your food will arrives at your table.</u> → In less than 15 minutes, your food will arrive at your table.

5 <u>Please be forgiving me, my wife, my chef and my café.</u> → Please forgive me, my wife, my chef and my café.

6 <u>According to Alfredo, one of Bennito's waiters, Bennito had to gives away free food only twice in all those years!</u> → According to Alfredo, one of Bennito's waiters, Bennito had to give away free food only twice in all those years!

Practice E

2 Then, fix the paper tray and paper rest to the printer.

3 After that, open the front cover of the printer and insert the colour cartridge into the cartridge holder.

4 Next, lower the lock lever to make sure the cartridge is in place.

5 Then, connect the power cord to the back of the printer.

6 Finally, plug the power plug into the power outlet.

1.2 VERBS

Practice A

2   3   5   7   9

Practice B

1 facing	5 take	8 bring
2 Let	6 waiting	9 to tell
3 have	7 smells	10 am leaving
4 gives		

Practice C

1 <u>respond</u> → responds

3 <u>have to stop</u> → has to stop

5 <u>be meeting</u> → will be meeting / am meeting

6 <u>holding</u> → is holding / will be holding

9 <u>operate</u> → operating

Practice D

2 Your tiny handwriting is giving / gives me a headache.

3 The lady teaching / who is teaching the girls to make patchwork quilts is Mrs Roberts.

4 Our college orchestra is taking part in the inter-college music festival.

5 My favourite restaurant specialises in northern Indian cuisine.

6 Biology deals with the study of living things.

Practice E

1 <u>A four-year-old girl lies in a hospital bed with a broken arm is causing a lot of concern among the hospital staff.</u>
→ A four-year-old girl lying / who is lying in a hospital bed with a broken arm is causing a lot of concern among the hospital staff.

2 <u>She speak a language no one understands.</u> → She speaks a language no one understands.

3 <u>Her gestures baffles everyone.</u> → Her gestures baffle everyone.

4 <u>"She is try to tell us something.</u> → "She is trying to tell us something.

5 <u>The press want photograph her but I won't allow it until she gets better."</u> → The press want to photograph her but I won't allow it until she gets better."

1.3 VERBS

Practice A

1 was challenged	6 was approached	
2 reprimanded	7 was developed	
3 were affected	8 has delayed	
4 was remarked	9 has planned	
5 were used	10 were involved	

Practice B

1 surprised	6 has used	
2 is shaped	7 have enjoyed	
3 was charmed	8 is pressed	
4 hugged	9 cooked	
5 was delighted	10 is also added	

Practice C

1 A, B   2 A, C   3 B, C   4 A, B   5 B, C

Practice D

(line 4)   <u>displaying</u> → displayed

(line 7)   <u>was appeared</u> → appeared

(line 8)   <u>were state</u> → were stated

(line 9)   <u>totalled</u> → was totalled

(line 10)   <u>would sent</u> → would send

Practice E

2 organised	7 scoring	
3 walked	8 to choose	
4 attracted	9 to read	
5 were divided	10 impressed	
6 selected / read	11 were awarded	

2.1 SUBJECT-VERB AGREEMENT
Practice A
1 are coming	5 projects	8 brother
2 know	6 is standing	9 carries
3 the men	7 is	10 is repairing
4 were		

Practice B
1 <u>box</u> → boxes
2 <u>admits</u> → admit
3 <u>have visited</u> → has visited
7 <u>are</u> → is
9 <u>are planning</u> → is planning

Practice C
1 either	4 I	7 Neither	9 is
2 or	5 Neither	8 nor	10 has
3 Neither	6 has		

Practice D
1 Neither Kenny nor his brothers are part of the band.
2 Neither of them has entered for the best performance award.
3 The singer, as well as the musicians, was greeted warmly on arrival.
4 Neither painting by that artist was commended.
5 Neither of them knows how to look after a baby.

Practice E
1 Neither of these ties matches my blue shirt.
2 Neither Grace nor her brothers intend to study overseas.
3 Either this house at the junction or the one next to it belongs to my manager.
4 Neither article on the efforts to protect wildlife gives a true picture.
5 The senior form teacher, along with her students, has painted a mural in the school canteen.

2.2 SUBJECT-VERB AGREEMENT
Practice A
1 appears	5 was heard	8 says
2 is	6 enjoys	9 was made
3 has	7 was	10 is
4 affects		

Practice B
1 None	5 A lot of	8 Any of
2 Anyone	6 Any	9 Every
3 Anything	7 Anything	10 Every
4 Everyone		

Practice C
3 <u>have been heard</u> → has been heard
4 <u>are</u> → is
7 <u>want</u> → wants
9 <u>were harmed</u> → was harmed
10 <u>are noted</u> → is noted

Practice D
1 <u>Every class were asked to be present at a special assembly in the hall.</u> → Every class was asked to be present at a special assembly in the hall.
2 <u>Everybody were curious.</u> → Everybody was curious.

3 <u>A lot of rumours was circulating as everyone filed into the hall.</u> → A lot of rumours were circulating as everyone filed into the hall.
4 <u>Any of the notion we had were quickly removed when the principal spoke.</u> → Any of the notion we had was quickly removed when the principal spoke.
5 <u>The teachers, as well as the students, was delighted.</u> → The teachers, as well as the students, were delighted.

Practice E
1 Everything about the operation of this company is being investigated.
2 A lot of the hi-tech equipment at the sports complex has not been fully utilised.
3 Every member of the hotel staff is instructed to give the best service possible to the guests.
4 Nothing concrete is being done to meet the needs of poor families.
6 Any of the women here is able to weave carpets.

2.3 SUBJECT-VERB AGREEMENT
Practice A
2 3 5 6 8

Practice B
1 is / was / has been	6 is
2 has	7 realises
3 looks	8 is
4 has	9 has
5 gives	10 is / was

Practice C
3 <u>member</u> → members	7 <u>believes</u> → believe
5 <u>works</u> → work	8 <u>zebra</u> → zebras
6 <u>traffics</u> → traffic	

Practice D
1 <u>Each of them were told to carry their bags to the customs checkpoint.</u> → Each of them was told to carry their bags to the customs checkpoint.
2 <u>Some of the women with young children was struggling to cope with their luggage.</u> → Some of the women with young children were struggling to cope with their luggage.
3 <u>Some of the officers was ill-mannered and unfriendly.</u> → Some of the officers were ill-mannered and unfriendly.
4 <u>Each passenger were given careful scrutiny before his or her passport was cleared.</u> → Each passenger was given careful scrutiny before his or her passport was cleared.
5 <u>After two hours, the exhausted traveller were told to return to the train to continue their journey.</u> → After two hours, the exhausted travellers were told to return to the train to continue their journey.

Practice E
1 All the property she inherited is mortgaged.
2 One of us is to blame for misplacing the keys to the office.
3 Each of the logs is sent downstream to the mill.
4 One of you has to take Lyn's place in the choir.
5 All the works of art in this museum are priceless.

2.4 SUBJECT-VERB AGREEMENT
Practice A
1   4   6   8   9

Practice B
1   are
2   haven't been
3   have enabled
4   have touched
5   were changed
6   were
7   were heard
8   are
9   have been praised
10   captivate

Practice C
1   skill
2   Help
3   There was
4   There is
5   Justice
6   There are
7   The suffering
8   There were
9   Violence
10   Education

Practice D
2   have increased → has increased
3   were → was
4   have led → has led
6   result → results
9   is → are

Practice E
1   Fog envelops the entire coast during the winter months.
2   There was great commotion in the departure terminal because of the flight delays.
3   The danger of a volcanic eruption has forced thousands to flee from their homes.
4   There was a variety of food and games at the charity carnival.
5   Depression affects many people who are lonely.

3.1 SIMPLE PRESENT AND PRESENT CONTINUOUS TENSES
Practice A
1   4   6   7   9

Practice B
1   are demanding
2   am looking
3   have
4   works
5   describes
6   doubts
7   is holding
8   live
9   affects
10   are laying

Practice C
1   are leaving
2   is coming
3   are still dressing
4   wake up
5   is
6   feel
7   takes off
8   have
9   am not grumbling
10   wish

Practice D
3   are demand → are demanding / demand
5   examine → are examining
8   am forgiving → forgive
9   signalling → is signalling
10   are describing → describe

Practice E
1   introduces
2   use
3   toils
4   helps
5   brings
6   manages
7   show
8   paints
9   exist
10   opens

3.2 SIMPLE PAST TENSE
Practice A
1   3   5   7   10

Practice B
1   got
2   is always finding
3   held
4   guides
5   is memorising
6   frequently studied
7   used to practise
8   almost frittered away
9   deals with
10   kept

Practice C
1   fascinated
2   swung
3   fought
4   was
5   gave
6   hired
7   takes
8   works
9   occupies
10   intends

Practice D
1   preferred
2   hoped
3   taught
4   disliked
5   occupied
6   takes
7   found
8   broke
9   fell
10   tease

Practice E
Photography took up much of Nick's time and energy. He derived a great deal of pleasure and satisfaction from capturing on camera the antics of animals in the wild. His pictures won him awards for his authentic presentation and originality.

Nick had inherited the talent from his father Martin Ross, a brilliant photojournalist. He hoped one day to produce documentaries both for the movie screen and for television.

Practice F
1   In those years when my father was in the foreign service, we were always moving from place to place and seldom had a chance to make good friends.
2   When Claire was about seven, her ambition was to be a doctor one day.
3   Kate's fears increased when she decided that the men on motorbikes were following her.
5   Early this morning, a car crashed into a retaining wall. The impact caused the motorist and her companion to be flung out of the vehicle.

3.3 PAST CONTINUOUS TENSE
Practice A
1   3   5   6   9

Practice B
1   were arguing
2   is attending
3   handed out
4   slipped
5   is taking up
6   was throbbing
7   graduated
8   was rummaging
9   roasted
10   arrested

Practice C
1   were coming
2   is moving
3   was demonstrating
4   were vaccinating
5   is frequently complaining
6   were shovelling
7   examine
8   was shouting / shouted
9   climbed
10   causes

Practice D

1	snow	6	was wondering
2	drove	7	dreamt
3	is thinking	8	was pulling up
4	prepares	9	is
5	was catching	10	is trudging

Practice E

1 While I was resting just now, I heard someone knocking at my door.
2 At midnight yesterday, Harun was completing his assignment when he noticed a sleek black car stopping outside his gate.
4 May bargained with the stall-keeper for more than 20 minutes this afternoon and finally brought the price of the shawl down to 10 dollars.
5 The audience was roaring with laughter at the jokes of the comedienne during the two-hour show last night.

Practice F

1 Mala was shopping when she realised that her purse was missing.
2 He was complaining about his workload the whole morning.
3 People were queueing up for hours this afternoon to buy tickets for the show.
4 At ten last night, I was still reading my history notes.
5 While Tom looked after the children, Betty had her hair styled at the salon.

3.4 PRESENT PERFECT TENSE

Practice A

1 B, C   2 A, B   3 C   4 A   5 B, C   6 A, C

Practice B

1 have looked after
2 chose
3 always encourages
4 was forever threatening
5 have risen sharply
6 have lived
7 was hanging
8 hasn't scolded
9 has already seen
10 has grown

Practice C

2 has discovered → discovered
4 just eat → ate
5 didn't announce → haven't announced
7 waited → have waited
8 yet see → yet sees / has yet seen
10 has bought → bought

Practice D

2	have often wondered	7	have earned
3	have changed	8	focused
4	were	9	threw
5	holds	10	has led
6	has just become	11	remains

Practice E

1 I have misplaced my house keys. I hope I find them soon or I will have to climb in through a window.
2 Sue has already distributed the booklets to the participants at the seminar, so everyone should have his or her own copy.

3 The workmen stacked up all our furniture yesterday because they are going to paint the house today.
4 Our friends haven't replied to our wedding invitation yet.
5 Peggy and I have been close friends since we were children. We enjoy doing things together like going shopping and watching movies.

3.5 PAST PERFECT TENSE

Practice A

1   4   5   7   9

Practice B

1	have emphasised	6	hasn't have
2	passed	7	has become
3	always disagreed	8	have fallen
4	had fascinated	9	had seen
5	haven't done	10	has inspired

Practice C

1	has been	6	found
2	had already flocked	7	stood
3	swept	8	swung
4	shouted	9	had never seen
5	had had	10	had already closed

Practice D

1 had heard → heard
4 had decided → decided
6 had took → had taken
9 ever hope → had ever hoped
10 had been drizzling → has been drizzling

Practice E

1	hadn't decided	6	have ignored
2	had taken	7	has willed
3	had burnt	8	has raised
4	had broken down	9	delights
5	hadn't given	10	had worked

3.6 PRESENT PERFECT CONTINUOUS AND PAST PERFECT CONTINUOUS TENSES

Practice A

1   3   4   7   9

Practice B

1	had planned	6	have cooperated
2	already saw	7	had investigated
3	had drunk	8	had rearranged
4	had been designing	9	have trimmed
5	has worked	10	had just been finishing

Practice C

1	has been restoring	6	had been queueing
2	had been showing	7	hadn't told
3	have indicated	8	has been making
4	had been painting	9	had already put up
5	has been running	10	had been waiting

Practice D

1 had been trying → have been trying
2 have all been working → had all been working
3 had been talking → have been talking
4 have been phoning → had been phoning
5 had been working → has been working

Practice E

1 Since early this morning, water has been gushing out of the burst mains and no one has come to repair it.
2 They came back from the forest covered with insect bites. They had been catching butterflies all afternoon.
3 I usually keep my letters in a drawer but now they are scattered all over the place. Someone has been reading my mail.
4 That lady has been staring at us ever since we sat down. I wonder whether we know her.
5 Kate had been postponing going to the dentist's for months but this morning her toothache was so bad that she had to rush off to the dental clinic.

3.7 SIMPLE FUTURE TENSE
Practice A

1   5   6   8   10

Practice B

1 will miss / are going to miss
2 be
3 climb
4 had just moved
5 is
6 hasn't / has not done
7 will have
8 will wait
9 had alerted
10 will be / are going to be

Practice C

1 will received
2 will being
3 am having
4 fall
5 going to approve soon
6 think
7 will froze
8 are going to close
9 will be officiate
10 has dominates

Practice D

1 am going to mail → will mail
2 already agreed → has already agreed
3 is going to scoring → is going to score
4 were washing → will wash
5 had been watching → have been watching
6 will insisted → will insist
7 isn't going to be reveal → isn't going to reveal
8 are going to came down → are going to come down
9 will taking → will take
10 has been searching → have been searching

Practice E

1 Their numbers rapidly dwindling in their native China. → Their numbers are rapidly dwindling in their native China.
2 Concerned Chinese scientists going to take steps to increase the panda population. → Concerned Chinese scientists are going to take steps to increase the panda population.
3 The Chinese government will intensified efforts to protect the young cubs, monitor their growth and feed them. → The Chinese government will intensify efforts

to protect the young cubs, monitor their growth and feed them.
4 Food will being of the utmost importance in this case, as the staple diet of these animals consists of young bamboo shoots which used to grow in profusion in parts of China. → Food will be of the utmost importance in this case, as the staple diet of these animals consists of young bamboo shoots which used to grow in profusion in parts of China.
5 These measures helped to safeguard the environment in which the pandas live. → These measures will help to safeguard the environment in which the pandas live.

3.8 FUTURE CONTINUOUS TENSE
Practice A

1 will be flying
2 was studying
3 have been rehearsing
4 will you be using
5 will be attending
6 have been working
7 are keeping
8 will be listening
9 will be preparing
10 Will you be taking

Practice B

1 will be watching
2 will soon be drilling
3 had been applying
4 will surely be attending
5 had been keeping
6 Will you be meeting
7 will be hosting
8 had been expecting
9 Will you be going
10 will be spring-cleaning

Practice C

1 are going to move → were going to move
3 you will be going down → will you be going down
5 not be sharing → won't / will not be sharing
8 The coach will be making → Will the coach be making
9 looking forward → are looking forward

Practice D

1 The reporters have been waiting all morning for the Prime Minister's comments about the situation.
2 The squads of soldiers were firing randomly into the crowd to disperse them.
3 The welfare committee will be looking into the complaints about the poor quality of food in the cafeteria.
4 We had better leave now as it looks like there is going to be a storm.
5 Everyone will soon be spluttering and coughing because of the thick smoke in the room.

Practice E

1 Our parents will be celebrating their 30th wedding anniversary this Sunday.
2 The lifeguards here will be put through rigorous training to ensure that they are fully prepared to deal with emergencies.

3 Will she be releasing the results of the competition to the participants soon?

4 We are going to speak to the doctor today about Dad's ear problem.

5 The sales season has hit the town again. Many people can be seen queueing up early outside stores to get the best bargains.

3.9 FUTURE PERFECT TENSE
Practice A
3   5   6   8   9

Practice B
1	will have made	6	has succeeded
2	had retired	7	will have damaged
3	will have just done	8	won't have accepted
4	has already gone	9	have turned
5	won't have realised	10	will have swum

Practice C
1	will have fitted	6	will rain
2	have seen	7	will have returned
3	lost	8	will have closed
4	will have established	9	have been cleaning
5	will have sold	10	had already left

Practice D
1 will rested → will have rested

3 have come → will come

6 will have grow → will have grown

8 were driving → have been driving

9 will already been served → will have already been served

Practice E
1 Southeast Asian countries will have experienced an economic recovery by the end of next year if the global situation improves.

2 Before the end of the year, welfare officials will have found foster homes for the orphans.

3 Our holiday will be ending / will end this week. We will have returned to the the business world by Monday.

4 The president will announce / will be announcing the names of the incoming board of the club at this evening's official dinner.

5 Mrs Thomas had never seen such strange behaviour before in her life.

4.1 ACTIVE AND PASSIVE VOICE
Practice A
1	delivers	6	will tie
2	took over	7	will be met
3	kept	8	was moved
4	was shut down	9	removes
5	are looked after	10	banned

Practice B
3   5   6   8   10

Practice C
1	put off	6	will be decided
2	was taken up	7	launch
3	will declare	8	was felt
4	is scheduled	9	smelt / smelled
5	employs	10	held up / was holding up

Practice D
1 Joan agreed with us that our volleyball team needed more training.

3 The pounding of drums to warn of an imminent attack woke up the entire village.

4 The marines are made to do difficult manoeuvres while they are in training with the navy.

5 Our plans for the evening was forgotten when unexpected visitors arrived.

Practice E
Wood is crushed into small pieces by machines. The pieces are mixed with water and chemicals to produce pulp. The resulting pulp is spun into fine sheets of paper by other machines.

When paper is recycled, the process is repeated. Different chemical processes are used to produce the various required grades of paper.

4.2 ACTIVE AND PASSIVE VOICE
Practice A
1	is tiled	6	are giving
2	was being created	7	are selling
3	by	8	was being attended
4	is produced	9	are introduced
5	with	10	with

Practice B
1	is being interviewed	6	was filled
2	was chatting	7	is keeping
3	is designing	8	are being added
4	is packed	9	were dazzled
5	was completed	10	are being checked

Practice C
1 The cafeteria was crowded with so many people that we couldn't find a place to sit.

2 The construction worker was struck by a falling beam while he was building the attic.

4 At 8.30 last night, technicians tried / were trying to reconnect the damaged power lines and restore electricity in our area.

5 The cupboard was crammed with so many things that everything fell out when I opened it.

Practice D
1 The demonstration turned violent and cars on the streets were being burned by the people.

2 Several shots were fired by the soldiers to disperse the mob.

3 Many demonstrators were overpowered with batons by the police.

4 Scores of detainees were led to waiting trucks.

5 The incident was being filmed by the TV crew despite the angry protests from the soldiers.

Practice E
The sound system is being set up by Mani and Chan. The lights are being tested by Pete and Halim to ensure they are working. The backdrop is being put up by Polly, our stage coordinator. All the props were completed by Polly and her team just two days ago. Now, everything is being checked to make sure there will be no last-minute problems on opening night.

4.3 ACTIVE AND PASSIVE VOICE

Practice A
1 have already registered
2 will have been felt
3 had not begun
4 has just been postponed
5 was supposed to rain
6 had been cut down
7 has already been told
8 will have been covered
9 has / have been delivered
10 were supposed to visit

Practice B
1 will have been lifted
2 had been looked after
3 had been shattered
4 will have undergone
5 are supposed to lend
6 are supposed to illuminate
7 has been ridiculed
8 have finally recognised
9 had briefed
10 will have spent

Practice C
(4) had not yet been exposed
(7) have gone
(8) is supposed
(9) has been laid
(11) have been prove

Practice D
3 Pat had been supported by her parents for two years before she was awarded a scholarship.
4 You were supposed to treat us to dinner if we did well in our exams.
5 A couple of passengers have cancelled their names from the waiting list so we are able to get seats on the next flight.
6 We submitted / had submitted our report to the chairman long before he asked for it.

Practice E
1 The club president has escorted the visiting dignitaries to a number of places.
2 We had been taught by Mrs Jones for five years before she returned to the her own country.
3 The candidates are supposed to be told the requirements of the interviewing board.
4 The agenda for the meeting will have been posted by the secretary to all the shareholders by Friday.
5 The city authorities have highly commended Stella for informing the police about the robbery she witnessed.

5.1 DIRECT AND INDIRECT SPEECH

Practice A
2   3   5   8   10

Practice B
1 "Those women,"
2 "so we'll come back later."
3 "I'm tired and hungry," said Sara,
4 "We'll be ready in half an hour."
5 "Hello Sandra,"
6 "Gradually," said Karen,
7 "My dear Kate,"
8 "Recently,"

9 said Sally to the doctor.
10 "and the counter is still closed."

Practice C
1 he, would talk   4 they, hadn't heard
2 That, fascinated   5 was, had
3 needed, us

Practice D
1 Sara had so many things to do, said Tom, that she didn't know where to begin.
2 The workers said that they might come for the meeting the next / following day.
3 Bill said to Julie, "My sister is going to visit you on Saturday."
4 Miss Wong said that the Chao Praya River provides the Thai people with water for consumption and irrigation.
5 Philip said to us, "You haven't missed much as the match has just begun."

Practice E
1 They told us that they would have submitted their designs by the following week.
2 Mrs Potts said to the manager, "Your salesman was rude to me."
4 Connie said to me, "I haven't worn an evening gown before."
5 A long time ago, said Mum, she used to read me bedtime stories.

5.2 DIRECT AND INDIRECT SPEECH

Practice A
1 The cashier said to Mrs Singer, "Do you prefer to open a new account?"
2 "How much did those shoes cost?" said Jill to Nina.
3 The principal said to the coach, "Isn't the school team playing on Friday?"
4 Simon said to us, "Where would you like to go for dinner?"
5 "Did you hear the doorbell ring?" said Mary to me.

Practice B
1 can, your   4 don't, that
2 you, took   5 why did, had wanted
3 Does, she

Practice C
2 Mum asked Linda if / whether she had finished her homework.
3 Mrs Lim asked us if / whether we wanted some lemonade.
4 Tom asked me when we were starting work.
5 Sally asked us whether or not the birthday cake looked lovely.
6 Eddy asked me why I wanted to see him.

Practice D
1 Ken asked the children why they were playing in the rain.
2 He said to his daughter, Sandra, "Do you like the dress I bought you?"
3 The science teacher asked us if / whether we knew how to set up the equipment.
5 We asked Jenny whether or not she had switched on the porch lights.

Practice E
1 . . . whether the invitation cards for the club dinner and dance were ready or not. / whether or not the invitation cards for the club dinner and dance were ready.

2 . . . if / whether she had got any replies.

3 . . . if / whether she thought there would be a good turnout.

4 . . . if / whether John had finalised the arrangements for the food.

5 . . . if / whether she was going to contact the committee members.

6.1 MODALS
Practice A
1	be	**6**	put
2	could	**7**	trying
3	should get	**8**	have completed
4	may be considering	**9**	must be placed
5	would be read	**10**	spray

Practice B
1	B	**2**	A	**3**	A, B	**4**	C
5	C	**6**	B	**7**	A, C	**8**	B

Practice C
1	be	**5**	taking	**8**	remember
2	be used	**6**	elected	**9**	want
3	running	**7**	cancelled	**10**	read
4	forgotten				

Practice D
2 Mr Nelson should be told the good news by Helen.

3 Your grandfather ought to be reminded about his next medical appointment.

4 About a hundred workers may be dismissed by the factory next month.

5 The tour arrangements have to be finalised by Julie this afternoon.

6 A buffet dinner for five hundred guests can be organised by Speedy Caterers in two days.

Practice E
2 must have been travelled → must have travelled

3 ought to leaving → ought to leave

4 can drove → can drive

5 should provide → should be provided

6 could planning → could be planning

6.2 MODALS
Practice A
1 ought to, ought not to

2 can't, can

3 shouldn't be, should be

4 shan't, shall

5 wouldn't have, would have

Practice B
1	A	**2**	C	**3**	C	**4**	B	**5**	A
6	B	**7**	B	**8**	A	**9**	A	**10**	C

Practice C
2 John can't be dismissed by the company without good reason.

3 The spicy food at the restaurant could not be eaten by my friend.

4 Steve might not be asked to explain his whereabouts yesterday.

5 The heavy rucksacks and poles needn't be carried by the girls.

6 You shouldn't be discouraged from attending evening classes by your employer.

Practice D
2 won't endangering → won't endanger / won't be endangering

3 shouldn't answered → shouldn't have answered

4 can't concentrated → can't concentrate

5 will not allowed → will not be allowed

6 wouldn't lying → wouldn't be lying

6.3 MODALS
Practice A
1   2   4   7   9

Practice B
1	A, B	**2**	A, B	**3**	B, C	**4**	A, C	**5**	B, C

Practice C
1	agree	**6**	Can
2	apply	**7**	be exempted
3	override	**8**	look over
4	be televised	**9**	this ointment be used
5	we get	**10**	Should Maggie be

Practice D
2 Shouldn't John have a fire extinguisher in his kitchen?

3 Will our team have a chance against the Red Riders?

4 Can the printer be repaired before Monday?

5 Shouldn't you use sunblock when you go out into the sun?

6 Couldn't Tina be contacted at her home yesterday?

Practice E
2 Would you like a cup of tea?

3 Can I pay by cheque?

4 Should we complain to the electric company?

5 Must you be a fussy person?

6 Can't our dog / it be sent to a friend's house?

7.1 PREPOSITIONS
Practice A
1	above	**6**	Between 20 and 25 youths
2	below	**7**	by
3	above	**8**	At
4	below	**9**	under
5	over	**10**	between

Practice B
1	at, by	**4**	over, under
2	below, above	**5**	over, between
3	at, between		

Practice C
1	A	**2**	A, B, C	**3**	C	**4**	A, B	**5**	A, B	**6**	C

Practice D
1	by	**5**	between	**8**	between
2	at	**6**	by	**9**	over
3	at	**7**	over	**10**	below
4	over				

7.2 PREPOSITIONS
Practice A
1	by	**5**	out of	**8**	in
2	into	**6**	of	**9**	with
3	from	**7**	by	**10**	out of
4	in				

Practice B
2   5   6   7   9

Practice C

1 That dolphin understands instructions given ⁄ English.
2 Do you know where these imported chocolates come ⁄?
3 Paul makes lovely miniature furniture ⁄ used matchsticks.
4 Joanna went ⁄ stocks and shares and now she regrets it.
5 I have been ⁄ touch with what has been happening in the scientific field.
6 Larry promptly put out the fire in the kitchen ⁄ a fire extinguisher.
7 Their son got ⁄ trouble during the time they were away.
8 Jennifer's creative work ⁄ glass and ceramic caught the attention of an art reviewer.
9 Her time ⁄ the world of modelling led to her setting up a modelling agency.
10 She eventually finished the project ⁄ getting assistance from her close friends.

Practice D
1 A	2 A, B	3 C	4 C
5 A	6 C	7 A, B	8 A

7.3 PREPOSITIONS
Practice A
1 with	4 at	7 against	9 for
2 with	5 with	8 of	10 to
3 like	6 from		

Practice B
1 A	2 C	3 C	4 A
5 A, B, C	6 B	7 B, C	

Practice C
1 Ever since her illness, she has had difficulty with her breathing.
3 Joe's dream is to go on a cruise ship with its own swimming pool, cinema, restaurants and video games arcade.
4 I love animals so I'm against all scientific experiments that subject them to pain.
5 The tour guide yelled to her tour group members not to sit too close to the edge of the pool.

Practice D
4 like	6 with	7 against
8 to	10 without	

Practice E

Ladies and gentlemen. Here ⁄on my right are the proposers ⁄for the motion 'Science has brought more evil than good to mankind.' On my left are those debating against the motion. Each team has come prepared ⁄with lots of 'ammunition' to 'fire' at their opponents. I think we are going to have an exciting time this evening because both teams have made it to the finals ⁄without losing a single debate along the way. I have been told they are ⁄like Mark Anthony and Brutus, two historical figures ⁄of such stature that they could sway crowds with their oratory, passion and logic. So let us give our finalists here all our attention.

7.4 PREPOSITIONS
Practice A
3 5 7 9 10

Practice B
1 for	5 because of	8 for	
2 about	6 on	9 on	
3 for	7 of	10 at	
4 of			

Practice C
1 B	2 A	3 C	4 A	5 B
6 A	7 C	8 B	9 C	10 B

Practice D
3 They were treated first because of their severe injuries. / They were treated first for their injuries were severe.
4 Jennifer dressed in black for a funeral.
5 The little boy ran to his mother for comfort.
6 We don't want to give Maisie the bad news because of her illness. / We don't want to give Maisie the bad news for she is ill.
7 He worked hard for the improvement of the living conditions of the poor.

Practice E
1 for	5 on	8 for
2 at	6 about	9 because of
3 of / in	7 at	10 about
4 for		

8 SUBJECT AND PREDICATE
Practice A
1 C	2 B, C	3 A	4 B	5 A, C	6 A, B, C

Practice B
1 The young thoroughbreds are trained by experts to become racehorses.
2 The chief minister declared open the conference with a brief survey of recent developments.
3 Brian scored the winning goal by heading the ball into the net from the side.
4 Ryan handed over the video camera and I continued filming the whales at play.
5 An enthusiastic crowd watched the players try to outwit each other at basketball.
6 Medical science has provided man with many answers in his quest for health and energy.
7 Little crystal vases which contained delicate orchids were placed on each dining table.
8 Four-year-old Nicole motioned to everyone in the audience to keep quiet.
9 He paid huge sums of money to enhance his image.
10 The wealthy recluse left a substantial portion of his estate to animal shelters.

Practice C

2 . . . snatched / and . . . direct object

3 . . . Edmund / very . . . verb

4 . . . gave / to . . . direct object

5 . . . since / hoping . . . adverbial

6 / Feel . . . subject

7 . . . to / and . . . indirect object

8 . . . studied / and . . . direct object

9 During / we . . . adverbial

10 . . . participants / tired . . . verb

11 . . . by / and . . . indirect object

Practice D

1 The royal symphony orchestra played two magnificent numbers at the international music festival.
2 He whipped the eggs into soft peaks and gradually folded them into the cake batter.
3 The new president chosen by the people is a man of vision and great courage.
4 The mouse scuttled across the room, sending us shrieking and running in different directions.
5 I didn't realise that time had passed so quickly and I had to go.

9.1 RELATIVE CLAUSES
Practice A
2 5 6 8 10

Practice B
1	, who	6	were
2	who	7	affects
3	gossip	8	, who
4	has	9	are to
5	had been awakened	10	is

Practice C
2 Miss Hill is the headmistress who the board has appointed.
3 The story is about Julius Caesar, who was a Roman emperor.
4 He is the psychiatrist who my patient is consulting.
5 We have e-mailed the actors who the director will audition.
6 She is holding her baby boy, who was born this morning.

Practice D
1 These are the performers who enthralled us.
2 She helps children who people have abandoned.
3 He was deceived by Lucia, who he had trusted.
4 We were the fans who made you famous.
5 I was defeated by Dad, who I usually beat.

Practice E
2 They are arresting the ship captain who is involved in smuggling.
3 We enjoy spending time with Grandpa, who tells marvellous stories.
4 She went to see the commander, who she implored to spare her son.

5 He is one of the people who has helped me arrange this carnival.
6 A woman claimed the child who the Lims had adopted.

9.2 RELATIVE CLAUSES
Practice A
1	, which	5	, which	8	which
2	that	6	is	9	, which
3	was	7	are surveying	10	has done
4	respects				

Practice B
2 4 5 7 9

Practice C
2 We are here to listen to your grievances / which we will explain to the management.
4 Friends took us to a bullfight / which we did not like at all.
7 They heard her story / which moved them to tears.
10 I gazed at the Pacific Ocean / which looked really peaceful.
11 Shaun went to your concert / which he enjoyed immensely.

Practice D
3 They gathered wealth, which failed to bring them happiness.
4 She is one of the great sopranos that have entranced audiences.
5 You must send us a copy which your principal has certified.
6 This is one of the projects that our company is financing.
7 I sent a report to a newspaper, which published it on the front page.

Practice E
1	, that	4	which	7	to have	9	which
2	which	5	has	8	, that	10	, that
3	, which	6	that				

9.3 RELATIVE CLAUSES
Practice A
1	, whose	5	questioned	8	whose
2	healed	6	is	9	are crumbling
3	need	7	whose work	10	needs
4	was known				

Practice B
1	, whose	5	build	8	whose
2	are	6	are ruining	9	famous
3	is	7	is	10	, whose
4	whose				

Practice C
2 It is an advertisement whose jokes children love.
3 Laura forgave her brother, whose coldness had hurt her.
4 Lion-tamers are special people whose authority the big cats accept.
5 We grieved for our favourite river, whose water had grown murky.
6 I've heard many songs whose lyrics need to be improved.

Practice D

2 He reminds me of a snake whose eyes hypnotise its prey.

3 I have always been the family member whose plans work best.

4 They were terrified of the man whose son they had bullied.

5 Ricky is the mischievous boy whose virtuous twin is often mistaken for him.

6 We make different types of bread whose quality is guaranteed.

Practice E

1 , whose	5 understand it	8 whose	
2 has	6 is	9 cherish them	
3 threaten	7 are	10 has	
4 includes			

9.4 RELATIVE CLAUSES

Practice A

1 The figures that the commercial artist drew look rather stiff.

2 She knitted him a sweater, which fitted him snugly.

3 Such movies are not for people whose hearts are weak.

4 Elvis Presley, who was a famous singer, led a hectic life.

5 The drapes which the decorator has selected do not appeal to me.

6 He was the greatest tragic actor that ever performed on stage.

7 My truck, whose tyres I had just changed, moved steadily on the wet road.

8 This is the lady who designs exquisite rock gardens.

9 We are heading for the Himalayas, whose lower peaks we plan to climb.

10 Our planet Earth, which man has polluted, is suffering will take centuries to clean.

Practice B

1 are	6 protects	
2 which	7 , which	
3 hitchhikes	8 were accepted who applied	
4 seems	9 that	
5 tutoring her	10 met him	

Practice C

3 decays → decay	8 looks → look		
4 differs → differ	9 was → were		
5 were → was			

Practice D

2 The boy who the gardener brought to help him has green fingers.

3 The Tans' bungalow, whose roof I have just repaired, is very old.

4 Celebrities that we see on television talk shows sometimes disappoint us.

5 King Mongkut, who was a wise Thai ruler, loved his country.

6 Many diseases which afflict people in modern times are related to stress.

Practice E

Vitamin supplements, which are sometimes neither necessary nor beneficial, are easily available nowadays. People who take them zealously should be warned of certain dangers. A man whose intake of natural food is already rich in vitamins can damage his health by taking too many supplements. For instance, the Vitamin C supplement which he takes in high doses to prevent infection may bring him heart problems. Vitamin A, whose importance to health no one can deny, is toxic when taken in much larger quantities than needed. Health writers, who readers tend to trust, have a serious responsibility in this matter.

10.1 ADVERBIAL CLAUSES

Practice A

1 B, C	2 A, C	3 A, C	4 B, C	5 A, B

Practice B

1 grown	5 under	8 more	
2 it's because	6 behaves	9 they	
3 to	7 wouldn't	10 difficult	
4 because of			

Practice C

1 You should install a house alarm as the number of burglaries is rising.

2 We can propose her name since she is eager to be on the committee.

3 Everyone was subdued because there had been a bomb scare.

4 The magazine will be launched soon since the market survey results are positive.

5 My aunt plants certain herbs as she believes in their medicinal value.

Practice D

1   3   6   9   10

Practice E

1 Umbrellas were unfurled because it had begun to drizzle.

2 We'll have to drop everything else since this is urgent.

3 Volcanic eruptions are useful as they make the soil fertile.

4 You shouldn't do that since you would be jeopardising your future.

5 Her eyes seem to have changed colour because she is wearing blue-tinted contact lenses.

Practice F

My next vacation will be special because I have saved enough to go abroad. I must choose the right destination since I may not be able to do this again for some time. I will not opt for Bali as many of my friends have been to that lovely Indonesian island. Katmandu in Nepal might prove too taxing for me because I have never done any climbing in my life. Granada in Spain might be the answer as it would be intriguing but not too challenging. I will go on my own because I do want adventure.

10.2 ADVERBIAL CLAUSES

Practice A

1 although	5 postponed	8 new	
2 been	6 were	9 not working	
3 don't	7 wealthy	10 crowing	
4 because			

Practice B

1   3   6   8   10

Practice C

1 A, C	2 B, C	3 A, C	4 A, B	5 B, C

Practice D

1	though	6	is screaming
2	impressive	7	as
3	we opposed	8	although
4	because	9	quiet
5	had done	10	have to

Practice E

1	unsuitable	6	I seem
2	is unlikely	7	does not
3	I am	8	are encouraging
4	have not	9	be leaving
5	never	10	it does

Practice F

We have not given up on you even though you have been silent for so long. You must be very busy but that is no excuse. All of us here miss you though you used to drive us insane with your deafening music.

Mum and Dad are well although Dad is not very energetic now. Joe pulled a muscle because / as / since he had not warmed up sufficiently before jogging at dawn. As for me, I am keeping virtuously to a new diet though I am often tempted to be naughty.

10.3 ADVERBIAL CLAUSES

Practice A

1	while	5	will go	8	were noticing
2	when	6	roasted	9	when
3	while	7	was travelling	10	is ripening
4	when				

Practice B

2	3	7	8	10

Practice C

1 A, B, C	2 B	3 B, C	4 A, C	5 A, B

Practice D

2 Jimmy was injured when his motorcycle hit a tree.
3 The vet treated the wounded bird while we watched.
4 We'll be thinking of you while you're sitting for the examination
5 I usually read a novel while I wait for my flight.
6 She was hanging up the balloons when one of them burst.

Practice E

1	when	6	was running
2	recognised	7	while
3	plucked	8	when
4	yelled	9	saw
5	while	10	I'm

Practice F

2 Time is running out while you are hesitating.
3 Jane angered her colleagues when she meddled in their affairs.
4 We will quote the spokesman when we write the story.
5 The guard eavesdropped while they planned the robbery.
6 Mr Mason was climbing a hill when his foot slipped.

10.4 ADVERBIAL CLAUSES

Practice A

2 The drainage is poor, so that floods are frequent.

---

4 He is used to hardship, so that this setback doesn't worry him.

6 They live so simply that we almost forget their wealth.

9 You have guarded your privacy so fiercely that nobody knows anything about you.

11 His gaze was so steady that I didn't suspect him of lying.

Practice B

1	extremely	5	might	8	so quiet
2	so	6	that	9	can
3	will	7	very	10	quickly
4	which				

Practice C

1	that	5	that	8	nobody
2	would	6	have	9	can
3	so	7	good	10	everybody
4	well				

Practice D

2	3	6	7	9

Practice E

2 He evicted his tenants at very short notice, so that they had nowhere to go.
3 Their wedding was so expensive that they were in debt for some time. / Their wedding was expensive, so that they were in debt for some time.
4 She wanted flexible hours so that she could spend more time with her family.
5 I worked steadily so that I might not panic just before the exam.
6 The view was so wonderful that we were speechless. / The view was truly wonderful, so that we were speechless.

Practice F

1	can	5	very	8	very
2	so	6	so that	9	that
3	so that	7	would	10	very
4	would				

10.5 ADVERBIAL CLAUSES

Practice A

1	considered	5	took	8	is
2	would defend	6	cannot	9	grew
3	offers	7	they'll	10	could
4	liked				

Practice B

2	5	6	7	10

Practice C

1 B, C	2 A, B	3 A, B, C	4 B, C	5 A

Practice D

1	had	4	stayed	7	couldn't	9	had
2	stood	5	are	8	have	10	will
3	passes	6	have				

Practice E

2 I wouldn't emigrate if I were you.
3 We'll tell you the latest news if you like.
4 We could have climbed the hill if the fog had cleared.
5 This house would stand firm if a herd of elephants charged at it.
6 I might have stayed if I had had job satisfaction.

Practice F

1	goes	4	would	7	are	9	were
2	have	5	been	8	tried	10	I'll
3	had	6	given				

10. 6 ADVERBIAL CLAUSES

Practice A

1 A 2 B, C 3 A, B 4 A, B, C 5 A, C

Practice B

1 3 5 6 8

Practice C

1	as	4	does	7	like	9	are
2	did	5	do	8	the way	10	have
3	the way	6	were				

Practice D

1 I will reconsider as you have urged me to do.
2 He is not boastful the way some men tend to be.
3 She won a gold for us as our sports reporters had predicted.
4 They are helping us move house like we did for their son.
5 The city is serene again the way it was before the raid.

Practice E

1	did	4	as	7	have	9	like
2	was	5	does	8	as	10	the way
3	like	6	is				

Practice F

2 The parade was magnificent like / as / the way I had imagined it to be.
3 I am enchanted with this place the way you were last year.
4 We are narrating the incident as / like / the way it was told to us.
5 Nobody else has understood my situation the way you have.
6 They often dance till dawn like / as / the way we used to do.

11.1 REPORTED CLAUSES

Practice A

1	had	5	be	8	should go
2	is	6	would	9	fear
3	he would	7	I can	10	whether
4	whether				

Practice B

1	is	4	was	7	didn't	10	suitable or not
2	are	5	was it	8	may I		
3	if	6	were	9	went		

Practice C

1 4 6 7 9

Practice D

1 They guaranteed that their method was foolproof.
2 She wondered if she was under surveillance.
3 He begged that his mother's life be spared.
4 They maintained that their experiment is successful.
5 We must check whether the rumours are true.

Practice E

1	whether	5	try	8	had said
2	I had	6	did	9	I could
3	had	7	should	10	change
4	is				

Practice F

2 He wondered if he could unify his people.
3 She proposed that they hold / should hold an inquiry immediately.
4 We were warned that Aedes mosquitoes are dangerous.
5 They're asking whether you suffer from insomnia.
6 Julie wants to know whether or not you're fluent in French. / Julie wants to know whether / if you're fluent in French.

11.2 REPORTED CLAUSES

Practice A

2 I can't imagine what you see in those people.   (thing)
3 We understand how they feel about us.   (manner)
4 He remembers who found him the job.   (person)
5 Everyone is wondering where you are hiding.   (place)
6 They asked when the interview would be held.   (time)

Practice B

1	who	5	where	8	why
2	why	6	when	9	where
3	what	7	how	10	who
4	how				

Practice C

1	who	5	did she grow	8	would you
2	are we	6	where	9	who
3	where	7	why	10	when
4	what				

Practice D

1 A, C 2 B, C 3 B, C 4 A, B, C 5 A

Practice E

1	what	5	what	8	what
2	she was	6	was she	9	when
3	where	7	why	10	he could
4	who				

Practice F

2 He found out who I liked and invited them to the party this weekend.
3 The little boy wants to know when he can ride in a spaceship and fly to Mars.
4 Step by step I learnt how an earthenware pot is made.
5 The old lady who is lost won't tell me where she lives.
6 I don't see why we must follow fashion blindly.

11.3 REPORTED CLAUSES

Practice A

1	he had	5	which one	8	whose
2	which	6	what	9	you would
3	whose	7	it is	10	who's
4	which				

Practice B

3 4 8 9 10

Practice C

1	which	6	you can
2	whose	7	which one
3	which	8	we are
4	whose problem	9	whose
5	who's	10	I would

Practice D

2 They will note whose expression shows signs of disbelief.

3 Of the three contenders, she could tell which one was the most resolute.

4 The shopkeepers daren't disclose who's been extorting money from them.

5 I saw the pistol and tried to think whose it could possibly be.

6 We've studied the projects and will decide which would benefit this country the most.

Practice E

1	who's	5	which	8	should we
2	what	6	which farms	9	whose advice
3	which aspect	7	who's	10	whose
4	who's				

Practice F

2 Journalists are speculating whose work will win the Nobel Prize.

3 After living in two countries, I can't tell which I prefer / which one I prefer.

4 He enquired which cuisine she preferred, Chinese or Japanese.

5 She told me whose biography she was writing.

6 We saw a huge footprint and could only guess whose it was.

12.1 ADJECTIVAL PHRASES

Practice A

3 Teens are the (years) between childhood and adulthood.

4 All of us loved the (stream) behind our house.

7 The cameraman photographed the (girl) in blue.

9 They want to interview (people) over 80.

11 You are speaking of (something) beyond my understanding.

Practice B

1	on	5	opposite	8	about
2	along	6	behind	9	below
3	within	7	outside	10	near
4	beneath				

Practice C

1 3 4 7 8

Practice D

1 A, B   2 A, C   3 B, C   4 A, B, C   5 C

Practice E

2 Carl is reading a novel about a brilliant boy.

3 He worked out at a gymnasium near his college.

4 The main character is a girl of tremendous courage.

5 I was received by a secretary in a bad mood.

6 These are delicious oranges from China.

Practice F

2 We held a barbecue one evening around mid-term.

3 She resented the constant comparison with her sister.

4 I resigned myself to a life without security.

5 Joan has a cottage within walking distance of the beach.

6 That was a moving tribute to our forefathers.

12.2 ADJECTIVAL PHRASES

Practice A

1 My brother is the (boy) wearing a leather jacket.

3 We learnt how to treat a (patient) suffering from typhoid.

4 She's studying the (factors) unifying her people.

5 He was kind to the (prisoner) quaking before him.

9 The director wants shots of the coconut (palms) swaying in the breeze.

Practice B

1	who smuggling	6	that unfolding
2	was travelling	7	would be voting
3	is tailing	8	has been rotting
4	are sipping	9	that sunbathing
5	were threading	10	which zigzagging

Practice C

1 He is the man making the decisions.

2 I have a friend living in Alaska.

3 They are students enjoying their vacation.

4 She's an ex-addict building a new life.

5 We're fighting the weeds growing in our garden.

Practice D

1 A   2 A, B, C   3 A, C   4 B, C   5 A, B

Practice E

1 3 6 7 9

Practice F

1 'My City' was a charcoal piece which showing vehicles perched one on top of another. → 'My City' was a charcoal piece showing vehicles perched one on top of another.

2 A watercolour entitled 'Family' fascinated many people who viewing the exhibits. → A watercolour entitled 'Family' fascinated many people viewing the exhibits.

3 It depicted a pink mum was comforting two blue, bawling children and a scowling dad in a grey suit. → It depicted a pink mum comforting two blue, bawling children and a scowling dad in a grey suit.

4 'Friends', a pencil sketch, portrayed a little boy and a television cartoon character were sticking their tongues out at each other. → 'Friends', a pencil sketch, portrayed a little boy and a television cartoon character sticking their tongues out at each other.

5 An abstract masterpiece by a three-year-old was a riot of daubs and blobs that bearing the legend 'Me'. → An abstract masterpiece by a three-year-old was a riot of daubs and blobs bearing the legend 'Me'.

12.3 ADJECTIVAL PHRASES

Practice A

2 She has natural (beauty) enhanced by subtle make-up.

4 I love that snapshot of (Miss Lim) caught in a frivolous mood.

5 Some people have (personalities) eaten up by ambition.

7 I admired the (table) set by the little girl.

8 That was a (remark) meant to cheer you up.

Practice B
1 He wears jeans torn at the knees.
2 She is tormented by eczema.
3 We rode in carts drawn by donkeys.
4 We've heard of the exciting experiments conducted here.
5 I can't understand the message scribbled on the board.

Practice C
1   4   5   8   9

Practice D
1	recommended	6	edged
2	concocted	7	cut
3	borne	8	worn
4	centred	9	marred
5	thrown	10	famous

Practice E
2 Next came the school song sung with gusto.
3 I had to smooth an awkward situation created by my boss.
4 She felt for the children abandoned by their families.
5 Tomorrow we'll meet the artist commissioned to do a mural for us.
6 You're looking at a man forgotten by the world.

Practice F
1	glued	6	nicknamed
2	ensconced	7	called
3	born	8	destined
4	filled	9	addicted
5	besotted	10	obsessed

13.1 ADVERBIAL PHRASES
Practice A
2   3   5   8   10

Practice B
2 They got into trouble because of their bad behaviour.
3 She was appointed because of her expertise in the field.
4 We lost money because of a sudden fall in share prices.
5 You weathered the storm because of the strength of your faith.
6 People get lost because of completely inaccurate maps.

Practice C
1 B, C   **2** B, C   **3** A, C   **4** A, B   **5** A, C

Practice D
1	need	5	the weakness	8 its
2	pride	6	travel	9 a bitter
3	because	7	because of	10 his
4	their			

Practice E
2 She's rather spoilt because of her doting parents.
3 You don't feel the strain because of your tremendous energy.
4 My little brother is lazy because of my inability to motivate him.
5 I did badly because of a foolish goal.
6 We must stop it because of its potential destructiveness. / We must stop it because of its potential for destruction.

Practice F
The jungle is my all-time favourite because of its uniqueness. I'll always remember its night sounds because of their mystery. I'm sorry the deer that came to our tent ran off because of my gasp of wonder at seeing it. I also remember the folk dances because of their enchanting grace. Last but not least, I'll come again soon because of my longing for the delicious food.

13.2 ADVERBIAL PHRASES
Practice A
1 He was not offended though mistaken for a burglar.

2 The film was well reviewed despite the director's lack of experience.

3 They've decided to employ him in spite of his brashness.

4 He made up his mind to punish the child although amused by her excuse.

5 She managed to work despite the unreliability of her computer.

6 The weather is still fine despite threatening to rain since morning.

7 The harvest was satisfactory in spite of the drought.

8 The room is cosy although cluttered with books and tapes.

9 He looked presentable in spite of his unusual hairstyle.

10 The hero was timid in behaviour though bold in words.

Practice B
2 The anthem is rousing though sung out of tune.
3 He is still agile in spite of his arthritis problem.
4 This issue is often neglected although vital for our economic growth.
5 She will be promoted despite her indifference to high position.
6 Pollution is still not taken seriously although hazardous to all forms of life.

Practice C
2   5   6   8   10

Practice D
1	despite	5	despite of	8	pines
2	though is	6	fill	9	forgiven
3	complex	7	its	10	is diffident
4	beautiful				

Practice E
2 She could concentrate on her work despite the noise around her.
3 We we tried to look optimistic despite being disheartened by the news.
4 He held his ground in spite of their persistence.
5 They were bored after a while although enthusiastic at first.
6 I was prepared for the worst though hopeful of a last-minute rescue.

Practice F
The lecturers have turned out to be approachable despite their initial aloofness / despite having been initially aloof. The famous Patrick de Jong's lectures are inspiring although incomprehensible at times. The 'orientation' of new students

by seniors was fun though marred by one case of rather wild ragging. I've made some good friends in spite of my lack of social confidence. We are a fairly quiet group despite dreaming of changing the world / despite our dream of changing the world.

13.3 ADVERBIAL PHRASES
Practice A
1 Jake attended vacation classes so as to graduate fast.
2 Meg entered a bookshop in order not to be soaked by the rain the street.
3 Father worked hard to make everyone's life easier.
4 She moved away so as not to inhale his cigarette smoke.
5 They always sit in front in order to catch every word.
6 Some people use long words to appear learned.
7 Ken has kept away in order not to be asked awkward questions.
8 He plans to reform so as to set a good example for his children.
9 The team will practise hard in order not to lose a third time.
10 I've been avoiding the subject so as not to have a confrontation with him.

Practice B
1 A, C   2 B   3 A, B, C   4 B, C   5 A, B

Practice C
1 They are taking firm steps to prevent another outbreak of cholera.
2 I'll do some of those duties so as not to overburden you.
3 We're here to help them and not to exploit their sad plight.
4 This is done in order to punish the criminals.
5 She's writing a book so as to dispel certain misconceptions.

Practice D
1 broke   4 and   7 seen   9 to
2 to not   5 attracting   8 has   10 bringing
3 not to   6 deem

Practice E
2 They have to tread carefully so as not to upset anyone.
3 She learnt to use the loom in order to weave silk shawls.
4 We must practise singing so as to have a good choir.
5 I turned my face away in order not to show my distress.
6 You are being unreasonable to try my patience.

Practice F
As far as possible, I plan each day so as to spend at least two hours with a good book. I take careful measures in order not to be disturbed. Sometimes I put on soft music to give myself a double treat. The music has to be without words so as not to / in order not to compete with my book. I need these quiet pleasures in order to feel complete.

13.4 ADVERBIAL PHRASES
Practice A
1 shedding   5 raising   8 their
2 terrifying   6 leaving   9 soared
3 amazing   7 stupid   10 honour
4 argued

Practice B
2   4   5   7   8

Practice C
2 He acted well, getting tremendous applause.
3 The bouquet arrived, creating quite a stir.
4 They've cancelled her show, disappointing her fans.
5 We succeeded, proving our critics wrong.
6 I scored three goals, surpassing their expectations.

Practice D
1 He has behaved rather badly, ruining the evening.
2 It rained heavily for a week, resulting in serious floods.
3 They held riotous parties, annoying their neighbours.
4 The reunion dinner was a success, reviving old friendships.
5 You brought in irrelevant points, weakening your case.
6 She took a long time to get ready, delaying everyone else.
7 Francis gave a wonderful speech, moving the audience to tears.
8 Dad came in a dinosaur costume, thrilling the children.
9 We took a short cut, saving ourselves a tiresome journey.
10 The little boy solved the problem, astonishing the adults.

Practice E
2 He treated them with contempt, undermining their confidence.
3 Her books are brilliant, introducing the reader to an exciting world.
4 They rejected his thesis, curing him of intellectual vanity.
5 This music is nostalgic, tormenting me with memories.
6 You challenged us, impelling us to develop our potential.

Practice F
You read magazines and discuss with friends, developing many ideas. Then you realise that the ideas conflict, preventing you from making a final design. You want a house that is modern and efficient, creating an ideal living space. You also want a place that is comfortable and traditional, encouraging relaxation. Finally, you make your decision, understanding compromise is necessary.

13.5 ADVERBIAL PHRASES
Practice A
1 He is quite calm when placed in a difficult situation.
2 They went into hiding after inciting the people to rebel.
3 The reports must be checked before being handed in.
4 She was humming softly while cooking in her new kitchen.
5 He began to counsel me after listening to my problems.
6 You must be careful when dealing with strangers.
7 I checked my bank balance before writing the cheque.
8 She kept smiling into the camera while being interviewed.
9 The gentlest creature can be vicious when cornered.
10 He was very healthy after having his tonsils removed.

Practice B
1 B, C   2 A, B   3 A, C   4 B, C   5 A, C

Practice C

2 A present is precious when given with real affection.

3 He sighed contentedly while having his neck massaged.

4 I was exhausted after playing with three lively little boys.

5 You must take care when buying a used car.

6 We need to think before agreeing to accept these responsibilities.

Practice D

1	calling	6	worrying
2	being X-rayed	7	learning
3	seen	8	being approved
4	identifying	9	torn
5	skating	10	hearing

Practice E

2 We can all relax after doing a good job.

3 They attended a special course before being sent abroad.

4 An injury is hurtful when inflicted by a trusted animal.

5 I was imagining all sorts of disasters while waiting for your call.

6 People often reveal the truth when taken by surprise.

Practice F

I began to fear English Language after getting low marks in the subject throughout the first term. Then, I discovered a new world while visiting an uncle during the holidays. I got to know and like the English language when introduced to 'Grimm's Fairy Tales' in my uncle's library. English became my friend after having been my dreaded enemy. Moreover, since then I've been able to turn to books when needing relaxation or knowledge.

14.1 NOUN PHRASES

Practice A

1 He has failed to impress them.

2 We'll miss having fun with you.

3 After a while, I managed to run the programme myself.

4 They did not even attempt to regain credibility.

5 Frankly, I enjoy watching silly comedies.

6 As children we hated reciting rhymes in front of the class.

7 Rita plans to spend August up in the mountains.

8 You really must stop blaming yourself.

9 They did offer to compensate us for our losses.

10 She regrets selling that old sofa.

Practice B

1	to see	6	to yearn
2	being treated	7	taking
3	to solve	8	flying
4	suggested	9	to safeguard
5	chose	10	discussing

Practice C

2 She resented being left to hold the baby.

3 They have promised to provide us with efficient staff.

4 Dad can't afford to send us to universities abroad.

5 He didn't mind working hard to give them a good future.

6 Every day she practises shooting the ball into the net.

Practice D

1	being ridiculed	6	being passed
2	confronting	7	having
3	seeing	8	loves
4	to act	9	decided
5	to lock	10	having

Practice E

1 B, C   2 A, B   3 A, B, C   4 A, B   5 C

Practice F

Comedian : Actually, I planned to be an actor. At school, I practised lines from Shakespeare's tragedies. I attended an audition once, trying to get the leading role in 'King Lear'. As I strutted and spouted, everyone present began to laugh / laughing uncontrollably. I wanted to play the tragic hero. Instead, I got the role of Falstaff in 'The Merry Wives of Windsor'.

14.2 NOUN PHRASES

Practice A

3 Their favourite occupation was hanging around malls.

4 My suspicions about the new hospital plans proved to be correct.

6 Their favourite pastime is playing chess against their children.

8 After a while, we became enthusiastic members of the group.

11 For me the major problems has been dealing with difficult customers.

Practice B

1   4   6   7   10

Practice C

2 His speciality was identifying fakes in the world of art.

3 The new schedule appears to suit everyone in the firm.

4 My role is giving everyone help when needed.

5 The experience seems to have done her a world of good.

6 His contribution should be counselling young couples with problems.

Practice D

1	to be	6	to win
2	drawing	7	to have
3	to vibrate	8	is making
4	staying	9	teaching
5	to understand	10	was whining

Practice E

2 Her weakness has always been making unrealistic plans.

3 His seemingly absurd idea proved to be perfectly sound.

4 The troubled people have come to trust and respect you.

5 What infuriates us is being treated like idiots.

6 For me the difficult part would be ignoring the sound of traffic.

Practice F

Our faces seemed to be just a blur to him. When we greeted him, his notion of a friendly response was muttering / to mutter something with a vague smile. One of our joys was taking / to take advantage of his absentmindedness. Sometimes, his melodious voice proved to be soporific and some of us slept happily right in front of him. One day, we were jolted awake by his calling out our names and saying,

"Shakespeare's Hamlet says: to die, to sleep . . . I say: A sure way to die is to sleep through lectures."

14.3 NOUN PHRASES
Practice A
1 We've spoken seriously about <u>offering her a partnership</u>.
2 Mum is satisfied with <u>being a full-time housewife</u>.
3 He persisted in <u>doing things his own way</u>.
4 She was sternly rebuked for <u>crossing the border</u>.
5 I pride myself on <u>keeping all my promises</u>.
6 They coaxed me into <u>changing my plans</u>.
7 Everyone must work towards <u>making this nation strong and peaceful</u>.
8 Sally felt remorse after <u>breaking the rules</u>.
9 The artist wants more time before <u>holding a solo exhibition</u>.
10 You can't attain lasting success by <u>bluffing your way around</u>.

Practice B
1 telling	5 without	8 besides
2 through	6 of	9 on
3 caring	7 seeing	10 restoring
4 starting		

Practice C
2 I was given the task of cooking for the entire family.
3 She drew the line at letting them choose a career for her.
4 He has problems stemming from having been ill as a child.
5 They quarrelled over dividing the ancestral land.
6 Sometimes, ragging is practised under the pretext of making new students feel at home.

Practice D
1 B, C   2 A   3 A, B   4 B, C   5 A, C   6 A

Practice E
2 She is totally justified in making that statement.
3 He impressed us by repairing both the cars.
4 I look forward to seeing you next week.
5 We're having second thoughts about promoting him.
6 There's no solution short of changing the whole system.

Practice F
1 learning	5 stopping	8 getting
2 sitting	6 without	9 obtaining
3 in	7 into	10 from
4 for		

15 SENTENCE STRUCTURE
Practice A
1 could, neither	4 neither, nor
2 either, or	5 neither, nor
3 should, question	

Practice B
1 neither	6 or
2 nor she	7 neither would
3 finished	8 he thought
4 either	9 Either admit the monks
5 nor	10 Neither the rescuers

Practice C
1 The rebels might either surrender or fight to the end.
2 Either they are caught in a traffic jam or they left late.
3 The medicine could neither heal her nor relieve her pain.
4 John neither wants to work nor to study.
5 They neither understood the boy nor approved of him.

Practice D
1 either	5 nor	8 can neither
2 Either	6 give	9 bring
3 or	7 I'll hit	10 or
4 neither		

Practice E
2 You should neither belittle people nor gossip about them.
3 The receptionist neither looked up nor responded to our greeting.
4 The machine would either make a horrid noise or break down.
5 Some reporters neither respect privacy nor care about accuracy.
6 Next vacation, Ken will either work on a farm or hitch-hike around the country.

16.1 REFERENCE
Practice A
1 It is, their	2 he, our	3 our, They are
4 they are, it	5 her, we	

Practice B
1 a rematch, The rematch
2 five products, The products
3 the instrument, her grandfather
4 A number of applicants, The applicants
5 The animals, them

Practice C
1 B   2 A   3 B   4 B   5 A

Practice D
2 Sentence (3) : <u>he</u> → 'My brother David' in Sentence (1).
3 Sentence (4) : <u>it</u> → 'the fridge' in Sentence (4).
4 Sentence (5) : <u>it</u> → 'juice or milk spilt in the fridge' in Sentence (5).
5 Sentence (6) : <u>we</u> → 'Dad, Mum and I' in Sentence (6).
6 Sentence (7) : <u>itself</u> → refers back to 'a fridge' in Sentence (7).
7 Sentence (9) : <u>The screen</u> → 'a touch screen' in Sentence (8).
8 Sentence (10) : <u>it</u> → 'The screen' in Sentence (9).
9 Sentence (12) : <u>them</u> → 'food items' in Sentence (11).
10 Sentence (14) : <u>it</u> → 'foodstuff' in Sentence (13).
11 Sentence (14) : <u>the hatch</u> → 'a hatch' in Sentence (8).

16.2 REFERENCE
Practice A
1 That
2 this wonderful form of relaxation
3 The place
4 the spectators

5 the game
6 that
7 the word in question
8 my opponent
9 These
10 The time limit

Practice B

1 the dishes
2 this talent
3 The prized possession
4 The four-star hotel
5 those

6 The procedure
7 That
8 the building
9 This service
10 These

Practice C

3 this unpretentious woman → Mary

4 it → what made me like Mary

5 us → The matron, the supervisor and I

6 The tearful little boy → Jimmy

7 That look → complete trust in his eyes

8 this → that Mary was a person with a heart full of love and compassion

TEST 1

A

(1) assigning → assigned

(4) could staying → could stay

(5) Stirs → Stir

(7) taking off → to take off

(9) making → is making

(12) wasn't grant → wasn't granted

(14) had disappearing → had disappeared

(15) manage → manages

(18) making → make

(19) testified → testifying

B

1 was given
2 has made
3 weren't told
4 has been rising
5 was used

6 experiences
7 causes
8 is
9 Do
10 were offered

C

1 astounded
2 had just made
3 will be
4 leaves
5 was deeply touched
6 seldom travelled
7 took
8 boarded
9 were determined
10 flew

11 had arranged
12 persuaded
13 produced
14 didn't think
15 realised
16 struck
17 was being battered
18 prayed
19 would manage
20 heaved

D

1 Dr Perez has been elected by the constituents as their new representative in parliament.
2 The police officer questioned the suspect until she broke down and confessed.
3 All new applications for car loans have already been frozen.
4 They will have completed the renovations to the house by the end of the month.
5 The reports for the annual general meeting were still being finalised by Jane at 2 p.m. today.

TEST 2

A

1 needn't finish
2 should be launching
3 might not have received
4 be repaired
5 would have been given

B

3 to → into
4 than → from
5 on → with

6 in → at
9 with → by

C

1 Anne asked us when we planned to go to Bangkok.
2 Mrs Larsen proudly informed my mother that her daughter had graduated with first-class honours in law.
3 The traffic policeman asked Mr Sims whether or not / if he knew that that was a no-parking zone.
4 Sam said, "Your chiffon cake is so good that I want another slice."
5 Bill said to Debbie, "Are you interested in joining the ceramic workshop next weekend?"

D

1 A   2 A   3 B   4 A   5 B

E

1 made
2 when
3 what
4 , whose

5 would
6 belongs
7 so

8 , which
9 whether
10 though

F

1 B, C   2 A, C   3 A, B   4 B, C   5 A, C

TEST 3

A

1 is hurt
2 are scolded
3 that
4 exuberant

5 that
6 rob
7 for he

8 waited
9 despite of
10 strong

B

1 spoken
2 sparkling
3 behind
4 crawling

5 roughened
6 under
7 hidden

8 without
9 riding
10 quoted

C

1 came → come

4 either → neither

6 Neither the youngsters → The youngsters neither

7 <u>was</u> → be

10 <u>Colin neither can</u> → Colin can neither

D

1 A, C   **2** B, C   **3** A, B   **4** A, C   **5** A, B

E

1 the instructor
2 an old table
3 a coat of white emulsion paint
4 participants
5 odd shapes
6 the coloured pieces
7 the varnish
8 participants
9 a beautiful fake-mosaic table
10 participants

TEST 4

A

1 of
2 should
3 was
4 didn't / couldn't
5 up
6 undue / unfair / destructive
7 was
8 and
9 had
10 was

B

1	C	**5**	C	**9**	C	**13**	D	**17**	C
2	B	**6**	D	**10**	D	**14**	A	**18**	B
3	A	**7**	C	**11**	B	**15**	B	**19**	D
4	B	**8**	C	**12**	A	**16**	B	**20**	B

C

1 The police were planning to raid the gambling den.
2 We'll photograph that building with a spiral chimney.
3 They supported him despite his bad record.
4 You must brief the agent taking your place.
5 He was furious when told of the fiasco.

D

1 David reminded us that we shouldn't make unkind remarks about others.
2 Jenny, whose piano skills are superb, won a scholarship to study at Trinity College.
3 My boss questioned all of us when some important files disappeared.
4 The packers worked so quickly that in half an hour they had packed and sealed the boxes containing our household items.
5 I will definitely help you if you encounter any difficulties during the course.

TEST 5

A

1	who	**5**	to	**8**	and
2	with	**6**	participate	**9**	the
3	and	**7**	at	**10**	of
4	or				

B

1	D	**5**	B	**9**	D	**13**	C	**17**	C
2	B	**6**	C	**10**	B	**14**	A	**18**	A
3	A	**7**	B	**11**	A	**15**	D	**19**	B
4	C	**8**	A	**12**	D	**16**	C	**20**	D

C

1 The chairman suggested that the money should be donated to needy children.
2 The football match was not postponed even though the rain was heavy. / there was heavy rain.
3 The Smith family lost a lot of money in the stock exchange because they were foolish.
4 Although we warned him of the consequences of his rash plans, Ralph still went ahead.
5 Mary is confident that she will get the majority of votes for the post of union president.

D

Interviewer : Why have you set your heart on studying medicine?

Student : It's not a decision involving only my heart. I've considered several other careers carefully so as not to make the wrong choice.

Interviewer : What makes you think you have the abilities and qualities needed to succeed in the medical field?

Student : I'd like to believe that love of science and my fellowmen will help make me a good doctor.

TEST 6

A

1 creating / causing / wrecking
2 the
3 when
4 having / forced
5 it
6 what
7 did
8 If
9 the
10 not

B

1	D	**5**	C	**9**	D	**13**	B	**17**	A
2	B	**6**	C	**10**	B	**14**	C	**18**	C
3	A	**7**	B	**11**	D	**15**	A	**19**	A
4	C	**8**	C	**12**	C	**16**	D	**20**	C

C

1 while I was trying to find a job.
2 that played against me at the chess club.
3 that I should talk to them about my problems.
4 although I was embarrassed about being unemployed for so long.
5 who is looking for employment.

D

1 by winning a scholarship to study in Texas in the United States.
2 not to copy 'wild Western ways'.
3 sending the whole family into shock.
4 raised among cowboys.
5 though somewhat annoyed with him for fooling us.